Roxy,
May Jesus draw you closer
to His amazing love for you!

Love
Ruth

BROKEN
HEARTS
HEALED

A STORY OF TRANSFORMATION

No one will ever take
your place in the
heart of God. Jn.10:10
Ruth McElwee

RUTH McELWEE

Foreword by WINKIE PRATNEY

www.xulonpress.com

Praise for

"Broken Hearts Healed
A Story of Transformation"

Dear Ross and Ruth,

It was so beautiful to get to know you and your family. You minister the love of Jesus in a transparent way that reaches many of our Alaska Natives. I always say, "A healed land begins with a healed people." You've demonstrated how brokenness can be transformed into something beautiful. You are a light in the darkness. You are an example worth following. Thank you for winning Alaska through love, honor and transparency.

Bill Pagaran
Carry the Cure, Inc. President
Broken Walls minister

The pain of childhood sexual assault is something that takes a lifetime to overcome. Ruth's vulnerability and honesty comes through her story. For all who have experienced this trauma I am sure that they will take comfort in knowing that God can redeem and use for His glory the tragedies that occur in our lives. Out of the ashes of despair Ruth rises as not only a survivor but one who thrives.

Yvonne DeVaughn
AVA (Advocacy for Victims of Abuse) Director
Evangelical Covenant Churches

This is a story of one little five year old girl affected by sexual abuse dynamics. But the story doesn't end there. More sad stories because of the results of neglect and abuse, but because of Jesus, redemption's story blossoms.

Dr. Clair Schnupp
NYM — Native Youth Ministries
Dryden, ON

"When you read the account of Ruth McElwee's life, and the tragic things that happened to her as a young girl, a phrase from Psalm 23 stands out to me very strongly where David says, "He restores my soul." Thank God for restoration. The McElwee's today are leading a flourishing ministry life and bringing people to the Lord. May you be inspired with this book."

With warm Christian love,
Leland Paris
YWAM Global Leadership

Ruth McElwee's book, "Broken Hearts Healed," graphically portrays God's determined love that pursues every individual. His desire was restoration from damage that sometimes cannot be recalled or diagnosed. Ruth's story of God's personal attention to healing and to restoring the ability to have whole, loving relationships amazed me. You will have to read the book to understand the impact.

Fran Paris
Co-Founder, YWAM Tyler, TX

Ruth is a gentle, compassionate person, guided by a thoughtful reflection on the Bible's relational truths. This led to wonderful healing and restoration within her. It has released her into wholeness and health in her relationships. Ruth (as you will read) has personally experienced this wonderful reality. From prayer, from close, personal relationship with Jesus, and from diligent, thorough Bible study, Ruth brings to the reader of this book the incredible opportunity of healing and restoration.

Ruth has another gift. She is a wonderful writer. She has natural, creative writing ability that links gracefully with her degree in English composition and literature. What is the result? It is a book that is easy and delightful to read. It gives the reader a wonderful communication of tested truths that Ruth has ministered into the lives of girls and women who longed for emotional healing and self-acceptance. She brings to her readers the opportunity to experience God's wonderful touch, His love, and His very practical principles that release them into the wholeness that Jesus intensely desires for them to have.

Larry Allen
YWAM -Tyler Training Director
Tyler, TX

The weakness of first-person accounts is that readers tend to think, "I can top that! Why, I once…" The strength of Ruth McElwee's book *Broken Hearts Healed: A Story of Transformation* is that right at the beginning she opts out of such a competition, freeing readers to share the ache of abuse… the betrayal of guilt, shame, and rejection… the lure of sexual acceptance. The sad truth is that few of us escape childhood and adolescence totally unscarred by such things. Through the love of a good man, and the healing of a faithful God, Ruth's life was transformed, her faith renewed, and the desire of her heart to serve God realized. Thank you, Ruth, for baring your soul. Thank you for freeing us to do the same. We, too, rejoice in the words, "They don't remember what you were, only what you are. Look what the Lord has done!"

Kay Marshall Strom
Author ~ Speaker

Ruth McElwee, along with her husband Ross, has been a pioneer with YWAM in Barbados, served with YWAM in Tyler. She has had a heart for the missionary call since she was a little girl; she has a story to tell, a story of broken hearts that can be transformed by the power of God's redemption. Many of us have broken hearts in different ways and you will learn from this book the ways of God and His healing.

Jesus is our healer. He can heal broken hearts as well as broken bodies and this book will help you understand His ways of healing.

Loren Cunningham
Founder of Youth With A Mission (YWAM)

Dedication

To my loving and faithful husband,
My rare treasure,
Ross

Acknowledgments

This book owes its livelihood to so many people along my life's journey, there is no way I can thank each one personally. The generous support and gracious friendships have made me who I am.

To God be the glory! I have insufficient words of thanks to Jesus Christ for saving my soul, redeeming my life and restoring my dreams.

To my precious children, Samuel, Rachel Joy, Isaac and Leah, you are my joy. I cherish the friendships I share with each of you. Thank you for all the sacrifices of your time, good meals and my company.

To my dear parents in Heaven, Oh how much I love you! Your amazing love in the tumultuous years of my life eventually led to my transformation. How thankful I am for all the answered prayers lifted on my behalf out of your own anguished souls.

To the many readers, friends, acquaintances and editors who inspired, challenged and corrected me I am thankful. You helped make this book the polished, powerful work that it has become.

To Debbie Millette and Susie Alkire, thank you for loving, praying and caring for me all those years, never knowing that Jesus would finally reach my heart. I have never forgotten either of you and the powerful ways that God used you to "spiritually mother" me.

To Charlene McCauley-Mayfield and Carolyn Walker Woodring, I am deeply grateful for you precious sisters, regardless of how many miles separate us. Thank you for all the years of special memories.

To Lori Paajanen, you are a gift of joy, encouragement and friendship. What delight it has been to walk with you and share life together.

To Terri Hibbard, I would not have known how to make this book come alive for the readers without your marvelous gift of editorial expertise and your friendship. Thank you for helping me make this book excellent.

To Ross, I could not have written this book without you. You are my best friend and greatest encourager. Thank you for all of your commitment to me for over more than twenty-five years. May the Lord grant us many more years of love and service together. I love you, my husband.

Foreword
By: Winkie Pratney

Dear Ruth,

I more than loved your book. I cried, I laughed, I loved God with you.

Many years ago I spoke in a little meeting about the Fall of Eve in the Garden and parallels of the story of Snow White to our own lost culture. (The purity and innocence of the kind young girl who loved the flowers and animals around her in the Garden. The proud Queen whose vanity spoiled her beauty and the tell-tale Mirror of truth that told her she was now no longer the loveliest in the Kingdom. The Huntsman sent out to kill the lovely girl who found he finally could not do it because of her trusting innocence and took back to the Queen a deer's heart instead. The transformation of the Queen into darkness and deception as the wicked Witch with the poisoned apple. That fatal bite that took the girl into the sleep of death and the thistles and thorns that grew up around her coffin. The lightning that fell from Heaven to strike the rock on which the Witch stood on the high mountain to kill those who had loved Snow White and the Witch's awful final fall to death that has no observable end. And the Prince who came to the coffin to kiss her back to life and took her back to his home in the Sky.)

My friends of Second Chapter of Acts were in the audience and sometime later I heard their Prince Song...

"Got a brand-new story though you've heard it a time or two
About a Prince Who kissed a girl right out of the blue
Hey, this story ain't no tale to me now
For the Prince of Peace has given me life somehow
You know what I mean
My sleep is over, I've been touched by His fire,
That burns from His eyes and lifts me higher and higher.
I'll be forever with Him right by my side.
He's coming again on a white horse He'll ride.
He'll clothe me and crown me and make me His bride.
You know what I mean. You know what I mean."

One of our most significant writers in New Zealand was Janet
Frame, an amazing woman whose book, *Owls Do Cry* touched me
deeply when I first came across it as a teenager in my mother's
lending library in my hometown of Manurewa. Attending a seminar
recently where four major writers discussed with an audience of other
authors in a national Writers Conference in Auckland, I missed an
opportunity to briefly share with them the impact this made on my
life and was an influence ever since. Damage done to us as children
can hurt us forever unless in some wonderful way we find rescue. For
Janet, a poem she wrote became a national prizewinning entry and
spared her from a mental asylums frightening lobotomy. Why I mention these is because in many ways your writing reminds me of hers.

Your gifts from God in poetry, music, singing and journaling are
different of course. Horrors and terrors that can fall on an unsus-
pecting innocent child for her had a different outcome and marked her
life forever in a way that you were instead kept and redeemed from
by the love and intervention of our Great Lover. You have something
to say and give that Janet never did.

Like her, what happened to you told a story in a way that multi-
tudes still need to hear, and all (who for some sad reasons were and
perhaps are still hurting) can find a kindred spirit in what was said
about what was done. All of us should hear the echo of what has
happened to God's poor world and what He can do to reverse the
ugly and the angry shadows to restore every Snow White from the

wicked Witch and the poisoned apple and to bring back the magic in the fairy tale to every Cinderella with amnesia.

~Winkie Pratney July 2015

Preface

*M*y words come slowly, mingled with tears.

"Mom, I feel that the Lord wants me to write my story, but I'm afraid it will hurt you. I love you, Mom, and it's important to me to have your blessing. If you don't want me to write this book, then I won't. You are the person that it could hurt the most and you know what this story is."

The phone is silent. I wait.

"Oh, Ruth Mary, you have to write this book! You have a calling to write. It is a calling from the Lord. There is no one who knew you in high school who could not say, 'Look what a marvelous work the Lord has done!' They would love it. They would find it hard to believe. You are an entirely different person."

Her affirmation continues and I am touched.

"I know that people will listen. Your words are so meaningful and come out so beautifully. You have a way with words, a way of saying things that touch people."

Editing is agony. Writing the book, my fingers flew over the keyboard as the thoughts came almost faster than I could type. The book was good.

But it wasn't excellent. It wasn't something that spoke into the reader's life. It was my story, told in a personal way but almost devoid of deep, inner emotions.

But all this personal, Why and how I felt…this is painful. I can somewhat casually read the other version, with only a few tears in places, but this….sharing and baring my soul….

This is travail. I can only work a little at a time. It's not that I don't know what to say as it is, *"Really? Do the readers need to know all that? And oh my goodness, is nothing left to vagueness, or to be unsaid."*

It's scary. Terrifying actually. To expose my heart…that is indeed vulnerable and excruciating. With the other version, I brushed aside people's comments, "Oh, Ruth, I am so sorry to hear how painful your life was." I justified in my mind, "It wasn't that bad."

But in editing, I can no longer deny the depths of the pain that I endured—the deep suffering of broken relationships, loneliness, rejection and the terribly distorted view of God, love, my parents and life. Only by acknowledging all that was lost, can I display the beauty of restoration through Jesus Christ.

Introduction

I hope this story touches your heart. It has been a book in gestation for over twenty-five years. I have not experienced the intensity of some people's abuse and there is a tendency to compare ourselves and minimize the pain we have endured. Yet the reality is, only God can truly measure pain.

As my husband said to me, "A person suffering third degree burns is not going to look at a victim with second degree burns and say, 'You have no idea what I've gone through.'" That statement gave me the confidence that I could be a "voice" for those thousands of victims who have been wounded in life and have never been able to share their pain. May this book be a catalyst of healing and forgiveness.

Disclaimer

I don't claim to remember all events perfectly but I have written this story to the best of my ability. Some names have been changed. My distorted perceptions and emotions were not a true picture of reality but it took years of pain and struggle before I uncovered those lies.

Table of Contents

———— ✳ ————

Part Three – Romanced

Part One

Bitter and Broken

Chapter 1

A Tangled Web

I stared at the stained glass windows with their designs of reds, blues, greens, yellows and purples. The sunlight pierced through the glass and made the colors sparkle. The organ music echoed from the high ceiling. I sat on the plush maroon pew and spread my right hand across the cushion while I traced patterns in the soft velvet only to smooth them out again. I breathed in the peaceful stillness. I knew that God was everywhere, but here in church, it was as if His Presence filled the room.

I sat in the sanctuary beside my mother and gazed at the wooden cross suspended behind the pulpit. *Could it really be true that Jesus loved me that much?* In Sunday school, I heard the Bible stories and I loved the powerful missionary stories. I thought to myself, *When I grow up, I want to be like that! I want to leave everything to tell others about Jesus!*

I sang the hymns while the words nestled in my heart. "Lord, speak to me," "Open my eyes to see" and "Fill my mouth with messages from Thee," became prayers to God. I wanted Him to use my life.

My dad's voice caught my attention. I didn't understand all that he said, but I enjoyed watching him preach. His hands moved with his words and it was as if Daddy was in a grand performance, except that he wasn't acting. I wanted to be just like him when I got older. I loved how his eyes sparkled when he laughed and filled with tears over something sad.

The blessing continued as my breathing quickened. I counted the last words over the congregation. "Amen." Weaving down the aisle between the elderly men and women, repeating appropriate "Excuse me's" along the way, I stood beside my hero, my dad, the Pastor. We smiled and shook hands as each person exited through the open doors of the large church. My olive-skinned complexion, deep brown eyes and long, jet black hair stood in sharp contrast to Dad's milky white skin, pale blue eyes and grayed temples highlighting his black hair. Finally, at five years old, I could attend the worship service and forever leave the walls of the nursery.

Like most children I was blunt and curious. My mother's answer was simplistic when I asked, "Where do babies come from?" She explained that a man's private part was like a stick and a woman's like a hole and the stick went into the hole to make a baby. The man and woman were married.

Mom said, "Ruth Mary, this is private and we don't talk about these things." I looked through the medical book at home and discovered the diagrams of various body parts. The descriptions of a stick, like a line, and a hole, like a circle, played a critical role in my development and perceptions.

That summer, for the first time ever, Mom didn't come with us on a short two week vacation. It felt strange and sad but Dad said, "Your mother is tired. She needs to stay home and rest." Daddy took my older siblings, George, Susie and Walt, along with me to a campground in the Ozark Mountains in Arkansas. The brilliant blue sky, warm sunshine and rugged mountains surrounded us with beauty.

One night I was lonely and missing Mom. Daddy held me on his lap in front of the campfire and we sat and watched the embers glow. His hands stroked my hair and he brushed the wisps away from my tear-stained cheeks as he sang softly.

On that same trip, Daddy took us to see The Passion Play — a re-enactment of the Life of Christ — at the outdoor theater. I watched mesmerized as the actors portrayed the story of Jesus. My eyes were riveted on the stage during the Crucifixion scene. At the exact moment of Jesus' death, out in the distant mountains, a large lightning streak split the sky directly behind the cross. It wasn't the dramatic effects on stage but the awesome God, Himself, Who made the pageant come alive for me!

Once we returned home, Daddy brought me into his room and taught me how to use the record player. He showed me some new records. They had stories from history about Jesus, Paul, William Tyndale, the Pilgrims and Jane Addams. There were stories of great hymns and the people who wrote them. Every day for several hours, I listened to the records by myself and sang aloud.

One day as I sang "Take My Life and Let It Be," I thought about how much God loved me and how I loved Him. I wanted my life to be consecrated to God. I didn't want to hold anything back from Him—not my voice, my feet, my hands, my heart or my money.

In a moment, I had an image in my mind of Africa and I felt in my heart that God wanted me to become a missionary when I grew up. Tears trickled down my cheeks and I knew that something special had happened. The experience was so amazing that like the Virgin Mary, "I pondered these things in my heart." I didn't tell anyone about my time with God, but somehow I knew that He had spoken to me.

I had no idea at age five, how long it would take before that vision would come to pass. I was unaware that there was an enemy of my soul plotting schemes to destroy that desire. The painful places that awaited me had not yet intruded into my idealistic, innocent world of loving God and trusting people.

When we came home from vacation, Mom told us she had diabetes. In order to help financially, she now wanted to be a teacher and no longer stay at home. Our church kindergarten program began at age six. So I was enrolled in a private daycare.

Dad wanted to implement change but the church board didn't approve of his ideas. Only one board member stood with him. The rest wanted to fire him. Dad knew his job wasn't secure. He considered leaving the ministry to sell records. Mom knew that he wasn't a good salesman and encouraged him to remain a pastor.

The daycare was run by a woman who was a relative of the board member who stood with Dad. I was the oldest child there and I didn't need to take a nap anymore so I was kept outside on a bed in an enclosed, screened porch. The outside air made it easier to breathe since I was still recuperating from being sick.

I didn't have anything to do but lie there until naptime was over for all the younger children. I was bored and all was quiet. So I ran my hands lazily over the pattern of the white, candlewick bedspread until I finally dozed.

My eyes, still blurry from sleep, opened and an old man stood by me. He didn't say a word but I looked down at his brown unzipped pants and his exposed privates. No sound escaped his lips. He took my hand in his firm grip and made me touch him.

It felt like a nightmare. I desperately wanted it to stop. Sickened and frightened, I wanted to close my eyes and pretend it wasn't happening. I wanted it all to go away. I didn't want to touch him. I didn't know what to do. And yet, paralyzed by fear, I couldn't make any noise. I didn't like what was happening but my parents had taught me to respect and obey adults, so I did not resist. In a matter of minutes, the door opened and his wife glared at us.

Her face reflected hate and horror as her eyes pierced through me. The disapproval and disgust penetrated into the depths of my soul. Guilt and shame washed over me. After all, *I touched him* so it must be *my* fault. In the devastating silence, the senile old man and his wife shuffled away and left me alone.

Later, Dad came and took me home. I told Mom what happened. Her reaction shut me down. "Ruth Mary, I cannot believe that." I interpreted her words to mean, "You are lying," and I closed off any further talk with her.

My father took me to another daycare in a different town. But that was only for one day because the drive cost too much. Then Dad let me stay with him at the church office, but that only lasted a few days, as well.

Is it my fault? Didn't my mom even accuse me of lying? No one talked to me about it and worse, my father stopped hugging me or showing me any affection. In a few short days, my world had changed and I didn't know how to fix it.

It must be my fault. After all, I touched him! No one hugged me, held me or said they were sorry. There was only the punishment of silence. No one said or did anything, I felt blamed — the anger grew inside me. I didn't know what to do about these new emotions. I felt dirty, ugly and completely rejected. I believed nobody liked or loved me anymore. It was terrible!

From that time on, I lived in my own private hell that no one knew about. I believed my daddy didn't love me anymore and I hated my mom for accusing me of lying. I didn't open up to them or anybody after that. I kept all my pain either to myself or I expressed it in temper tantrums. My emotions felt like I was on a roller-coaster. Sometimes I was happy and other times I was furious. Most of the days I was lonely and felt lost in my own little world.

With nowhere else to send me, my parents returned me to the same daycare. I felt extremely lonely and very angry. At naptime, I was kept with all the other kids. My bed was the last in the row, near the wall. I turned my back to ignore the happy children. As I lay on the plastic mattress, I unfastened my two barrettes and smashed them together as if they were male and female and silently let the tears fall. It wasn't a sexual act. I wanted to hurt the man who had hurt me. I wanted someone to make it his fault. But sadly, no one seemed to blame him.

In the late 1960's, no one talked about sexual abuse. Because Dad no longer displayed any physical affection towards me, I perceived his distance as shame, rejection and punishment. I turned all my inward turmoil on the man whom I once adored.

I often exploded in anger and rage. I threw temper tantrums, screamed and yelled. When I was in college, reflecting on my past, my mother said, "You hated me but you despised your father." Sadly, that was often how I felt most of my life even through high school. But I wrongly believed that they also hated me. It wasn't the abuse that hurt so much as it was the way it was handled.

My father had his own agony. The man who abused me was related to the only man on the church board who stood with him. Dad felt trapped between losing his job and wanting justice for his daughter — the struggle of thoughts of wanting to murder the abuser, and the condemnation of the guilt for *wanting* to murder the abuser.... *What kind of pastor could you be to want to murder someone!* What an incredible burden to have carried!

My innocence was being stripped from me and I felt defenseless. The following Spring, I crashed my bike while riding around the

31

church grounds. The tall Mexican janitor came over to check on my scraped knees as I exited the bathroom. As I stood there with tears in my eyes, he pushed himself against me and I felt the hard, red brick wall as it pressed into my back. He was too close. I felt trapped.

"You're such a pretty, little girl. Come back here in an hour."

He shoved a large fistful of loose coins into my hands. I had no idea what he wanted but I knew enough to know that it wasn't nice. I cringed from his touch. The odor of his sweat mingled with my tears. I bolted home as soon as he let me go. I had no intention to return. All the emotions inside me churned as fear gripped my heart once again. I burst into the door of my home and poured my story out to Dad.

I sobbed and shook as I relayed what had happened. Even then, Dad didn't hug me. I felt bad that I had forgotten my bike. My father told Walt to get it. Then he spoke these devastating words, "You are never to go to the church again by yourself."

Once again, I felt as if I had done something wrong and was being punished. It wasn't fair! I despised my favorite person and now I was banned from my favorite place—church!

I began to think, *"Maybe since I am 'a pretty little girl,' it really is my fault."* If I were ugly, maybe the man at the daycare and the janitor would have ignored me. I kept believing, "do unto others as you would have them do unto you," but I didn't realize that people would not always act kindly towards me, especially adults. I had been taught to respect adults and I naively thought that meant adults were nice.

Shortly after this incident, Susie and Walt got Dad to play a game with us in our bedroom. Susie and I shared a room as did George and Walt. It was a fun time together, even though, as usual, Dad won the game. He told Susie and me to get in bed and we did. Into the silence, from across the room, she said, "I dare you to dance naked in front of the window."

She had never dared me to do anything before and I don't remember if I protested at first or not. All I know is that I got out of bed and danced naked. The bedroom door opened, the light switched on and Dad saw me. Shame washed over me once again. He told Susie to leave the room. Without another word, he turned me over his knee and spanked me with his bare hand.

I crawled back under my covers. Susie returned to her bed and said nothing. It was the first time I ever went to bed naked. I was furious at Dad and at Susie. I felt deeply ashamed, rejected and in physical pain. All I wanted was to feel better. I didn't know that there was a name for what I did that night, but later I learned that it was called "masturbation." That false safe place held me in its shackles until I went to college. Almost every night that was where I went to feel comfort and yet at the same time it was mixed with guilt and shame.

Rage boiled inside me like a smoldering volcano. My personality fragmented and I was lost in a fantasy world of violence. I played with dolls and stuffed animals until after a few seconds of being "loving," I spanked them and vehemently punished them. One time Mom caught me "spanking" my dolls. Her look of shock and anguish embarrassed me so I didn't hurt the dolls again. I was extremely distraught but somehow, I learned to survive.

My idyllic childhood had shattered. Relationships once held so tenderly in my heart, now only stung with rejection, pain and anger. Shame and guilt mixed with the pleasure of masturbation began to weave a tangled web in the depths of my soul.

Chapter 2

Faulty Foundations

*I*n the first grade class, the pink and blue cardboard "tails" hung beside the chalkboard. Our teacher finished explaining that "tattling" would be punished by wearing the tail. We needed to learn that "tattling" was not nice and that it was wrong.

"Class, I'm going out to run an errand. Stay in your seats and do your work. I will be back in a few minutes." The teacher's heels clicked on the sidewalk as she exited the room. Because I lived in south Texas our classrooms were in two long one-story buildings connected by a sidewalk. We had mild weather and we never had snow. Christmas presents were a new bicycle, roller skates or a scooter.

Immediately, Ramon jumped up from his desk, ran outside the class to the back side of the school building and for fun, threw a rock into the room. The window was opened so he didn't break the glass. He wanted to see if he could get away with the prank. He hurried into the room, flipped over a small desk and sat down.

Heels clicked and the teacher returned. I promptly spoke up, "Miss H., Ramon got out of his seat while you were gone and he knocked over a desk." I didn't tell the part about throwing the rock because I figured the evidence on the floor was obvious and I also assumed that she would ask him, "Is that true, Ramon?" Then he would lower his eyes, mutter the rest of the story and the punishment would be given out accordingly. I did have a crush on him but I still felt that what he did was wrong. After all, our teacher had specifically told us not to get out of our seats and he had disobeyed.

Unfortunately, the scenario I expected didn't occur. Instead of punishing Ramon, Miss H. looked at me. "Ruth, we do not tattle in this class. I have already taught you children that tattling is wrong. Please come here."

From my perspective what Ramon did was wrong because he disobeyed, but from the teacher's perspective what I did was wrong because I tattled. I reluctantly walked to the front of the room as all eyes stared at me. She pinned the pink cardboard tail to the back of my dress. If we had stayed in the classroom, it would have been bad enough; but, oh no, that day our class was scheduled to visit the upper grades.

I couldn't believe it. I was the student who never got in trouble. I stood in line with my fellow students and hoped that nobody would notice my tail. No other girl had a tail pinned to the back of her dress and so of course, I was different. I felt my cheeks burn and I fought the tears. I refused to cry and I willed myself invisible. Even though I was embarrassed, I was also angry at the teacher. Our first grade glass visited both of the classrooms where Walt and Susie were. I thought for sure that they saw me. The dreaded tail swayed against the back of my knees.

After school, I tried to tell Susie and Walt about the tail but they just laughed at me. They yelled, "Stop lying," as they pedaled away on their bikes, leaving me to walk home alone. I figured since they didn't believe me, my parents wouldn't either so I never told them.

We lived nine miles from Mexico and my school had many Mexican students. Before school one day, a few of my Mexican classmates and I played on the jungle gym. As we watched some white children playing off in the distance, my brown-skinned friends suddenly looked at me and asked, "*What* are you?"

Their question puzzled me. I thought I was "white" like my other peers but obviously I was wrong. Dad was white and Mom was of Lebanese descent. I always thought of Mom as "white." I knew we weren't Mexican so their question made me feel strange. I was much darker than my mother or any of my family due to genetics and my perpetual tan in the Texas sun. I couldn't answer their blunt question but I began to realize my Middle Eastern background separated me. I didn't define people by the color of their skin but I guess they did. Both white and Mexican students teased and rejected me.

Adding to my sense of being different was the story of my birth which always seemed weird to me. Every time I asked about my birth, this story was repeated. It went something like this. My mother had me in a hospital in San Antonio. According to her, the nurse brought me into her room, looked at her, and walked back out with me still in her arms. She came in a second time, looked at the bracelet with my name and then at my mother's bracelet with her name, and proceeded to walk out of the room again. The third time she came back in, looked at both bracelets, looked down at me, handed me to my mother and said, "Well, I *guess* she's yours."

Around age seven, I learned that when I was conceived, I had had a twin. This baby died in the womb. When I asked about my twin, I was always told, "It was just a piece of flesh, no larger than a quarter." I never made a connection about a "baby" being any bigger than that. I didn't ask more questions but I continued to wonder. *Why does a woman get so fat? Who could get excited over that small a thing? This baby is like the size of an insect.* Consequently, I never experienced all the maternal desires for children that so many girls seemed to naturally possess.

Babies terrified me from the standpoint that I was afraid of life and death. I thought if I accidentally dropped a baby, it would die. I liked reading the children's books but I didn't ever think about having children. I wanted the "Prince Charming" romance of being in love and those Disney movies and fairy tales always ended, "And they lived happily ever after." None of those romantic characters had children. I didn't grow up around babies. I was only around babies three times before age eighteen. The women I knew were career-minded or elderly.

Once we stopped at a Mexican market. Dad said we only had a short time, but we could each choose one wooden puppet. It was unusual to get presents. I knew I had to choose quickly. So I grabbed the first puppet that caught my eye. It was a colorful, war-painted male Indian puppet.

"Is that the one you want?" Dad asked.

"Yes, Daddy," I said excitedly.

"Are you sure that's what you want?"

"Yes, Daddy, I'm sure."

"Okay, then." He sighed.

He didn't seem happy and I didn't know why. But he allowed me my choice.

Within a few minutes, Susie showed Dad her choice. She held a pretty, Mexican girl dancer with two long black braids, dressed in a white peasant blouse and a long green skirt, trimmed in gold. As I looked at her puppet, I wanted it. It even looked like me. I was so disappointed because in my excitement to choose a puppet, I never saw the other aisle and I didn't realize that there were more puppets to choose from. I only saw the aisle with male puppets – Indians, musicians with guitars and matadors with red capes. George and Walt chose the other two styles. I pleaded with Dad to change my choice but he was firm.

"Susie chose that one. You already chose the Indian."

I pleaded and cried but Dad held a strict view about his concept of "fairness." All four of us were to be treated equally in life, as much as possible. Dad refused to change his mind about the Indian puppet.

I kept the Indian. I grew afraid of it and tore out its black hair. The Indian's face was angry and painted for war. I didn't like the way it looked, especially in my semi-dark closet. I wanted to destroy it. I didn't want to remember that I made the wrong choice and if I hadn't been hasty, I could have had a pretty puppet like Susie's.

That experience left a deep impression on me. *How was I ever to know what choice to make if I didn't know all the options and once made, could I ever change my mind?* I grew indecisive and constantly afraid of making the wrong choice.

Whether intentionally or not, I grew up with a sense that "choice" had very little to do with life and specifically with God. God was Sovereign and that meant there was no such thing as choice. This view of God formed early. Though He was good, amazing, loving and all things wonderful, in my mind, because He was God, He decided everything that happened to us. In fact, even God had no choice but to love everybody. If He didn't, He wouldn't be God. It didn't occur to me until years later that no one was holding a gun to God's head saying, "You MUST love them."

The invisible enemy of God used my life experiences early on to forge a wall of rejection, fear, and abandonment. But as seeds take time to ripen, so my life's unfolding drama and trauma took time to develop.

As a child, I was ignorant of any spiritual reality that wasn't God or angels. In my mind, the devil was in hell alone, waiting for people to get there. I knew nothing of a demonic realm. Angels had no place on Earth — just in Heaven. This painfully distorted theological view left me exposed to many lies of the enemy and much heartbreak to come.

Prayer was a simple part of my life. I didn't pray out loud but I silently talked to God a lot. I knew, with my childlike faith, that He could do anything. He was God. Nothing was too hard for Him. I even had evidence of His great power. One Saturday, my brother Walt got lost. He bicycled all day and by nightfall, he still hadn't returned. We were so afraid. I prayed so hard that God would keep him safe and bring him home. God answered our prayers. We later found out that he was more than ten miles away from home! Late at night, Walt finally stopped at a gas station and a man gave him some food and called the police.

The next day Dad and Walt retraced the route as they drove back to get his bike. They were amazed that in places Walt had ridden only feet away from deep canals. In the darkness, had he had ridden closer, he could have fallen in and drowned.

This experience only strengthened my childlike faith that God answered prayer and that He always listened and cared. I knew that He watched out for Walt and that God helped him to come home. I was so happy on the inside. I knew God had answered my prayers. There was no one else like Him.

I had another time when God answered my prayer when I cried out to Him. Often I played outside and one day I pretended that the "spies" chased me. I ducked into a tiny closet, big enough to hold a few garden rakes, and the door jammed. I tried to get out. I started to panic. I screamed for help and my dog constantly barked. No one heard me. Soaked in sweat, I crouched in the dark closet and sobbed uncontrollably. In desperation, I cried, "Oh God, help me! Open this door, please!"

Once more, I wrenched the knob and the door flung open. I gulped in fresh air and welcomed the sunshine. I thanked God. It felt great to be outside, free from the closed in feeling of the dark closet. I knew once again that God was near me and that He *did* listen and care.

Even though there were deep experiences of God's love and care, there were also places in my heart that were deeply wounded and that I couldn't talk about to anyone. The damage from being abused and left to figure out all my emotions by myself was traumatic and affected me in some unusual ways. Everything I saw reminded me of private parts. The first grade train of alphabet letters above the chalkboard, glared at me. I was sickened! There it was again. Lines and circles—every letter needed either a line or a circle and sometimes both. I couldn't get away from the images. It was as if all of life was a reminder of sticks going into holes and I hated it.

I looked at all the lined-up brown paper bag lunches. Someone had sprawled a strange "W" with two minuscule O's at the base of the points. On further examination, I discovered someone had drawn a pair of breasts on the bag. Ordinary objects, all composed of lines and circles, crashed into my shattered and scarred conscience as life reeked of saturated "perverseness." My brokenness left me embittered against anything of beauty or creativity. I never told anyone what I saw because I thought that my perceptions were true and that everybody saw exactly what I did. Because no one ever explained that the elements of art consisted of circles and lines my reality assaulted my eyes only with sexual images. I constantly replayed painful memories accompanied by fear, rejection and punishment.

A few years after I was abused, Dad called me into his room. "Ruth Mary, I just wanted to tell you that Mr. R. is dead." Utter silence. *Good, I hope he's in hell.* Instantly, I felt horrible and guilty. *We as Christians are supposed to love everybody like Jesus does. I shouldn't hate anyone so much that I would want them in hell.*

Relief flooded my heart that the abuser was dead. Dad continued speaking, "What he did to you... he probably thought that you were his girlfriend." I didn't say anything but I thought, *"Yuck! Is that what happens with a boyfriend?"* Then I was angry because it felt like Dad didn't blame this man for what he did to me. Dad said, "He didn't know any better." The patterns of rejection towards Dad were only more firmly established because of his explanation. I knew that someone had to be blamed because touching private parts was wrong and since it wasn't the abuser's fault, then it must have been *my* fault.

Nevertheless, from that point on until I was sixteen, I had no more conscious memory of being abused or of the incident with the janitor. My mind repressed anything associated with my abuse as I fully entered the Denial stage of grief because the trauma was too much to bear consciously. It was as if since the abuser was finally dead, I didn't have any more reason to be afraid of him or to remember the janitor. Even though I didn't consciously remember the abuse, the consequent damage to my self-esteem and broken will continued to wreak havoc in my relationships, perceptions and emotions.

The enemy used a true life event to distort and pervert my relationship with Dad by haunting me with a consistent dream. Fear paralyzed me as the nightmare brought such crushing torment. Subconsciously, I re-lived the abuse from the man at the daycare but since my mind had blocked that event, it only surfaced in my sleep.

Though nothing ever happened sexually in the nightmare, the intense fear was so great that I knew if I didn't wake up that "my father" would sexually abuse me. In those feverish moments, Dad wore a pair of brown pants and chased me. He acted like he was insane and when I ran to my mother, she laughed at me. This dream seemed so real and I couldn't figure out why it wouldn't go away.

I awoke screaming and ran to my Mother's side of the bed. I never told either of them what I dreamed. I either crawled into bed beside her or I stood at her bedside. She gently tried to coax me to let Dad comfort and reassure me. Even though Dad spoke calmly and lovingly in the darkness, I was too tormented by the twisted, distorted nightmares to trust him. Instead, I climbed out of their bed and returned to my own.

After a while, they thought I was just trying to get attention so they locked their door or just ignored me. I learned not to scream but just go to the bathroom, turn the light on and calm myself down. Many times to my embarrassment I woke up only to realize I had wet the bed. Sometimes I stood in the bathroom with the light on for several minutes until my breathing settled and I relaxed enough to go back to bed.

In their defense, I never told them what the nightmares were until I was out of college. It was only then that I heard the truth. One Halloween at a different church, when I was four and we lived in another part of Texas, Dad dressed up in brown pants and acted like a mad man. He chased me and I was terrified and tried to run to Mom but she was laughing because she knew, as did my siblings, that Dad was dressed up and acting. The abuse morphed with the real life event and was used by the enemy to torment me from the time I was five until I was twenty-one years old.

At seven years old, I loved to play barefoot out in the lush green yard. It was a beautiful day in the warm sunshine. I gazed up at the light blue sky with its floating wisps of clouds. My thoughts wandered as I spoke out loud. *"Jesus, You did miracles of feeding the five thousand and of healing all the people. Do You still do miracles today? That would be so neat if those things still happened."*

Into my reverie, came a sudden shrieking of metal. I turned around in time to see two cars crashed in front of my house. One car rested onto the sidewalk about twenty feet from where I stood. I rushed inside and got my parents. But by the time I came back out, the other car was slowly driving away. I stood at a distance as a strange woman sat on the sidewalk and wept uncontrollably. I felt awful. The thought of causing an accident filled me with fear and I made inner vows. *I never want to drive because I could hurt someone or even kill them*!

Fear wrapped around me like a poisoned vine. I had had nothing to do with that accident but in my mind, I had to be responsible. It was unfounded guilt and false accusation but I couldn't understand those emotions at the time. The enemy's schemes of destruction were being firmly planted in my heart with each event of rejection, torment and confusion.

Chapter 3

Sticks & Stones and Twisted Theology

I have always been a word person. Even as a child, I took what people said quite seriously. Whoever said that "sticks and stones may break my bones but words will never hurt me," obviously didn't live in my world. I knew that phrase intellectually. However, realistically, words did hurt, sting and bruise my heart. I would need ample amounts of grace, love and affirmation poured into those wounded places before they could even begin to heal.

When I started first grade, I had to go to a speech therapist. I sat in the school library aware that I was in a special session and that I was different. I pronounced my "s's" more like "*th*'s" and other letters were equally hard for me to say properly. The pretty female therapist spoke soothingly to me, "I need you to practice swallowing like I showed you every night at least one hundred times. You currently swallow backwards. You'll also need to say "la la's" like I showed you twenty-five times at night. These are your exercises. Here are your tongue twisters that you must practice saying every night as well."

The hardest was "She sells seashells down by the seashore." I had to consciously and slowly think about each word to get it right. I know that the words, "specific", "shoulder" and "soldier" were also difficult for me.

It didn't make sense to me that I "swallowed backwards" since I ate and drank and "swallowed" my food like everybody else. I certainly didn't vomit so I didn't understand how I could possibly swallow backwards, but apparently I did. I tried to change my speech patterns. The need for these exercises didn't seem to last long, whether because I gave up or the speech therapist only visited our school one time. My parents were convinced that if I didn't get professional help, I would never be able to speak properly so they took me to an orthodontist who fitted me with a permanent metal, two-pronged mouthpiece. As I touched my tongue to the sharp points he said, "When you do that, stick your tongue on the roof of your mouth, where it is normally supposed to be."

It was somewhat painful. I learned to ignore the physical pain, even when my tongue was scratched and scraped from the prongs. My peers expanded their insults from "witch" due to my black hair and my laugh that even my mother said resembled "more of a cackle," to "vampire," complements of my "fangs." The pain of hurtful words was not as easy to ignore.

Being a Preacher's kid came with the unspoken, hidden expectation that my halo must always be perfectly in place on my head. Most of the time, mine seemed to dangle at my ankles. Other church members faltered or stumbled, but our family was supposed to be "perfect." I saw my mother that way for many years. She never seemed to do anything wrong and she exuded impeccable manners and flawless grammar. Whenever she would start to get frustrated with me, she would stop, then speak quietly and without emotion—"That's enough."

In my child's mind, she might as well have said, "Shut up!" because that's how it felt. She never used profanity and she didn't actually say, "Shut up." She was controlled, unlike me who often lost my temper, shouted and cried. She never apologized for anything (because she didn't seem to do anything wrong) and my life couldn't compete with her "perfection."

It was so hard to relate to her. She shared almost nothing about her childhood. It only made her more distant in my heart. I knew that God was perfect and that I wasn't. It seemed that somehow my parents were, though.

Even though I experienced hurt in their actions or words, they never offered an apology. It was as if because Dad and Mom were my parents, they were the authority and as a child, I was always wrong.

Many times there were corrections of "Ruth Mary, you shouldn't do that. Oh, Ruth Mary, we don't act like that." The emphasis Mom put on behavior was in relation to being the "family name" and not that "We're Christians," or about pleasing God. It felt like our social status as the preacher's family had to stay at "near perfection." The pressures to always be "good" and maybe even "better" were fraught with fears of failure, fear of mistakes and fear of what others might think about me or our family. In our home, it didn't seem like an atmosphere of freedom most of the time.

I knew that God was the Highest Being in the Universe and to disobey Him was serious and sinful. Because of the ways that I was treated in the years following the abuse, everything associated with God and church began to drastically change in my mind. This terrible distortion of God was more firmly fixed by the tormenting nightmare and the wedge that the enemy had jammed between my parents and me. Love was lost between us. Duty, obligation, performance and religion seemed to be the most important reasons for good, moral behavior. Obedience was based on fear of punishment and shame, not on relationship or a love for God and a desire to please Him.

This Creator of the Universe was no longer the God of love, affection, kindness and relationship. I now treated all of that with contempt. I knew the Ten Commandments. I was so full of the "fear" of God that I didn't think I could get any more afraid of Him. Once at supper, I wanted to share something exciting that had happened at school. I thought my father had finished praying and eagerly jumped into my story. When I realized the mistake, I ran from the table, went and hid in the dining room curtains and bawled.

Dad tried to unwind me from the folds of material but I circled and curled them tighter around me. Eventually my tears stopped; I came out of the curtains and sat down silently to eat. There was no discussion on my part and I am not sure that anyone even knew why I had had such an emotional outburst.

My heart wrestled and tried to comprehend— *How could I have possibly interrupted the prayer to the God of the Universe? Talk about rudeness. It was one thing to interrupt a mere adult human, but to insult the Highest Being...He must be so ashamed of me.*

I imagined God to be like the big head on "The Wizard of Oz," with a loud, booming voice and nostrils that emanated fire. I quivered before Him like the cowardly lion. It was as if He bellowed, "I Am the Almighty God! Bring Me the broom of the devil," and I shot through the window of the Throne Room to flee from His awesome Presence.

Halloween was not viewed as a holiday that had any negative spiritual connections so I went to my school's Halloween carnival. At the fish pond, I won a tiny green plastic frog. I liked this toy and for a number of days I played with it. Then the thought hit me, *I like it so much, I must have made it a god. I must be worshiping it. Didn't the Egyptians worship frogs and God sent plagues on them for their terrible sins?* I threw the frog away. I learned not to "like" anything too much because then it would become an idol.

My father did not preach this kind of God. On the contrary, he forever preached about a God of love and mercy but I couldn't put *"holy"* into anything practical. Simple past-times and pleasures always held potential danger of idolatry—whether that was my desire to be a famous actress, singer, dancer, or in later years, a poet and writer. Dad told me once, "Fame and fortune aren't always good things. Many good people have been led astray by having too much money. Some people, when they become famous, even turn their backs on God."

When I heard these words, they dashed my hopes of ever becoming famous. I should never want to aspire to be someone excellent enough to be recognized because then I might walk in pride and if I did, God wouldn't be pleased with me. I came to the conclusion that it was enough to be a "nobody" for God because then I never had to be afraid of turning my back on Him. It also seemed to mean that making too much money was bad and so how could I ever be rich? What would be "too much money"?

For Dad, it seemed that we always had "too much." Nightly he prayed and thanked God for our food and for how fortunate we were because so many people, especially children, all over the world had so little. I used to get so angry inside and feel guilty. It made it seem that we were stingy and should give even more of our toys away. I never felt like I could be happy and enjoy what I had. By comparison to my peers, we were poor. We could have qualified for free school lunches but Dad was always of the opinion that if we could afford it, we should pay because other people were far more needy than we were.

Dad's childhood was a broken one. His father drowned while teaching some boys to swim and my grandmother was pregnant with Dad when she got the news about her husband's death. She eventually mentally divorced herself from reality. My dad lived with her until he was nine. Then he lived in an orphanage until he was sixteen and his mother lived in a mental home for the rest of her life.

Dad knew that there was no such person as Santa Claus. At Christmas, a small group of church folk came to the orphanage. They sang carols and gave a few gifts to the children. So, with his background of having virtually "nothing," of course, our family always had "too much."

Our home was not one in which we talked much about private matters. I don't recall Mom talking with me about changes in a girl's body but I do remember that Susie told me about them. Whether Mom asked her to do that, I don't know, but Susie was closer to me than Mom.

One night, I listened to the news and heard a new word.

"Dad, what does *rape* mean?"

"Go ask your mother."

I walked out in the kitchen. "Mom, what does *rape* mean?"

"Look it up in the dictionary."

That was her typical answer when I wanted to know something. I pulled out the huge, maroon dictionary and read the definition to myself. I already knew about sex from the sticks and holes, Mom's explanations and the medical diagrams. I figured that rape must mean sex between a black man and a white woman since the news said, "a black man raped a white woman." I didn't tell anyone what I thought; I assumed I was right and since my mother had no desire to continue the conversation I never shared my wrong definition with her.

My parents were always interested in furthering our education so we had opportunities to watch Audubon movies, read National

Geographic magazines, tour museums and visit various historical places. We were surrounded by good books; classics lined the bookcases on the walls of our home. Mom taught all of us how to read before we ever started school so we were always ahead of our peers when it came to reading, vocabulary, comprehension and communication. The world of books fascinated me and I could spend hours in the library or reading at home.

My uncle took our entire family to see *The Sound of Music* in the theater. It was the first movie I ever watched and it became one of my all-time favorite movies. I wanted to be an actress, play guitar and ballroom dance just like Julie Andrews. Eventually I wanted to become a nun. I thought of how close "Maria" was to God and that drew me. I had no idea what "being a nun" fully meant and again, I never told anyone that, either.

I continued to form my own ideas about God, religion, money and the future. The words people spoke took deep root in my heart. I viewed these perceptions as correct and since I lived in a private world, no one interfered or knew what ideas and concepts I had begun to develop and believe.

Chapter 4

Crumbled Popularity — Ugly and Unloved

*W*e moved from Texas when I was in fourth grade. Although the two-pronged mouth piece and the teasing of "witch" and "vampire" didn't follow me to West Virginia, in my heart I had begun to believe I was ugly, unloved and unworthy of being loved. In West Virginia, I was in for deeper challenges to my tattered sense of self-worth.

I was weird enough since I moved from the South to the North. One of my classmates politely took time to answer my questions in a detailed manner. It made me feel special so I told him, "You speak very nicely."

Some of the other students laughed and said, "Haven't you ever seen a black person before?"

I hadn't or at least I couldn't remember ever seeing someone black but color never bothered me. He had a nice voice and I was so used to being rejected in Texas that it felt good to have someone talk to me. But then I was embarrassed because no one seemed to understand that I was being polite and my compliment had no bearing on the color of his skin.

Another boy taunted me, "*What* are you?"

I chose to stay silent and withdraw into my cocoon. My first day at school and already I was rejected. I didn't look white but I didn't look black either, so once again, I was the "odd one." I felt so different from everybody and I definitely looked different as I stood in my thin yellow cotton dress with knee high white socks and laced shoes. Those pale colors only emphasized my dark tan.

At the end of the day, the fourth grade teacher reminded my neighbor, "Oh, Anthony, don't forget to walk Ruth home."

There were a few snickers and then another boy piped up, "Hey Anthony, are you gonna get some?"

The tension in the room was thick and nothing else was said but it felt dirty. I didn't know what he meant but I had a feeling it wasn't nice. I was ignorant of the sexual innuendo but it was only a short while before I clearly understood all the sex talk. The sexual knowledge and "experiences" of my peers seemed to be "normal" in this new place.

Anthony walked me home but I was so shy, nervous and used to walking by myself that I didn't walk beside him. I merely followed him home at a distance of about ten feet. I never talked to him and even when he walked me to school the next day, I still followed behind. After only a few days, I memorized the roads and I walked by myself for a long time after that.

I liked Anthony and thought he was cute. A lot of girls did. He had a girlfriend in fourth grade but I had a huge crush on him. In the neighborhood on the weekends, all the kids played in their yards and sometimes I joined them. I was still shy but somehow I opened up to get to know Anthony.

Over time my crush got so intense that one day I walked home and ran up close to him and said, "I love you, Anthony." He quickly dashed my romantic endeavors and flatly stated, "Ruth, I love Julie." Though I was inwardly crushed, I didn't let go of my infatuation and I held onto hope that our friendship would eventually develop into a dating one.

By the time I was in sixth grade, I knew all the sexual innuendo that was a daily part of life at school. I knew that rape wasn't about color but about forced sex. It was one of the worst things to ever happen to someone and it was so full of shame and ugliness that even talking about it seemed wrong.

The teachers either ignored all the sexual language or the students talked in places and tones where they weren't heard. I found the minds of my peers saturated with sex. Even simple comments could be twisted and distorted to be perverted.

Even though I didn't consciously remember what happened to me in Texas at the daycare, in one strange and unusual conversation as Anthony sat in my yard, I told him that I had been molested. His face was strangely wicked. "Did he rape you?"

Sickened, disgusted and repulsed, I vociferously retorted, "No!"

Again, I pushed the traumatic memories deep into my subconscious and once again forgot that first violation of my will. Not only did I forget what happened in Texas but I forgot that I had told Anthony that I had been molested. Anthony heard those words and the enemy of my soul planted seeds in Anthony's heart for the future. Anthony and I spent lots of time together as he talked in my yard. That development of our friendship took place over the course of a few years and I genuinely gave my heart to him. I reveled in the fantasy that someday we would date, get married and live happily ever after. Anthony became my world and my only future.

The entire friendship was a scheme of the enemy to plant seeds of abuse where I believed I had made a special friend. Those seeds took three years to germinate in his heart and the fruit produced was deadly poison in my life.

The first week at my new school I had a life-changing experience. The teacher set up a filmstrip and gave me the privilege of reading the captions since I was the new student. Instead of reading I said, "I don't see any words."

My classmates' heads jerked up as they stared at me and silence filled the air. My teacher fiddled with the knobs and asked me, "Can you read it now?"

I was embarrassed and anxious. "No, I can't see any words." She adjusted the filmstrip but no matter what she did, I didn't see any words. Finally, she asked Anthony to read the filmstrip and he rattled off the sentence without hesitation. I was devastated. I couldn't see anything that he read. Shock and deafening silence filled the room as I tried not to panic. She sent me to the office and I tried to read the eye chart. The uneasy stillness filled the office as the school secretary asked me for my father's phone number. I gave it to her and Dad came to the school and took me home. Within a short time, I had my first pair of glasses. I was never asked to read the filmstrip again and for a short time the kids weren't even sure if I could read.

In fifth grade, I became more popular and was voted President of my class. We made some of our own rules. One of them was that there would be no name-calling. As I walked home one day with a girl in my class, I told her about a boy in our class and I referred to him as "Shaggy." I liked his long, blond hair and the way he flicked his hair out of his face. He wasn't sloppy with his hair or his appearance. I had a small crush on him and I made up this affectionate term to express my feelings for him. I thought there was nothing wrong with what I said to her and I didn't mean anything negative by it. She became more agitated with me until I finally stopped talking. I didn't have any idea why I bothered her so much unless she had a crush on him too. I didn't tell her that I had a crush on him. I guess I imagined that she knew I liked him.

The next day, a strange class meeting was called. The conversation that I'd had off the school grounds, while walking home was presented to the entire class. I was accused of "name calling" and of being a hypocrite. I was devastated by how my classmates reacted. At the end of the meeting, I was impeached. It was my senior year before I ran for any office again.

Music was integral in our home. My parents encouraged Susie and Walt to join the band. Learning the discipline of playing an instrument was deemed a worthy pursuit. Susie played the flute and Walt, the trombone. I wanted to learn to play the French horn. The first band instructor I had required that I learn to play the trumpet first. Christmas came and my parents gave me a trumpet. I was sad because I had never wanted to play the trumpet and now I knew that I had to continue because they had spent money on it.

I wanted to become a cheerleader but my father insisted, "No daughter of mine is going to wear those short skirts." He never even gave me permission to try out. So, once again, I complied. Complied is an inaccurate word because I rebelled internally time and time again. I never verbally communicated what I wanted because I didn't have the emotional energy to combat the strong personality of my mother or the seemingly unmovable stance of my father.

I was teased about my glasses and called, "Four eyes." No one could see my eyes because my mother purchased tinted lenses that got dark in the sun, so that I could get a pair of sunglasses for "free." The problem was that they always stayed dark. Then in junior high, I got braces. Additionally my orthodontist put me in headgear that went around my face. Later, he gave me headgear that looked like the skeletal insides of a football helmet. I appeared as if I had been in some major traffic accident. I hated it but I didn't have the backbone to protest.

I was verbally accosted with, "Breaker, breaker, you got your ears on?" because of the strange apparatus on my face. I endured all this silently as my parents and I existed in the same house, along with my siblings. Slowly I crumpled inside.

Daily, at the bus stop, the boys barked and howled at me because of my name, "Ruth." They found it particularly funny to bark at me like "Ruff, ruff, ruff." I hated how they treated me and often I wanted to "meow" back at them, but I never did. I cringed and tried not to cry as this was their daily "bullying" of me.

I hated my name. I hated everything about me and I hated not being liked. Finally I quit waiting for the bus and I walked over a mile to the school. Because it was located on the "other" side of town I had to choose either passing a barking dog or crossing in front of the local beer joint, typified by a few loitering drunk men. Both choices filled me with fear.

Once I finally got the braces off, my orthodontist insisted I wear a new kind of retainer made of hard rubber. I had to bite down on it for eight to twelve hours a day. When I asked the orthodontist if the retainer could be worn at night, he said, "No, it needs the pressure of biting for the teeth to stay in place." Although other patients had clear ones, I ended up with a solid black one.

As I look back, I'm sure the black retainer was probably cheaper, as were the tinted sunglasses. Mom was always trying to save money and I guess our preferences weren't considered. Susie, four years older and more assertive, simply refused to wear the black rubber retainer. Though I hated wearing it, I didn't argue. My peers now added a new name to their arsenal of insults — "Sh— Mouth."

I had such low self-esteem and I felt so ugly and unattractive. Mom said I was lazy and in some ways she was right. I threw my clothes on the closet floor or shoved them under my bed. I never kept things neat and tidy, except I always made my bed every morning. Susie's side of the room was always orderly and clean so I felt like a slob and sometimes was even called one.

On the other hand, my inner life was fighting defeat. From daily being bombarded with all these names, I eventually began to believe that I was ugly and unlovable. To be labeled "a dog" by my peers made me believe I was not worthy of love. I interpreted their actions to say, "You are so ugly, no human would even want you. No boyfriend will ever be interested in you."

The mirror reflected all the changes of puberty with large pimples, oily hair and now with everything else, my facial hair began to darken until I had a painfully visible mustache. The jest became, "Ruth is really a man in a woman's body."

There was one other girl who had a mustache but she discreetly got rid of it. I never knew there were creams that removed facial hair. Mom brushed away my concern about my mustache and said liltingly, "Oh, Ruth Mary, it's such a little thing."

I wore hand-me-downs and as a result, many of the clothes were not complimentary to my skin tone. One day I had on tan pants with a beige turtleneck and I was outside when my mother stepped out on the porch and called, "Ruth Mary, get in this house immediately!" Her tone of voice was sharp and loud which was unusual. Her face contorted in such a disapproving glare. I was clueless as to what I had done now. As I ran to the porch, she looked at me, "Oh, good gracious! I thought you were out there, *naked*!" I was hurt by her preposterous accusation since I was a teenager, but obviously tans were not colors that flattered me.

Mom often told me, "You look sick without your make-up." She meant that I needed some blush and lipstick but because of my low self-esteem, I interpreted her words to mean, "You are ugly." I used to imagine that if I ever did get married, I would get up early, wash my face, brush my teeth, put on my make-up and crawl back into bed.

Mom tried to get me to think about the future and my domestic responsibilities. "What are you going to cook for your husband — TV dinners?"

"I'm going to marry a chef and he'll cook." What she didn't know was that I took her words into my heart and the enemy plunged the darts into the already deep wounds and maniacally twisted them to further inflict damage, pain and torture.

Quite often, I stood in front of the mirror, either talking to myself, singing, or just looking at my reflection. One time I made up a song. "I love me, I love me, I love me." Susie and Walt remarked disgustedly, "Ruth Mary, you're so vain." I didn't really believe what I sang but I so longed for someone to say the words and for me to believe that they meant them.

I discounted compliments. I couldn't believe that people were sincere. I felt that all compliments were only lies or manipulation. The daily barrage of insults confirmed what I had come to believe about myself. I was ugly. Because I believed all the negative words there was no room for any compliment to take root.

Chapter 5

Poetry, Peer Pressure
and a Ruined Reputation

round age twelve I began to write poetry. I was good with words and it was nice to have a healthy way to express my feelings. Every year our family put out a newsletter for Christmas in which my mother highlighted the achievements of each child. I read the accolades of my siblings—how well they were doing in school, the awards they had received, the honor's courses they were enrolled in, their musical abilities and talents.

Then I read with hopeful anticipation what she had written about me. "Ruth Mary is 13, with all the teenage symptoms— of spending hours on the phone talking about boys, of not wanting to be associated with her Dad and Mom and we long for the day when she will no longer treat us as strangers, etc."

It shocked me and cut deeply. Even Dad came to my defense. "Why would you write that? Why didn't you talk about her poetry?" Gratefully, that was the rough draft and it was revised but as far as I was concerned, the damage was done. When I read those words, I believed that was truly what my mother felt towards me. I felt rejected and that she was ashamed of me. It was as if all the misperceptions I held inside my heart and head were confirmed in those words. Though the paragraph was changed, as far as I believed, the "new" one was just for social purposes.

I gave up. Worn down by all the teasing, the insults and the seemingly constant rejection, I didn't care about being a "good Christian girl" anymore. Without ever feeling that I would be accepted and affirmed by my own family, I became desperate for attention, even if that meant losing my reputation.

Then surprisingly, in seventh grade, Anthony began to pursue me for more than a friendship. I couldn't believe it. He was good-looking, popular, a star athlete…and he noticed me. For the first time in my life, I fell in love. I worshiped the ground he walked on. I lived for his smile, his acknowledgment, his attention.

I had adored Anthony since fourth grade. We had talked in my yard for years and I believed that he liked me. In seventh grade when he wanted to make our friendship more than platonic, I was hesitant but hungry to feel loved.

Only once Anthony said, "I love you."

I retorted, "No, you don't."

"You're right. I love your body."

Even though my conscience was pricked, I still met with him. I didn't care that he had a steady girlfriend. I convinced myself that I must be special to him because he met with me even though he dated a cheerleader. I vowed to myself, *I will be his wife someday and we will live happily ever after.* I made an idol of him and refused to see his glaring abusive ways. I pretended nightly that someday we would get married and be blissfully in love for a lifetime. How deceived I was and how long it took before I saw the truth. What a toll my idolization of him cost in every area of my life.

From seventh to eighth grade, I met him in the woods or at his house and I did anything and everything to keep him happy — gave him money, let him cheat in school looking over my shoulder, allowed him to call me names and even fondle me in public and in private. I went "almost all the way" — except "technically" I was still a virgin. I wanted so much to eventually date and marry him. I gave him my money, my heart, my allegiance, my body….everything that I knew I had to give. He wore me down little by little and more and more I hated myself for it. He ruined my reputation, called me all kinds of names and used me any way he pleased.

One day, Anthony came to my house to mess around with me while my parents were gone. I didn't want him there because it was too risky but he came into the house anyway. He wanted his buddy to see him coming into my house so that Anthony's stories about me would be believed. Later that night, as was my habit I wrote about the events in my diary. A few days later, I accidentally left the small spiral notebook lying on the floor and left for school.

My parents found the diary and read it. When I got home, my mother confronted me. I was livid that they had read my diary. My mother told me, "You go upstairs and tell your father these are all lies. These are dreams you made up."

I started to protest, "But Mom, those aren't lies! Those things really happened."

"I know they did, Ruth Mary. I know how wicked you are...but your father is crushed. He doesn't believe that you would do those things. So you go upstairs right now and you tell him those are dreams that you made up and those things never happened." *Her stinging words made me feel like I was the worst sinner that had ever lived.*

"You want me to lie to him?!" I was incredulous.

"You will go upstairs now and not another word. Do you hear me?"

I couldn't believe that she wanted me to directly lie to Dad but she was firm. I felt so angry at her for reading my diary and then for demanding that I lie about what was in it.

She was adamant. I walked upstairs into his room. He was teary-eyed and shattered. "Dad, the things I wrote were just dreams. They really didn't happen."

"Really, Ruth Mary?"

"Yeah." I didn't stay around to talk anymore. It felt weird that my mother insisted that I lie to him but I did what she had ordered.

Ironically, a few days before the diary incident, Anthony had this conversation with me. I had been so betrayed by him that I hadn't written this down yet. It was too painful and I didn't want to believe it.

"So, are you going to 'go all the way' this time, like you promised?"

"I can't. I am so sorry, Anthony. I have to save that until I'm married."

"You're just a tease. This is the third time you have promised me you would and you still won't. You know if you turn me down this time, it's over, don't you?"

With my heart cracking I trembled, "Yes, I know."

I kept my virginity and he walked away—and out of my life—for awhile.

My heart shattered in a million pieces.

All the name-calling was bad enough but the ruined reputation, the loss of respect and the low self-esteem combined to make life a living hell for me. I needed to be known for something, anything. I wasn't an assertive, strong, opinionated girl like my sister nor was I able to compete with my brother – the nerdy, geeky genius.

Anthony had been my world and I had stooped lower than I would've ever dreamed. As a defense and self-protection, I became the most sarcastic, cutting, bitter, rebellious, flirtatious girl. I hardened my heart so that no one was going to get to me again. I epitomized the easy, cheap girl consumed with sensuality and sexuality. Provocative clothing, lewd jokes and endless sexual bantering were my daily hallmarks.

It was awful! I woke up every day plagued with suicidal thoughts. I wanted out of the terrible pit I was in but I didn't see any hope. It was excruciating to attend church as the preacher's kid. I tried to block out everything Dad said as I let my bitterness seethe. But when we sang certain hymns, I fought to hold back the tears.

I knew all too well, I had blown it. I couldn't go to God and tell Him that I was ignorant. I knew what I had been living was a life of deception, full of sin. I was miserable and my only defense was to keep getting harder. I couldn't afford to let people know I had real feelings so I learned to stifle them.

I was a tremendous loner who wrote poetry that was dark, suicidal, depressing or the other extreme of romantic fantasies. I also wrote for pure joy about beauty, creation and anything I wanted to. Poetry was my one place where I dared to express deep-felt emotions and it was something that made me unique. No one else would or could ever write exactly like I did.

I went to church camp every summer for a week from the time I was in fourth grade through eighth grade. Even though I was only at camp about a week, inevitably God met me. I was several hours away from my town and no one knew my family. Most of them didn't know that I was a preacher's kid or if they did, it didn't matter to them. I cried, wept, prayed and rededicated myself to God. I basked in His love and forgiveness and thought that I had changed. But when I returned home, the temptations were just as strong and the same culture of sexuality, popularity, vying for attention, struggle to not get hurt all bombarded me and once school started again, I was back to the "old me." I felt desolate and full of despair. I knew enough of the truth of God and felt miserable while living in sin. The guilt overwhelmed me at times.

Chapter 6

Prejudice and Fragmented Faith

arie was my best friend. She was overweight and funny. I adopted her mom as if she were my own. My mother always seemed old to me, because she was ten years older than my friends' mothers. Marie's mom smiled and laughed when I was around. She seemed to like my company. Marie was an only child and I didn't have to compete with her siblings or anyone in her home.

My mother was a teacher in another town and I rarely spent any time with her. In Texas after she began working, it always seemed that after we ate supper she spent the evening focused on her schoolwork, grading papers and preparing lessons. She talked about her students but they were just names to me and in a lot of ways, I was jealous of them. She spoke so proudly of some of them. Many times I felt that her students were more important to her than me.

I thrived on my friendship with Marie and her mom. She treated me like a second daughter and to Marie, I was like a sister she never had. We liked one another a lot but the more I hung around Anthony, the more distant I made myself from Marie and her mom. I was ashamed of what I did with Anthony but I didn't want to give him up, either.

One Christmas season while shopping together, Marie showed her mother a beautiful ring. "Mom, do you think Grandma would buy this for me? I *am* her only grandchild."

"Marie, I don't know. How much is it?"

The saleslady responded, "It's five."

I got so excited and I discreetly took Marie's mom aside. "Mrs. T., I can buy that for Marie. I have five dollars in my purse."

Her eyes smiled at me and she gently spoke, "Ruth, it costs five hundred dollars, not five dollars."

Five hundred dollars! I was flabbergasted. We didn't have that kind of money in our home and certainly not for a piece of jewelry. Once again, the reality of our financial status shocked me compared to many of my classmates. I was nowhere close to being in their league.

Marie had a crush on a certain basketball player in the same way that I did towards Anthony. Only with Marie, she was only obsessed with talking about him. While she merely dreamed of dates with Jay, I actively made my dreams happen after school, in the woods and other deserted places. She started smoking and I knew that I wanted none of that. Though I didn't see the hypocrisy in my choices, I knew that smoking and drinking were bad, even illegal. No one ever came to the school to talk with us about the dangers of sex, like they faithfully did every year about drugs, alcohol and smoking. In fact, nobody ever said anything about petting, making out, or anything sexual. We all just knew that it was embarrassing if you got caught.

One time, Marie smoked inside our house. I insisted that she shouldn't but she brushed aside my concerns. Marie was in the bathroom when Mom walked in the door. The smell of cigarette smoke wafted in the house.

Mom interrogated me immediately. "Ruth Mary, *YOU* have been smoking!"

"I have not!" I forcefully denied her accusation.

"Yes, you have. Don't lie to me."

"I am not lying." I stared at her through fiery, angry eyes. Neither of us was going to back down.

"Let me smell your breath."

I furiously breathed heavily in her face, outraged that she would continue to accuse me of smoking. Satisfied that I didn't have cigarette breath, she said nothing. Marie stepped out of the bathroom and admitted her guilt. Mom was deeply saddened and her tone became soft toward her as she said, "Oh, Marie, you shouldn't do that. Your mother would be so disappointed and ashamed."

My mother's tone changed as I knew it would. She never seemed to talk to anyone the way that she talked to me. She was compassionate and kind and genuinely concerned about Marie. Only after Marie left the house, did my mother do something extremely unusual. She actually apologized to me!

"I'm sorry."

I was shocked and moved by her genuine sadness at accusing me of smoking. I spoke gently as well and also apologized to her. It was one of the few times ever in my teenage years that we were nice to one another.

We talked briefly about my concern for Marie and her smoking habit. Marie's mother smoked and I guess that made it harder for Marie not to smoke. I did not want Marie to make choices she might later regret and I wanted her to be "good." I knew that I wasn't "good," but I only saw my own faults and sins at that time. It wasn't easy for me to see that other people had shortcomings, too.

Marie went home but she didn't stop smoking. It was only a brief amount of time before our friendship ended. She hung around people who smoked and she made other friends, people who didn't like me, so I ended our friendship. At the time, all I did was find another girl to hang around with. There were many times in the years that followed that I sincerely regretted my choice to reject Marie.

A new girl, Vicky, came to school and she seemed more mature than Marie. She had a crush on a black guy and eventually they got together. It was a secret because her Dad was prejudiced. Vicky seemed to be attracted to one guy after another. She often burned people with her words. I didn't like some people either but I never had the guts to say things to their faces, just behind their backs.

She often ended up in fights with girls. I didn't like the words people used to tease me but I had been taught, "Sticks and stones may break my bones but words will never hurt me." I cannot say that phrase was true, but it was a rule that I was supposed to learn even back in elementary school. I was supposed to "turn the other cheek" when someone insulted me. Once again Bible verses and childhood sayings were meant to keep me from getting hurt but they never did.

My heart was bitter, angry and full of self-hatred. The wounds from the ugly words bled deeply in my soul.

The emphasis of sin always seemed to be on what I did, not necessarily anything that I thought. I am sure that I saw myself as "better" than most of my peers because at times I only thought mean things but I didn't say them. I watched Vicky fight back and not just take the insults and I wished I could be that bold and courageous. I wanted to stand up for myself. Instead, I felt like chopped liver or a dog, not worthy of even being considered human.

In eighth grade, I had a class where we got to "role play." We were given a scenario— like a drug addict or a teenage pregnancy— and the next day we acted it out impromptu. We were told, "There is no right or wrong answer." I deliberately chose to play the parts of the immoral people because I wanted to experience what those situations felt like. I loved the acting side of it. I got to express myself as various characters and to shock people with my ability to "become" the character. I wasn't hindered from being on stage because of wearing glasses, since there was no stage where we needed to perform.

I always looked to see actresses wearing glasses and it seemed that I could never find any. As a result, I felt that since I wore glasses, I would never have the opportunity to be on stage. I relished the chance to act during "role playing."

What bothered me was that there was never a "set" answer— everything was acceptable since it was all relative to the situation at the time. How little did I realize the seeds of doubt that were being sown and the shift away from the foundation of God's absolute truth! It seemed that God, church, and all that religious instruction had no bearing in real life and that we could choose for ourselves. But it gnawed at my conscience since I knew that God was more than that. I knew that He created everything and that Jesus did die on the cross and that the Bible was true. But it seemed that no one who was a Christian was popular. The few Christians I did know were geeks, weird, and not well liked.

In Science class, we debated creation vs. evolution. For fun, I chose to take the evolution side. The girl on the creation side was a shy but real Christian, and she just insisted that "the Bible says so."

So, I challenged her, "What if I don't believe the Bible?"

"Well, then you're stupid."

That ended the debate and the class broke out in laughter. They all laughed but I began to question. *If she can only answer, "The Bible says so," and nothing else, then how do we prove the truth to those who don't believe the Bible?* I began to believe and embrace the humanistic viewpoints and to turn away from the faith I once had as a child. I certainly wasn't innocent any more so it became easier to pull away from God. I had a lot of fragmented ideas of "faith" but it was still what I knew. To have it so attacked and dismissed made a huge impact on my life.

I challenged all that once was held "in faith" in my childhood heart. I questioned, *Did God really love me? Or did He just "have to love me" to do the right thing?* I thought if I could hear how He felt, it would be something like this. "I am really angry at Ruth. I really am mad at her. But I can't be angry at her…because I took all My wrath and put it on Jesus." I then imagined Jesus as He leaned over to the Father and said, "Father, You took all Your anger out on Me so now you can love Ruth." It made it feel that even God didn't want to love me, but He was obligated to because Jesus took the punishment. Now the Father God "had to be happy" with me again. That convoluted perception plagued my thoughts many times.

The confusion regarding God, religion and tradition began to build inside me and I already had enough baggage that no one else knew about. I didn't talk to anyone about my issues because I was ashamed and I figured if I did try to share about my life, I would be rejected.

I joined a girls' group by invitation from Susie's best friend. I saw those older girls as pretty, well liked, dated and popular. I thought if I joined this group that would happen to me. It made me feel special to be invited into the secret society. The group had many religious symbols scattered throughout the meetings and public ceremonies. Membership came only by invitation. I was excited to submit the name of my friend, one of Mrs. J.'s daughters. Mrs. J. was my black English teacher.

There was stunned silence. Shock and awe accosted me. How dare I have the audacity to mention her name! The vote came up with one "black ball" and she was rejected. Afterwards, both Susie's best friend, and our elderly supervisor, a gentle woman, came to me to explain, "We don't allow that."

The more I questioned, the more irritated and dumbfounded I became. "You mean just because she's black?" That was the gist of the discussion and it was also the last time I ever went to a meeting. I never wanted anything more to do with a "religious" organization that was rooted in prejudice.

I knew that God made all people and loved them, "red and yellow, black and white, they are precious in His sight." I was sick of all the prejudice against people because their skin was a different color than mine. It was wrong and I didn't like some of these girls anymore after that. I saw them as prideful, stuck up and thinking that being white and having money made them more important and better than others. It wasn't that way with all of them, but I still wanted nothing more to do with this secret society.

While a member of the girls' group—though I was no longer sexually pure, I was still a virgin—and there was enough of a religious focus to keep me that way. Once I no longer associated with that group of girls, I didn't have the same social constraints. Everything became more muddled and confused. Now I was friends with guys, both black and white, and I was disliked by girls, regardless of skin color. I constantly felt like I was laughed at and held in scorn and derision by all parties.

Life changed again once I entered high school. I took a speech class and we had our choice of topics to address. I firmly believed in justice and I composed a speech all about prejudice. The student population in my school was 60% white and 40% black. I wrote a speech advocating boyfriend/girlfriend relationships between the ethnicities. I didn't want people judged by the color of their skin and in my speech I mentioned love not seeing skin color. I didn't understand what a huge target I put upon myself for daring to speak out against such a taboo subject, not only in school but in our community.

So I wrote this speech about Prejudice. I shared it in class and promptly sat down. The black guy behind me said, "You should put that in the school newspaper." He was a grade ahead of me and I was surprised that he thought it was that good. So I did. I submitted it without my parent's knowledge. I didn't submit it against them; I just didn't share my life with them and this was no exception. I had no idea the ramifications I set in motion or the ways that my words and feelings would be misunderstood.

The day it came out, I passed my old junior high English teacher, a church member, and I asked her what she thought of my article. She seemed flustered and irritated as she responded, "Ruth Mary, God made the bluebird to lie down with the bluebird and the redbird to lie down with the redbird."

She walked on and I didn't say a word. Inwardly, I seethed and wanted to confront her. *So who did God make the parrot to lie down with?* I thought of the parrot with its vibrant colors of red, blue, green and yellow and how striking and stunning it was. The mixture of colors in this bird weren't a problem for God, why should a mixture of colors in dating be a problem?

Chapter 7

Shattered Dreams,
Betrayal and Deception

As a sophomore, when I thought my life couldn't get any worse . . . it did. I found myself in a situation, once again just being called "a tease." This time it was by a black guy. I knew Anthony would never take me back, and I felt sick and tired of it all. So, I said, "Yes."

I clenched my teeth to keep from crying out, "No!" Every fiber of my being screamed at the top of my lungs as the tears silently trickled down my cheeks. My heart ripped in two and something died in me. Afterward he looked at me with his taunting grin, "You just lost your virginity."

Emotionless and numb, I looked away from him, stared at the ceiling and thought, *Who cares?* I hated me and I hated life. As I walked home, I stopped in the middle of the sidewalk and told God, "If I'm supposed to feel guilty . . . let me feel it."

There was complete utter silence. It was the most horrible and terrifying moment I had ever experienced. I realized that I had seared my conscience so badly that I couldn't even feel conviction anymore. That shook something in the core of who I was. It felt that I had crossed the point of no return when it came to God. Losing my virginity as a preacher's kid was to me, the unpardonable sin. There was nothing left for me to live for.

Later that night, my mother reminded me, "We're going to the local theater to watch, "Of Mice and Men." I sat beside her in the dark community theater and the guilt came. She could never know what I had done. If she had made me lie two years before to Dad and I hadn't gone "all the way" then, what could she possibly feel about me if she knew this? I realized I started to bleed and I went to the bathroom at intermission. The shame, the brokenness, the awful feeling of suicide seemed strangely appropriate as I watched the horror of John Steinbeck's story and there was a part of me that wished I could die, even as the innocent, beautiful blond died in the strong arms of the mentally challenged farm hand. But I was afraid to die because I believed that only hell awaited me and that was more terrifying than just staying alive and surviving.

All my childhood I carried the notion of someday "I'll get married and live happily ever after." I hung onto "Cinderella" and "The Sound of Music" as my all-time favorite movies. I believed that I would be a virgin. I held onto those shreds of a dream until the fateful day. From then on, I felt like I had nothing else to live for. I believed I was "used goods" and that no guy would ever want me. No one would see my heart. I couldn't even allow myself to see my heart. I didn't allow people to see me cry and the harder I got, the easier it was not to cry.

Supposedly, Vicky had gotten together with the same guy about two weeks before. Both of them kept giving me two different stories. He insisted, "I got into her pants." She promised me firmly, "He did not!" I was torn between wanting to believe her and determining if he had lied to me. I wanted to trust both of them but I knew I couldn't.

One weekend Vicky and a female friend showed up at my house. My parents weren't home. At first, I was glad that she came to see me but the more the three of us talked I realized that she wanted to physically fight me. Vicky's friend kept wanting her to fight me and I am not sure why. I was good at being silent and I guess that only irritated her more. I only wanted to know if Vicky had had any sexual relationship with this guy.

I had never fought in my life and I wasn't interested in fighting now. She kept trying to bring our argument into something physical and I kept it at just words. Finally, when I refused to physically fight, she came clean. "Yes, I fooled around with him. I didn't want you to know because I wanted you to be like me—no longer a virgin."

I went into my house and securely locked the door. Immediately I went upstairs and called the guy that I had lost my virginity to. He finally told me crassly and with a laugh just how far they had gone. So, no, she hadn't had sex with him, which was what she kept telling me. But I was crushed. I felt betrayed and broken. Why didn't she tell me how they had parked and made out a few weeks before I was with him? Why did she lie to me? It was too late for me to ever be a virgin again.

I was devastated. I expected guys to use me and lie to me and treat me disrespectfully, but this was my *female* friend. I knew, as well as she did, that I would never have had sex with him, if she had told me that they had already been fooling around. That was the deepest betrayal I had ever felt or experienced. She and I were bitter enemies and I turned only to a few guys as friends and female friends were not even a part of my life anymore.

I was consumed with inner hatred. Every person that I had wanted to please, I had hurt and been hurt by. In the wake of my fury, I had destroyed several relationships. I was on a self-destructive path and I lashed out constantly with my words and actions. I was angry and full of shame. I didn't pop pills, slash my wrists or starve myself but I did intentionally hurt myself.

Often, I locked all the doors when I was alone, turned on music and in the dark living room I picked up the fire poker and continually beat myself on the arms, legs and back—places where no one would see.

I vented my pain in tears and silence. I hated myself even more than I hated everybody else. There was no room left for love. I felt like an empty shell and when the music stopped playing, I was spent— physically and emotionally. I had no hope in my heart or life and survival was all that mattered to me.

Survival was just making it through another day since I knew if I committed suicide I would have to stand before God and I feared hell. I merely existed, without purpose, meaning or direction. I had reached rock bottom with nothing left to live for. I was totally ashamed of who I was and what I had become.

I had always wanted to play the part of the Virgin Mary in the Christmas pageant. Instead, I was given the part of the announcing angel. Ironically at age sixteen, I got to play the part. Appalled and ashamed, I didn't want to but there was no other girl in the church old enough. I sat in the candlelit sanctuary next to the Christmas tree, decorated with religious ornaments, looked down at a doll and tears silently glistened in my eyes and dribbled down my cheeks.

Afterwards, one of the women of the church came to me, "You played that part so realistically. It was so loving and touching. It was beautiful!" She was totally ignorant that the tears were from a broken heart. I was no longer a virgin and God and I both knew it. I was overwhelmed by the sense of blasphemy with my horrid secret and its shame.

It was February and I hadn't had a period in three months. After I lost my virginity, I met with the guy a few different times to have sex but there was never any dating relationship. I even gave him money at times and I am not sure but he might have been doing drugs. There was no love between us and I was just a broken girl who met with an abusive guy. I had missed periods in the past but I never had a reason to be afraid of being pregnant, until now.

I pondered my predicament. *Do I jump out of the window and try to commit suicide or do I go downstairs and tell my parents what's going on in my life?* I didn't know where to turn. I had tried talking to a counselor on the phone anonymously but that wasn't the answer either. In a moment of sheer desperation, I chose to walk downstairs and tell my parents the truth about my life.

The disclosure was a nightmare as I had to share the reality of where my life had gone. The deep pain that I felt towards myself and the horrid isolation of carrying all these burdens was one thing but now to have to tell my parents, and particularly my dad, the pastor, about the sins that I had committed was almost too much to consider. I would forever be a fallen daughter, no longer a virgin and the consequences of that scarring both on my parents and on me felt like it would haunt me for the rest of my life.

I walked quietly downstairs into the living room where Dad sat in his chair. I tried to gather my strength. Mom was downstairs in another room, but still within hearing distance.

"Dad, I need to tell you something but you won't be able to handle it."

He lowered the newspaper and looked at me.

"I'll be able to handle it."

"No, you won't. You're a pastor and you're my father and you won't be able to be objective."

Quietly, he folded the paper and placed it on the floor. "I can handle what you're going to tell me."

He stood up and called for my mother and I backed away into the hall agitated and questioning if I should disclose my fear and shame. The three of us were near the stairs.

The silence was deafening. I mulled over the words and I kept wondering if I really was making the right choice to be honest. I hesitated and continued to stress the point that he needed to be objective but he kept assuring me that whatever I had to tell him, he could handle. I didn't know any other way to say it. So I blurted out,

"I think I'm pregnant."

The shock and pain shot through Dad's face and his body contorted on the stairs as he collapsed and broke into tears. I had never seen him look like that. Seeing his crumpled body and hearing the anguished weeping ripped my heart even further. I was afraid that he was going to die right there. Then when he didn't, I was scared.

"Mom, is he angry? Is he going to hurt me?"

"No, he's not going to hurt you. You hurt him. You broke his heart, Ruth Mary."

My mother's words cut deeply. There was nothing more to say. Once again, I was met with silence and I had to carry my own pain, shame, guilt and fear alone. I tiptoed passed my Dad, walked upstairs to my room, lay down on my bed and wrote out a prayer to God. "Dear God... Well, I went down and told them everything. Dad looked like he was going to have a heart attack. Now they know. After all these years of hiding, it's all out. I am sorry for the pain I caused them but I am so glad that I don't have to continue to live in deception." (It turned out that I wasn't pregnant.)

The shock of my sexual involvement caught my father totally off-guard. The rage I felt toward my parents only intensified because they had evidence two years prior that I wasn't innocent and, yet, my mother had insisted that I lie to my Dad. So, by the time I lost my virginity, I was angry at how much they had lived in denial about who and what I had become.

I was angry because if they had dealt with my rebellion two years before when Anthony used me then rejected me and broke my heart, maybe I would have kept my virginity and gotten the help and healing I needed. I didn't always know what was wrong with me but I had told them for several years that I needed to see a counselor. Mom brushed my words aside as being "so melodramatic." I wanted their help back then, in my own strange and twisted way, but Mom closed off that chance when she insisted that I lie to Dad.

In spite of all my mixed emotions of rage, anger, regret and shame, I was also extremely sorry and sad that I had hurt them and that my life had turned out like this. The hatred that filled my heart only seemed to increase and abound. It was as if I experienced another death, not just of hopes and dreams but of a more severe loss. This was the death of my soul.

My parents had thought that I was going to tell them I was hooked on drugs or alcohol because of my extreme rage and mood changes, my struggling grades and my attitudes toward life. I had become so distant, angry, deceptive and withdrawn that other than eating with them at night, I barely even spoke to them. Silence ruled in our house now that all my siblings were gone, and that silence was certainly not golden.

Dad commented, perhaps a few days later, "I thought you were going to tell us that you were on drugs."

I didn't mean to laugh but that was so far from any temptation for me that I quickly dismissed it and assured them that I had never taken drugs and that I had no intention of doing that. I was totally shocked that they would even think that. But I imagined from their questions, that taking drugs would have been a lesser evil than having sex.

I am grateful that all through those years, I never once smoked a cigarette or took drugs. I only got drunk once when I was eighteen and I drank because it was legal. I held a high regard for the law and I was ashamed when I found out that sexual misconduct as a minor is also considered illegal. Had I have known that, perhaps that temptation would not have become a stronghold in my life. I knew it was against God's law, but I had long since abandoned that.

The grace of God on little children to forget traumatic experiences was something that I had received. Other than the one brief conversation with Anthony I never consciously remembered any abuse by the man at the daycare. Nor did I recall the incident with the janitor. Those memories were removed and I had forgotten them for years.

Out of the pain of my emotional honesty, within a week, Dad took me to see a Christian psychologist in a city about fifteen miles away. My sessions were private and I was alone with him. I told him if he were a preacher, I would refuse to talk with him. He wasn't a pastor but he asked me, "If I am a Christian psychologist, will you talk with me?" I reluctantly agreed.

I kept a small notebook and wrote down my thoughts when I didn't want to talk. He tried to help me put some of the pieces of my life back together. I assumed these sessions were expensive and I quit seeing him after six weeks. I can't remember all that took place but there were some major breakthroughs.

It was my third session when Dad met privately with the psychologist. I had no idea what they talked about. We sat in the car and Dad said, "We moved from Texas because we hoped it would help you to forget about what that man did to you."

I pressed myself against the car door, to stay as far away from Dad as possible, as I always did. His words puzzled me. I was so shocked and dumbfounded that I jerked my head sideways, looked at him and said, "What man? What are you talking about?"

He turned to look at me with a pained expression.

"Ruth Mary, don't you remember? Mr. R., the man at the daycare." This was the first time Dad had talked to me about being abused, except when I was in his room in Texas when he told me the abuser was dead.

All was quiet as Dad turned the key and we headed home. Memories flooded my mind –all long forgotten. Puzzle pieces floated in. Yet, there they were. All lined up, pain after pain, abuse after abuse. I watched a slow movie with blurred images. As they came into focus I re-lived it all—haunting and tragic. Finally, the present faced me as I stared at my hands in my lap. Everything was clear but now that knowledge had come too late. I saw what I had become – a cheap, easy girl who was "used goods."

The countryside sped by and silent tears slid down my cheeks. The snow swirled outside as I pressed my forehead against the icy window. Winter encased the world in white with huge snowdrifts along the edges of the road. Everything was a perfect reflection of my life-barren, empty, cold and lifeless.

After a time, Dad ventured to speak. Once again, Dad tried to explain even as he had when I was seven. I guess he thought I would understand now that I was sixteen. "Mr. R. was senile. He probably figured that you were his girlfriend." Something was different in the way that Dad talked. He sounded old and tired. There was only deep sorrow and sadness in his voice, not accusatory towards me but broken. It felt as if he were a long way away, reliving something that I had quite forgotten.

After a while he continued, "His wife knew that he was senile and we knew that he was senile." *I couldn't believe it!* My twisted mind accused, *"They knew what this man was like as a child abuser and they all put me in that daycare anyway!"* Unfortunately, what had begun as the slightest possibility of healing now ended with tremendous hurt and confusion. I thought the definition of senile was "perverted," but I never shared that. I was twenty-five before I understood that senility is not synonymous with being sexually abusive.

The Christian psychologist and I met every week. After each session, he asked me if I would like to come back. It was a strange feeling to know that I could make a choice about whether I wanted to be there or not. One time Mom took me and she pointed out a girl from my high school wearing a school jacket. "Look Ruth Mary. Do you want to say "hi" to her?" I brusquely told her, "No!"

The last thing in the world I wanted was for anyone to know that I needed psychological help. I couldn't believe that my mother would even suggest such a thing. Besides, that girl was there because her parents were getting a divorce—not because she herself was the problem. It was the only time Mom took me and I was mad at her, so angry, because she refused to talk with the psychologist privately. Dad had already had one session with him but Mom let me know, "Ruth Mary, this is nothing that your father and I have done. This is all you. We have provided you with everything you need. It is not my fault for how you have chosen to act." Again her words slashed huge wounds into my chest. I knew that she had to have done something wrong in her life, hadn't she?

No matter what person I looked at, no one's sins could be as bad as mine. I was a preacher's kid from a solid Christian home and I knew better. These other people didn't know God so their sins couldn't be that bad. But mine, mine were "inexcusable." That's how I felt around my mother.

Ironically, Dad said I still had to come to church and Mom also insisted that I was part of the family and "you will be there." With each level of rebellion against God, being in church became more unbearable. The last few years with Anthony, I was gripped with guilt and shame so church just about killed my heart. But now that I had lost my virginity, I had to choose to harden my heart in order to cope with the devastating shame and loss of everything I once lived for.

I hated being in church. I hated the shame I carried and that I had to still had to "play the part" of the preacher's kid when my heart, life and actions were totally against everything that church stood for. I actively thought wicked, ugly and awful things and I deliberately churned angry and judgmental thoughts throughout the service.

On rare occasions, we sang a few hymns that touched a deep chord of my childhood that was now only mist in a dream. At those moments I gripped my hands on the pew in front of me until my knuckles whitened so that I could remain standing and get through the song. The tears burned but I refused to shed them. All those glimpses of my once innocent childhood mocked my tortured soul.

Life didn't become better immediately. The sexual strongholds were well forged by then but I still clung to a hope that Anthony would eventually want me again. During this same time, my sister casually remarked to me, "Dad will someday become senile." The enemy deviously took those words and hammered more nails into the coffin of my soul. I felt trapped and distrustful and wondered, *What will happen when my father finally touches me again?* My father had never sexually abused me but the enemy of my soul kept that as a constant threat and fear to hold me in bondage.

It felt like the only time I got attention from either of my parents was when I was angry, disrespectful or in trouble. There were the few times a year, Christmas and my birthday, when the unspoken rule was to "be nice and loving one to another." So, I did get and give hugs then.

Once guys knew I was "used goods" with a black guy, only a few white guys wanted anything to do with me. The black girls considered me a threat to their chances with the black guys. My reputation went downhill rapidly. The black guys thought I would want to be with them all, just because they were black. I didn't and I wouldn't, though their hands tried to wander just as much as Anthony's. My rejection came because I had dared to cross the unspoken "color" line.

One time Dad stated emphatically, "I don't care if he was black, white, brown, green, purple or pink with polka dots—you sinned!" At that moment, I wanted to throw my arms around my Dad and hug him. He understood what I did wrong and I knew that I had sinned, having nothing to do with skin color. Unfortunately, at that time, I said nothing.

The horrible relationships I had with my parents were volatile, harsh, cutting and totally without love or respect. At an unusually vulnerable time I made some comment about my future and getting married. I was lighthearted in the moment, which was extremely rare but that pleasantness was immediately squelched when my mother looked up at me. "Oh no, Ruth Mary! You can never wear white at your wedding."

Her harshness took my breath away and what little desire I had barely shared was demolished in that one quick declaration. I was reminded of my "used" state and I knew in my heart that no man would ever marry me. I hid behind a mask of bitterness to minimize the sting of her words and I retorted just as harshly.

"If what you two have is a marriage, I don't want one." I always saw them as nitpicking and the atmosphere was extremely tense. In my observation, Dad was "married" to the ministry, Mom was "married" to teaching in another town and the kids were "just there." I felt like we were hypocrites and I wanted nothing to do with God or church. (The truth was that my parents were living with a daughter whom they dearly loved but could not reach. There were many other issues in our family but I couldn't see them. In retrospect, I felt like I was the scapegoat because I was "the rebellious child.")

I overheard a girl in my class once talking about her mother. "My mother is a slut." Those words went all through me. I could never make such a degrading statement about my mother's sexual purity. I hated her, sad to say, but as for her fidelity and morality, my mother and father were saints. When I heard this girl trash her mom, I made an inner vow, *I will never have a daughter, because I could never look at her and hear her say to me, 'Why not, Mom? You were a slut at this age. Look at what you did.'*

Although I did not realize it at the time I believed the constant lies that satan fed me. Once I fell for the various temptations, he was there to forcefully condemn me and fill me with despair that my life could change or that my sins could be forgiven. It was many years before this vow was renounced in my life.

Chapter 8

Hanging by a Thread

*B*y the time I was sixteen I had composed one hundred and eighty poems. I wrote practically every day. I expressed my deepest emotions as my poetry ran the gamut in style, topic and vocabulary. I escaped into a world of feelings and a place to bare my heart. It was easy to write and I thoroughly enjoyed it. I only let a few classmates read my poetry, along with my sophomore/junior English teacher, Mrs. J. She took a deep liking to me and it was mutual. For some reason, I always called her "Grandma," though she wasn't old.

Mrs. J. often laughed and affirmed me. I don't know what I did to deserve her friendship but she thought I was a delightful student. I thrived in her class under her praise. I knew that she believed in me and going to her class was one of the highlights of my day.

She encouraged me in my writing and my peers told me it was good, but I struggled to believe it. Then one day a "real" poet came to our school. I stubbornly kept my work to myself until the last minute but Mrs. J. insisted that I show the woman my poems. So, I took my large black notebook to her and waited as she read through many different selections. She looked at me and said, "You've got the gift."

I was awkward and pondered, "What "gift" does she mean?" I was too embarrassed to ask so I stayed quiet. She wrote a list of different poets for me to study and she wrote, "Show, don't tell." I also didn't quite understand how I was supposed to "show and not tell," but none of that mattered to me at the moment. For the first time in my life I was being validated for something significant that none of my siblings had ever done. I felt amazingly powerful and special. Maybe there really was something more than just my own satisfaction in writing? Maybe someday I could become a poet or an author? This woman poet said words to me that were life-giving, even though I didn't thoroughly understand them. A long forgotten dream of a little girl to "be somebody and make a difference" began to curl its way up into my heart. It was as if a breath of life was breathed into my soul.

The summer I was sixteen I began to repent. I left home to work in Virginia. It was there that I met some true Christians. The dorm mom was in her early twenties and she introduced me to Christian "contemporary" music. I listened to Keith Green, Amy Grant, Ken Medema, Second Chapter of Acts, Phil Keaggy and many other Christian artists. When I listened to the biblical lyrics I learned that God did not desire all the evil things that had happened to me but that there was a devil and he was out to destroy me. I discovered that there was choice involved in my life.

It was an incredible summer and I voraciously drank in God's love for me. I didn't get sexually involved with any guy—I was too hungry to find out more about God. I was fascinated with Jesus Christ. He loved me and I couldn't get away from that sacrificial, unconditional love. My soul was famished. At the end of the summer, I spent money to purchase a lot of Christian albums and returned home with a new resolve and a new hope. I listened to the music and I loved it. Anthony lived close by and I gazed out the window and thought about him. This time, though, my thoughts were prayers. I hoped that God would reach him and change his life. I prayed diligently for his salvation and longed for the day when he would understand how much Jesus loved him, too.

My father didn't like the music and he wasn't open to listen to the lyrics. As he saw me staring out the window, in a moment of great frustration, he bellowed, "Christian? You aren't a Christian!" It was like a bucket of water quenching the embers of a fire that had begun that summer. With that judgment thrown at me, it wasn't long before I put the albums in the closet and I returned to my former self. It didn't matter that I had experienced a heart transformation and that I really did want to follow God. I had many areas that needed to be sanded but my heart had changed....or so I had believed.

After that accusation, I decided that no one would ever believe that I had changed so there was no point in trying. It didn't matter that I had received psychological help and a summer of saturation in God's love, because the man whom I believed would speak truth, had just been used by the enemy to throw shovels of dirt onto my smoldering hope.

Because of my parents' views about education, they placed me in an honor's track in high school, which meant I had to take upper level math and science courses. Although I struggled with math in earlier years, in high school, it only got worse. One time, I spent several minutes at the chalkboard trying to figure out a problem and as I kept writing, some students began to chuckle, which only increased my anxiety. When I finally gave up, the entire class burst into laughter and then the teacher pointed out that several steps back I was supposed to multiply by zero and anything beyond that was superfluous.

I tried so hard to get things right. I felt so stupid. No matter how diligently I tried to do the homework, nothing made sense. I was so tense at test time that I forgot which formula went with which problem.

I felt like a failure. At the end of the year in Algebra II, my teacher quietly consulted with me.

"You actually failed my class. However, you have tried so hard that I am going to give you a D -, but I wanted you to know that you really made an F."

I was crushed and I couldn't hold back the flow of tears. An "F" was unheard of in our family. I knew she was right. I never asked my parents for help—they were not a part of my life and hadn't been for a long, long time. I asked my peers for help but nothing seemed to connect. A similar thing happened in my science class. I didn't understand Chemistry. I copied the work of my team whenever we did experiments. I even cheated on the final, only to realize that I failed the test anyway. This sense of failure spilled over into every area of my life and it unraveled my final threads of significance and value. I felt even more worthless and hopeless.

Chemistry was a combined class of juniors and seniors. Anthony and his brother were together. His older brother held me with contempt and harassed and barked at me daily. He always made fun of my name, "Ruth," and instead of saying it, he pretended to bark like a dog. He made me feel ugly and despised. When I was in seventh grade, he asked me to do something sexual with him, since I was involved with Anthony. I refused.

One day, a small group of us talked about the musical *The Sound of Music* and in my complete ignorance, I commented, "I always wanted to be a nun."

Anthony's brother exploded, "You can't be a nun—you aren't a virgin!"

I was cut to the quick and silenced with shame and humiliation. Yes, everybody knew I had a bad reputation . . . but to blurt it out. Inwardly I cringed but outwardly, I said nothing. His explosive reaction continued. "You're not even Catholic."

Up until that moment I had had no idea that I had to be Catholic to be a nun and I hadn't given conscious thought about virginity, though that made perfect sense as well. I left myself wide open for that backlash but the words also cut me to the core. I was so ashamed and I had nowhere to hide. As Anthony's brother ranted, I realized that my desire to be a nun was an affront to his religion.

I didn't think of Catholics as being that different from Protestants. My father was not a man to preach on hell-fire and brimstone as many other pastors did. He didn't have any exclusionary views that our denomination was the only one that would be in Heaven. He had no problem with Catholics, Baptists, or any other Christian denomination. He also had no problem with women pastors and for his time he was liberal, in a godly, biblical way. My dad passed on his views to me, whether consciously or subconsciously, and I found it strange and sad to think that some church goers thought their denomination would be the only one in Heaven.

From the time I was thirteen, I found that God often touched my heart when I attended Church Camp in the summer. Looking back I could see the pattern, whenever I could get away from my hometown and people who knew me, I could escape my private hell. I discovered that God was still there and He loved me. God would get a hold of my heart, plant some seeds and then watch me spurn Him again once it was no longer "popular" or accepting to be "weird." There were incidents when He would answer some of my strangest prayers. At one point I saw nothing wrong with alcoholism and abortion but I did struggle with the idea of rape. I told God that I wanted Him to show me how someone could love Him if they had been raped and if their life had been so painful that they turned to alcohol in order to numb it.

Amazingly, the summer of my junior year when I was seventeen, He brought two strong, devoted Christian girls into my life. One was a rape victim and the other was a recovering alcoholic. As I became more acquainted with their lives and their love and devotion for God I could not deny that God had answered my accusations and that He was real and intimate with these girls. This reality both amazed me and made me jealous. *Would God ever love me like that? Could I ever receive His love for me?*

During that summer and the next, I was involved with the same guy. I wanted to be dated by him but he wasn't interested in dating me. He was already dating another girl while still "getting together" with me. That seemed to be the story of my life. I was always good enough in parked cars and paths in the woods, but never in public. It made me wonder, *am I really that ugly?*

I knew the relationship wasn't what I wanted and I was saddened but at least I got undivided attention. He threatened not to be my "friend" anymore so I had sex with him. How needy I was—so desperate, clingy and fragile. Each time I thought I would be accepted and I crossed the line sexually with a guy, the friendship forever changed and it was almost impossible to have any interaction other than a sexual encounter.

During my junior year, I approached Anthony and hoped he would take me back. We did have sex and my romantic notions were filled with his taunting, accusing, abusive language and actions. It was nothing that even resembled my fantasies. I told myself, *he must've really been hurt by my betrayal of having sex with someone else and therefore, I guess I deserve this.* It is pathetic to think what lies I made myself believe. After two times, I never approached him again nor did he approach me. Inner vows that I would marry him someday hung on a fragile strand of a spider web of lies, deceit, abuse and fantasy. All I had left were broken dreams and a broken heart like a million shards of glass from a shattered mirror. My perceptions of who I thought Anthony was, turned out to be nothing but delusions. I lost all self-respect and I felt reduced to being worse than a prostitute. Anthony, like other guys, asked to borrow money from me, right after we had sex. I hated myself and felt cheap, used and less than human.

The ups and downs of broken relationships continued. I took far too many risks. My rage often focused on my parents as I discarded the psychological counseling. There was no positive relationship to build on so I kept seeking to find attention in the arms of guys. It deeply humbles and amazes me at how powerfully God protected me. I can't count the number of times I fervently prayed, "Oh, God, please don't let me be pregnant." I used birth control as did most of my partners but that never stopped me from the fears of consequences. My heart was so hard and blinded to the life of a baby that I shudder to think what my choice would have been had I gotten pregnant.

The summer of my junior year, I was chosen to attend a special week of Girls' State. Every year one girl was chosen from the upcoming senior class. Various members of the school faculty decided which girl went.

It was a week of learning about government and the political process. Upon returning home, I was required to give a speech to a women's organization. I enjoyed speaking. Unfortunately, my mother was not invited by any of the ladies, since she wasn't a member of the club, so none of my family ever heard my speech.

My mother talked with me as I effervesced about my speech. I asked her why she wasn't there. I saw the hurt and disappointment in her eyes. "No one ever invited me." I was sad for her, disappointed for me and angry at the stuck-up women for overlooking her. Everyone else thought that somebody had invited her when nobody had. It was a rare moment in my mother's relationship with me that I saw her genuine hurt that she wasn't there for something that was special in my life.

At the end of my junior year, I vied for the position of Editor for the Yearbook. I was determined that I wanted that responsibility. It was the first time I had run for any class office since fifth grade when I was class president and I got impeached. The class voted for me to be the Editor and I won the title. I attended a college for a week to learn how to produce a yearbook. I was absolutely thrilled and I began to hope that maybe I wasn't as disliked or unpopular as I used to be.

I knew that I only had one year left of high school. I had carried my fantasies of Anthony and they had crumbled before my eyes. I wanted to try some new things and I felt desperate enough to become assertive and give myself a chance to be an adult as at the beginning of the school year, I turned eighteen.

Chapter 9

Accomplishments, Anguish and Answers

After years of trying to fit in with my peers and receiving many wounds in my heart, I made a strong, bold decision to finally change. I turned eighteen and realized I was now an adult. I deliberately initiated loving attitudes and actions towards my parents. For a while, every day before I left for school, I hugged each of them and said, "I love you." They didn't know how to react or respond. Dad was not used to hearing those words so he said, "Thank you, Ruth Mary." Occasionally, Mom said, "Thank you, Babe." I don't recall that they said, "I love you," back to me but I didn't care. I didn't do it to get anything from them.

No one knew how to handle me. I was finally not in any more math or science courses and I was older than most of my class. I was an adult, in certain aspects and I saw clearly the immaturity and emptiness of so many people's lives. It was as if I was awakened to the truth and I didn't want to go back to the lies anymore. I had a lot of changing to do and it wouldn't all happen overnight but the process of healing had begun.

It was my senior year and I came out of my "shell" of ugliness. I endeavored to be different and more assertive. I had endured playing the trumpet for five years and I always felt like a failure. I decided to quit band and instead, I finally joined chorus. Because I was the yearbook editor, band was going to conflict with that period, anyway.

My band instructor told me persistently, "You have the potential to be a great trumpet player." Like so many other positive words in my life, I could not believe them or him. My ability to trust a sincere compliment was greatly hindered. One time I finally looked at him and said, "No, I don't think so. Besides, I love to sing. You have never heard me sing before." At the end of the year after he heard me sing, he signed my yearbook, "To an outstanding vocalist who still has the potential to be a great trumpet player."

That was my year to begin to gain some small sense of self-worth, achievement, independence and confidence. I was able to finally speak up for myself and tell guys, "No." The year was lonely as I had burned all my relationships with girls and most of them with the guys as well. I branched out to try new things, as this was my last year and it felt like my last chance to make a difference in high school.

Throughout the year I wrote poetry about feelings of being a drug addict, suicide, teenage pregnancy, death—all things I had never experienced but had a sympathetic understanding about. When I shared my poems with my peers many told me, "You write as if you know just how I feel." I wrote every day in school and I never struggled with words. It just flowed.

I developed my friendship with Mrs. J. She had been my sophomore and junior English teacher, a black woman who I dearly loved and affectionately called, "Grandma." I wanted her to be my senior English teacher. Unfortunately, that was not to be the case. The teacher of honor's senior English wanted me in her class and she appealed to the principal so that my schedule included her as my teacher or miss out on being in chorus.

I treated this teacher with such disrespect but I also knew, as did the class, that she dishonored me. She was a church member and she insisted on calling me, "Ruth Mary." That was my family name only; none of my classmates ever called me that. I was eighteen and she pointed out my behavior and asked me, "What would your mother think of that?" She insisted on bringing church, religion and Christianity to bear weight on me. Finally one day, I talked with her quite bluntly after class.

"Mrs. S., I have never claimed to be a Christian. My father may be a pastor and I had no choice in being a preacher's kid, but I am not a Christian….and I am late for class." She was stunned.

I heard about a poetry contest that included sixth through twelfth grades that spanned our county. I was eager to submit some of my poems until a discouraging incident occurred with my senior English teacher. For one of her assignments, I spent several hours looking up words in the dictionary making sure they were just the right ones to express my feelings. I even added a few of my poems into the work. When I turned it in to be graded, I felt confident that it would be well received.

When I got it back from this teacher, I asked her eagerly what she thought of it. "I think you just opened up a dictionary to try to impress me." That stung. I put out my poetry, an extension of my identity, and she had nothing positive to contribute. I determined I wouldn't even enter the dumb poetry contest. When I shared with my former English teacher what happened, she was livid at her fellow teacher.

Mrs. J. told me emphatically, "If you don't enter your poetry in that contest, then I will." So I agreed to enter.

Years before when I expressed that I wanted to be a writer, my father said, "You can't make a living at it." Those words interpreted in my mind equated to, *You're not good enough at it*. The poem I entered told the story of a couple on a romantic date on the beach. In my mind, it was a honeymoon scene but I never directly said that.

Prior to the contest, I let my parents read it. Mom may have said something positive or she may have stayed silent. But Dad completed reading it and said critically, "There's only one thing that concerns me. You don't mention anything about marriage." In my stubborn state, I wasn't about to tell him that I wrote it with that in mind so I either got exasperated or stayed silent.

During the contest, I felt imprisoned as we were not allowed off the school property. The hours dragged on with the judging process. A senior from another school let me read his poem. I was impressed and told him that it reminded me a lot of Edgar Alan Poe. He said my poem was good. I told him the reason it was taking so long was that his poem was going to take first.

Finally the spokesperson said, "The first place winner for the County-wide Poetry contest from 6-12th grade is...." I was so stunned, it took me a few seconds to realize they called my name. I went down and got my certificate. I walked passed my senior English teacher with a smug expression and Mrs. J. was so proud of me. Unfortunately, Mrs. S.'s opinion of me never changed but mine didn't change towards her, either.

There was a nice looking male teacher who told me, "I felt sorry for you today because I wanted to tell you that your time here was going to be worth it." I had griped and complained about everything all day long. I found out later that my poem, "Reflections," had been diligently researched and studied by the judges because they thought that I had plagiarized. Apparently, for most of the hours of the day these judges pored over poems to discover "mine" in the midst of some already published poet.

Some of the judges said, "It has to be plagiarized, because it sounds just like something Emily Dickinson would have written."

~ Reflections ~

We went to the beach together
you and I.
I threw bread on the shore
for the birds
And you covered me with sand.
We ate sandwiches,
Potato chips, and drank pop. We rested,
lying beside each other.
We tanned dark in the afternoon
you and I.

You covered me with lotion,
I tickled you.
We rode the waves together
without any fear.
We made sand castles but the
water washed them away.

Evening came and we took a walk
along the shore.
The water lapped at our ankles
and you put your arm
Around my waist, and I put my arm
around your waist.
The wind blew my hair around
and you laughed.

We watched the sun set over
the quiet sea,
And we walked back to our spot.
We built a fire,
You played your guitar and you
sang songs to me.
You lay down and I massaged your
tired back
You wrapped your arms around me
and hugged me.
Our lips met and we kissed
you and I.

We shared love on the beach
by the moonlight,
With the salty sea breezes
blowing over us.
We were lost in our own
very passionate, raging
Tempest on the sand together
you and I.

I went home and did something strange. I told my mother this long story about how the day went and that in the end I didn't win anything.

She seemed genuinely saddened. "Really, Ruth Mary?"

I looked at her and grinned, "No, Mom, I'm teasing you. I took first place in the county!"

It took her a few minutes to believe me. She was happy and so was I. Later, she came downstairs to the living room and placed a book, *The Treasury of American Poetry,* on the floor in front of me.

I asked, "What's this for?"

"Look at it."

I looked at the cover. I kept prodding her, "What's this for?"

She kept insisting, "Just look at it."

So, quizzically, I opened it. She had inscribed, "To Ruth Mary with love from your Dad and Mother. May your name be found in these pages someday." That gesture was so beyond anything that I had ever imagined. Never had she given me a gift unless it was oblig-atory—birthday or Christmas—a gift I treasure to this day.

There was beginning to be a restoration of my relationship with my parents even as God had begun to soften my heart towards Him again. My parents and I talked more freely than we ever had and Dad especially opened up to me. He shared some of his own painful childhood and though it shocked me I was moved by his honesty. It was as if he no longer had to appear a "perfect" father but he could be someone who could at least understand some of my pain. In one particularly vulnerable moment I looked at Dad and asked him some-thing that had plagued my thoughts for the last two years.

"Daddy, did I do the right thing when I told you and Mom about my life? I hurt you both so badly. That night I was either going to tell you or I was just going to jump out the window... and commit suicide."

His arms wrapped around me as he cried out, "Oh, Ruth Mary! You did the right thing. You needed help so badly and we didn't understand." He and I shed a few tears on each other's shoulders. The weight of guilt began to fall from me. It was reassuring to know that even though I had made life hell for them, they still wanted me. I think it totally shocked Dad to see how desperate my emotional state had been at that time. I don't believe they had any idea the self-hatred that I had carried for all those years.

I had another significant event happen my senior year. On the same day as my senior prom, I had the opportunity to sing the

National Anthem at a semi-professional football game held in our local football stadium. I sang *a cappella* and when I finished singing, the applause sounded thunderous. I was elated and my voice rang out over the stadium in strong tones and with great confidence and joy.

Though that was a tremendous boost to my self-esteem, only a few hours later I experienced the sadness of the senior prom without a date. I walked home from the stadium, changed into my formal gown and Dad drove me to the dance where I entered, alone. I watched all my classmates with their dates and the loneliness engulfed me. A black guy, also alone, asked me to fast dance so we did.

Later in the evening, my parents came. Dad always took Mom to the Prom when my siblings were in high school so it wasn't something unusual for him to take her to my senior prom. It was held close to Mother's Day and they arrived in their formal attire. Dad made it a point to slow dance with me even though neither of us knew how to slow dance. I was strangely grateful because the emptiness of the evening bothered me. Dad later returned to the school and took me home. It was a sad night. It was a place of shame for me to have no one to take me to my Senior Prom.

How strange that in one day I experienced the height of confidence, accomplishment and affirmation as outwardly I was improving. Yet, that same night I was stricken with grief and sadness as the loneliness of my inward life played itself out at the Prom—rejected, alone and isolated.

For years I had played out fantasies in my mind of how Anthony would finally date me at eighteen. It never happened. The guy who stole my virginity asked to borrow a dollar from me one day. I coldly asked, "When are you going to pay me back the one hundred dollars you already borrowed?" I had worked hard babysitting and had lent that money to him two years prior when we had been together. My caustic comment caught him off-guard and shamed him. I was sick and tired of the way I had been treated and how I had allowed myself to be treated. I had hoped to leave high school with a new and different reputation. Sadly, no matter how hard I tried, it was next to impossible to gain respect again. I had lost something so valuable that I could only bite back tears and leave the halls of high school with all its shattered dreams.

At my Baccalaureate service, I stood and spoke a few words to all my soon-to-be graduating peers. "I know we're all getting ready to graduate and go our separate ways. I know that no matter where your life takes you, God will always be there and He will always love you. He can forgive you and I know that because He has forgiven me. This song has become my own and I sincerely hope that it will be your song as well. I hope, like me, you will choose to walk with God."

I sang "I'll Walk with God" as a solo. I closed my tear-glistened eyes and sang it like a prayer. My voice reverberated throughout the gymnasium as the anointing of the Lord fell upon me. After the program, one of my classmates came running outside to find me.

Breathless, she caught up to me, "I never knew you could sing like that. You have a beautiful voice!"

It was bittersweet. All those years I hid behind low self-esteem and a ruined reputation. Sadly, I had so much more to offer of myself. I thanked her for the compliment and walked away. They were words and experiences that came far too late for me. I was glad I got to sing but it was so much more than that to me. As I sang the words, God knew I prayed for my fellow classmates—me, the preacher's kid who should have pointed them to Jesus Christ all those years—and in the end realized wasted time, lost souls and damaged relationships that hopefully in eternity would finally be healed and restored.

Later that summer I worked in another state at a camp when my parents called me and told me that they were moving. I ran outside in the dusk and rejoiced because my old life was over. All that lay ahead was a hopefully clean slate in college.

Part Two

Redeemed and Restored

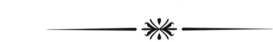

~ Victorious ~

I think you thought you had me,
feeding me those lies
I felt so empty
and helpless
I wanted just to die.

But you didn't count on losing
and you figured
I was wrapped in your spell
Then I laughed and told you
to go straight back to hell.

And since that day God's changed my life
He's brought the sunshine
and He let it rain
I've still felt sadness
grief and pain,

But the Lord has never let me down
and even though I've been deep
He's pulled me from the stormy sea
and placed dry ground beneath
my feet.

I smile, laugh and sing
I sometimes cry tears of joy
For on one dark day
a Son was given to save this world from sin
A victory was won
and you, satan,
have lost again.

Chapter 10

Searching for Truth

*D*eciding my future was not easy. One possibility was to study Voice and I was excited when a voice instructor from a small state college wanted me to study with him. When I discovered that one of his former students was used for sexual favors, in exchange for voice training, my parents encouraged me not to go to that school. They told me, "If you have such a wonderful voice it will get noticed in your university."

I did take one semester of Voice for beginners at my college and that was the end of any public singing for me. I did have a beautiful voice but I didn't have the assertiveness or the confidence to push myself into learning more. Another dream died—I wouldn't become a famous singer.

I headed to college, not because I wanted to, but because my father said, "What are you going to do, flip hamburgers for the rest of your life?" That comment was strange to me since I had never flipped hamburgers but I knew that he meant without a college degree I couldn't get much of a "decent" job, in terms of making money. No one in our family was going to be less than a college graduate so I made my plans and embarked on the next journey.

Within a few months of my high school graduation, my parents moved from our little town to a totally different part of the state. Around that time, Anthony came home from his state college where he had hoped to play football. His former girlfriend was pregnant.

He took responsibility (though in my frenzied fantasy I was devastated) and he married her.

I couldn't believe the twisted turns my life had taken. Everything that I had hoped, planned, dreamed and desired lay mangled and mutilated at my feet. Surely, this was not what my life was meant to be.

I was lost. I had planned my whole life around Anthony ever since fourth grade. I had secretly hoped that we would go to the same college because then I figured he would date me. Now that he was married, I knew that I would never have a future with him. It was all over. All my nights of pretending, imagining, hoping and believing were wasted and futile. I couldn't turn back the clock. With all my unfulfilled fantasies dashed, I threw myself into my college classes to try to ease the pain.

Though I was almost nineteen, I was terribly insecure. I didn't even know how to write checks or keep a bank account, much less live life on my own. I was terrified of failing college because I was afraid I wasn't smart enough.

There was a whole new world and I was filled with fear and anxiety. I was obsessive about my studies, even to the point of exasperating my peers because I didn't want to take a few minutes to visit them. Thankfully, I relented because they had decorated their room, made a cake and threw a surprise birthday party for me. I hadn't had a party since I was eight!

I was so surprised and happy. It was so sweet of these girls to make me feel special. I also felt terribly guilty for how stubborn I had been with feeling that I needed to go study when all along they had planned this party. It was a kind gesture.

Throughout the first semester I went to the first class of every day thirty minutes early so I wouldn't be late. I ate every meal and tried to do everything right. I looked at college as a chance to truly change. There were a few people there from my hometown but for the most part, I was surrounded by total strangers. It was a painful learning and growing experience but at the same time, quite rewarding. I made the Dean's List the first semester and I was shocked. I was never an honor's student in high school, though when the scores were added, I barely missed graduating with honors. That saddened me because throughout high school I believed that I was a miserable, failing student.

Within the first weeks of college, I made a bet with a girl that I could last longer without a guy's kiss than she could. I had never tried to be self-controlled in that area and I wasn't sure I could do it but we set the limit at a month. I realized later that she set me up to go on a date (which I did) but I never kissed the guy. She lost the bet. When I held it and kept that bet for over a year, I was stunned.

Ironically or perhaps, providentially, I joined a Christian campus group as I realized that I needed support and fellowship as well as God's help. As much as I had hated being known as the preacher's kid in my hometown, I now found some sense of identity, internally speaking. My family background anchored me in the increasing storm and crashing waves of humanistic, anti-God and anti-Christ philosophies and evolutionary beliefs. My college courses were saturated with the "goodness" of mankind and the dorms were playhouses of partying. They hosted a virtual sexual smorgasbord of every perversion and appetite imaginable. To become a disciple of Jesus Christ in this environment was like being a salmon relentlessly swimming against the current. It was not for the faint-hearted.

In one of my Psychology courses, the feminist professor emphatically stated, "If the church doesn't like the way we teach sex education, then they should teach it themselves!" I thought, *You're absolutely right. If nothing else came out of your mouth all semester, at least this was definitely truth.*

I was becoming someone new as the transformation that begin my senior year of high school continued. It was as if I was inside the chrysalis with old habit patterns, mindsets and beliefs slowly beginning to dissolve.

I found joy in not living for sex or guys. However I still had the habit of comforting myself with masturbation. Due to my roommate's confrontation one night, "What are you doing? Are you okay?" I felt ashamed. I quit that habit but she had already made the decision to room with another girl. I was left with remorse and rejection. As a result, I focused solely on my grades with only a few friends thrown into the mix.

My mother wondered why I wasn't taking part in all the other activities and opportunities that college offered but I was too afraid of ruining my grades. I felt compelled to study all the time and therefore I couldn't afford to attend football games, go swimming for fun or take time to enjoy myself. In essence, my life was consumed with learning, classes and homework. I looked at education as a necessary evil toward my future and fun didn't play a part in my life.

By the end of my sophomore year, I came to the roots of all that I held dear and treasured in my childhood. I had begun a journey to search after God in my freshman year. The reality was that He continued His relentless pursuit of me by placing Christians in my path. They befriended me, cared about me and they didn't want me for sexual purposes. I made honest friends in guys, something new and rare to me.

I was still lonely and hoped for a boyfriend. I wanted to be found attractive and desirable in a good way. Surely, there would be someone who would want to take me on dates, call me on the phone and be seen with me in public? That didn't happen, though.

Unfortunately since I relied on myself and in my own strength, when I did "lose" the bet, I lost tragically. It appalled me that I was so beguiled. Through a series of unfortunate events, I ended up going out with an anonymous, perverted phone caller. Somehow after the perverted speech and my talking to him, don't ask me how, I softened and ended up going out with him. I know even in writing this, it sounds ludicrous, but it shows the degree to which the enemy had me bound in deception.

This man had lied to me all about his life and by the time I was in the car with him I prayed silently that God would get me back to my dorm. Some sexual things happened and I hated that too, but thankfully, he fell asleep and I stayed awake all night long, silently and fervently praying. No one knew where I was, or who I was with and I could have just become another statistic.

Thankfully, in the morning, he drove me to campus. I got out of the car and never looked back. My college never looked more beautiful. He had no idea what room was mine but I knew he had my phone number. He planned for me to meet him at the library the following weekend, but by the time Sunday came, I felt a strong urge to go see a girlfriend of mine that had been in high school with me. I had such a good time with her and it was evening by the time I returned to my dorm.

I got a phone call from this man and he was angry at me because he had waited for me at the college library and I never showed up. The library was always closed on Sundays. As he got angrier and I tried to apologize, he blurted out that he was indeed, married. I was furious and almost sick at my stomach. Even as immoral as I was, married men were always off-limits. I also was deeply ashamed because I realized that I had been with a complete stranger who was significantly older than me and the experience left me realizing how potentially dangerous it could have all been. It was too much for me to consider. I praised God for His protection and I never saw that man again.

After that incident, I got sexually involved with a supposedly "Christian" guy. He was weird and once again I was so deceived. He told me all about his mental abilities and how he was gifted. He gave me these outlandish stories of something with his intelligence and working with the government. It was scary because he was so believable. He was the only guy who ever tried to mix God and casual sex.

We no sooner finished having sex and he had the audacity to turn on Christian music. I couldn't believe his hypocrisy. I knew that sex outside of marriage was sin but he acted as if he and God were so close that having sex with me didn't matter. He and Jesus were still just fine. I knew that God was holy and that we had just sinned—I didn't want to think about God.

When this guy abruptly broke up with me, he told me that he had found another girlfriend and he no longer was interested in me. Later, I realized that he was mentally unstable which was why he lived at home and came to college to take courses. My first roommate had dated him a year before and one day I talked with her and she let me know all about his mental issues. I had been deceived once again.

My new roommate, Joan, was even more bizarre. She was super-intelligent and yet she had few friends. Every weekend Joan went home to be with her parents. I found that odd. She spent hours mesmerized in front of the TV watching soap operas. I had been addicted to one soap opera when I was in junior high. Because Dad worked until five and Mom didn't come home from teaching until about that time, I was on my own alone in our house. My parents would have never approved of my filling my head and heart with adultery, immorality, compromise and foolishness that took place daily before my eyes.

I became addicted once again to that particular soap opera. It was so bad that one time neither Joan nor I wanted to leave our dorm during a fire alarm. (It had gone off consistently at the same time two days in a row.) Reluctantly after the blaring continued and fellow students came to bang on our door, we trudged down the stairs and got out of the building. There was no fire after all. Had there been a fire, we would rather have perished in the midst of the saga on the screen than flee to safety.

I made some good Christian friends and I often spent time over in the guys' dorm. The five of us would study, talk, laugh, and just hang out together as there was no other good place to visit. On occasion Joan made snide comments about how often I was with "my guys," but unlike my checkered past, it was all perfectly innocent.

I was teetering on the edge of becoming a fully committed Christian. More than once Joan talked about hours of conversations and the laughter and sexual teasing that she and the jocks had over the phone and in the dorms. I wasn't all that interested in her phone calls.

Once, I came back from visiting the guys and Joan was on the phone, supposedly carrying on a conversation with one of the many jocks on campus. From several feet away from my door, I heard a piercing, incessant shrill as Joan laughed and carried on. It took me awhile but I was repulsed when I realized that she was talking to a dead phone! I was so shocked I didn't know what to do. Because her classes were so different than mine and her afternoons were filled with television watching, the closer I drew to God, the less I found in common with her. I never saw her study and there was no way that I could stay in the room with a television going and concentrate. In the end, we shared a room and not a friendship.

For my entire sophomore year, I thought I had built an honest relationship with Joan, only to discover towards the end of that school year, that she had filled hours of our time with lies. With the prank phone caller, he had lied to me about his age and his marital status and my one boyfriend was mentally unstable and had lied to me as well. Joan's dead phone call conversations were the last thing that I felt I could handle of being deceived anymore.

It gripped me with an intensity that wouldn't let go. I walked down to my college dorm lobby and stood there in agitated and empty silence. *What is Truth, anymore?*

In the recesses of my mind, I had heard that phrase before. I couldn't remember where or who said it, but there was something about it that was so profound. I contemplated and searched my memory and tried to recall any of my literature selections, but nothing seemed to jump out at me.

These words seem like they should be so familiar. I became more confused as I felt these words had deep significance but in all my indoctrination in a secular university, for the life of me, I couldn't remember. *Who said those words? What is truth?* I was shaken as if there were a cloud over my mind....and if I could just reach far enough back, maybe, I could remember.

Then, so faintly an image came into my mind. I saw a man in a robe with long hair. He was standing before a ruler, "What is truth?" the words repeated in soft waves. Then as gently as a lullaby whispered the thought, "I am the Truth." There came an echo from my childhood, *"I am the way, the truth, and the life."*

Of course! Jesus Christ before Pilate, before His crucifixion. Suddenly it was all so simple and yet it seemed like eons since I had heard that sweet Voice. I needed to get outside to think. Something or Someone was drawing me and I didn't want to run away. I wasn't sure how to feel but I knew that I had been stripped in every way possible. I had lost my sexual innocence. I had been deceived by those I trusted. I was the fallen preacher's daughter, haunted by the skeletons of my past. I wanted truth more than anything. I needed truth when every day I was being trained in lies. But to face the truth meant that there was no more hiding or excuses.

I needed simplicity. I had run from the truth all these years. I vehemently despised it and dared God to keep on loving me. Along the way, I encountered real Christians and I couldn't handle their unconditional love. It tore at me and I attacked them verbally. Though it was my second language, I deliberately used profanity around them.

One or two times I used God's name in vain, until one of my friends directly confronted me about it.

"Ruth, I love you. I'll put up with a lot of what you say but when you start to trash my God, that's it." I was ashamed and apologized. I knew that the love of God would break me more than any insults, sexual abuse, rejection or anger. I fought with everything not to be loved. I was no longer worthy of that love and yet, I really didn't want to live eternally without God either. What a quandary to be in!

Chapter 11

Radical Repentance

That night, February 22, 1984, I turned my life over to Jesus. I wanted Him to be Lord of every area. I was tired of running my own life without God when I desperately needed His love and forgiveness. I needed God. I had always needed Him, but for so long I had pushed Him away. Like the "Prodigal Daughter," I questioned would He even take me back?! I didn't just want a prayer answered to get me out of a difficult situation. I wasn't looking for the emotional charge of a church camp prayer and I wasn't trying to manipulate God to get my way. I did all of those in the past. There had been times when I tried walking with God, but I didn't have an attitude of total surrender and once the seeds sprouted, they shriveled and died. This time was different—I finally wanted what He wanted.

I fell to my knees out on the track field and began pouring out my heart to God. I wanted a new life. I laid my heart bare with all its rebellion, deception, brokenness and sin-stained life. *I can never be a virgin again. I can never be pure again . . . but oh, Jesus, if You will just take me as I am, if You can do anything with what's left of my life, then I give it all to You.*

It was radical. It was extreme. I meant every heart-felt word as I wracked with sobs in the dark, starless night. I had run so long from the Only Answer . . . salvation and surrender to Jesus Christ. I felt His heart of love for me, which only made me cry harder as He gently and lovingly took me to a place of forgiveness and peace. I found comfort and solace…and then budding in my heart was Joy! It was a deep reminder of all the years of the love of God, the mercy of God, the power of forgiveness . . . and it was something that grew with each day of fervent commitment and devotion.

He took me just as I was and I began a new life. I was sincere. I was committed to finishing my college degree since my parents were paying for it. I was finishing my sophomore year. Over the next two years I was transformed. I focused on my schoolwork but I also joined a daily Bible study, prayer and fellowship group. I wasn't interested in anything sexual with any guy, not even a kiss. I wanted to be pure. I poured my longings into Jesus. There was nothing that I couldn't or didn't talk with Him about. This was incredible. Friends who had witnessed to me off and on for the last two years couldn't believe I had changed. They were incredulous that God had gotten a hold of me and I was just as surprised and shocked as they were.

That summer, I became a church camp counselor at the same camp I had attended years ago. At the end of the summer, God gently confronted me with an area that was painfully real. I admitted how incredibly lonely I was for a male companion. I was brought face-to-face with the lie that I had believed. I cried as I acknowledged, *I really do want to be married, Lord.* I had convinced myself that no one would have me. Then I rationalized my desires into being "single" for Jesus. That way I wouldn't have to deal with the pain and shattered hopes of no longer being sexually pure and innocent.

Once I returned to college my junior year, I developed even closer friendships with my brothers in the Lord. Because I wanted to be married someday, I found myself capable of "falling in love" with them. Obviously, these times of infatuation happened only one at a time.

It started with John. My freshman year, he met me and wanted to get to know me. I gave him permission to call me once a week but other than that, I focused on my studies.

John grew up in church. He was a good guy but eventually he fell in love with one of my friends. John's roommate was Ted.

Ted was blond, cute, sweet and a total gentleman. He was strong in his walk with Jesus and he stood out in the crowd as a committed believer. Ted called us all to accountability. Once when I was visiting in the guys' dorm, Ted reminded me that it was time to leave because "we don't want to give the appearance of evil."

I was shy and ate alone. Ted came and got my cafeteria tray and brought it over to his table of about four guys to eat with them. From that point on, I always ate with them. We all teased that someday Ted would be a preacher. He had a spiritual maturity about him. His hair was thinning and he looked almost bald in places but he was only twenty.

I was searching for answers when Ted met me. He shared passionately against the murder of unborn children and I was open to listen. He showed me a Keith Green ministry newsletter with pictures of aborted babies— something I had never seen before. Those three photographs both convinced and convicted me. I repented of my views on abortion and for my willful ignorance.

God used my friendships with these Christian young men. They befriended me my first year of college and we kept getting closer throughout my four years. During the first two years, they interacted with me on a daily basis but I was still having seasons of running from Jesus. I have no doubt that Ted and John prayed diligently for my heart to change.

Next there was Alan. He was John's friend. Alan had become more committed in his walk with Christ due to John and Ted's influence. He worked in the cafeteria and I smiled and laughed with him. He was friendly but shy. My crush on him was brief. We laughed about liking each other. "Ruth, I'm flattered. I really am. But, well, I mean you're pretty and all. It's not that. It's just that I look at you more like a sister in the Lord. I think that it is better this way." So, Alan and I remained friends. He focused on studying, being a diligent worker and growing in his walk with Jesus. He was a part of our "group." We enjoyed his lighthearted playfulness and his caring heart for people. Even though he'd grown up in church, he hadn't been discipled. He joined John and Ted for Bible study and prayer in their dorm room on a daily basis.

Then there was Stan. He was studying to be a nurse. He was sensitive, easy to talk to, fun and a good friend. Eventually, he fell in love with a girl and only after it was "safe" to tell me how he felt, did he share his feelings. "You know, Ruth, there was a time when

I really liked you. I thought maybe we'd have a future together. But I never told you. You liked Pete and we were all such good friends that I didn't want to risk it. I didn't know if you liked me that way. I am so glad that you and I have only ever been just friends. It's better this way."

I met Craig. He liked me but we both knew that it was better for us to focus on friendship. Ted befriended Craig as had the rest of my guy friends, and within a few months, he repented and asked Jesus into his heart. Craig was a young believer and he was hungry to learn everything he could about God. He was radical in his conversion and sometimes he was so full of zeal that he reminded me of Paul in Scripture. He had a good sense of humor and he loved learning and deep intellectual discussions. He and Stan also joined Ted's Bible study.

In the midst of these friendships, there was Pete. He was older, a graduate of our university and still single. He was a strong Christian and he mentored us. We all looked at him as "the older brother" and he cared for each one of us in prayer, encouragement and when he visited us on campus. He was a body builder and he encouraged me to take weight training. I took one class and thoroughly enjoyed it but, unfortunately I didn't keep up with it. Pete was handsome with long brown hair, tanned muscular body and he loved to laugh. He was older, owned his house, had an established job and I was definitely falling in love with him. He was friendly and knew lots of people. He found creative ways to witness about Jesus.

Pete often told me, "I don't think many people are called to be missionaries, anymore." (I struggled with that because I believed that God had called me to be a missionary. Yet, I had begun to give my heart to Pete and to hope that the day would come when he would fall in love with me.)

He and I shared deep feelings for one another but they weren't to the exclusion of ministering to other people. Our group was outward focused as we longed to see God change the lives of our fellow students. We all prayed several hours weekly, both individually and corporately, against all kinds of evil that blatantly displayed itself on our secular, humanistic campus.

Pete told us, "I'm not going to date or kiss a woman until God tells me, 'This is the one.'" That was a new concept for me and since I was deeply attracted to Pete, I made that my commitment as well. Pete singled me out as a close friend. Every Monday he called me and we talked for about two hours. We spent all day Sunday together at church services and every day he came to our Bible study and prayer time held in my dorm room. That study was open to anyone who wanted to join us. We desperately sought God for revival on our campus and we were fervent in our desires for holiness. We allowed God to use us as examples, witnesses and as true believers. It was awesome to grow in our faith.

There was no compromise in Ted's life. He only listened to Christian music. Ted had his own car and he drove the guys and me to church almost every Sunday and sometimes in the middle of the week. This commitment involved a forty-five minute drive one way. We all grew together in prayer, Bible study, worship and teaching. God was the center of our conversations.

We all admired Ted. I felt especially blessed to be in the "inner circle" of relationships with "the guys." For the most part, I was one of them. Other girls were seen as feminine, attractive, and potential dating material. As Ted and I spent more time together, he called me, "Roo." After a trip to Israel, he gave me a necklace with my name in Hebrew and a bracelet. He had purchased gifts for some of the guys but I was the only girl in college that received a gift. His kindness made me feel special.

I sincerely believed that he liked me as more than a friend. Once he had his arm around me and there was romance in the atmosphere. Instead of embracing me, he stopped and looked into my eyes. "Roo, I don't want to do anything that wouldn't please God. If I'm not the one for you, then I don't want your husband to feel bad about this. I don't want to hurt you or for either of us to get hurt." I admired his stand for God but I was saddened because I knew that unless God spoke to him, Ted would remain nothing more than a close brother in the Lord.

I had a Christian roommate my junior year. She was beautiful with curly, long brown hair, green eyes and a knock-out figure. She was feminine, friendly, fun and flirtatious. Within a few weeks, she and Ted were dating.

I couldn't believe it. All the guys were physically attracted to her. John tried to explain things to me. "Ruth, we all like you. You're like one of us. You know, one of the guys. But Alicia, well, she's.... a woman. She's beautiful. You know what I mean. She's…feminine."

The more John sought to explain, the more he stuck his foot in his mouth. After awkward chuckling, he finally broke off the conversation. I bit back tears. Each one of these godly young men was aware of me as a spiritual sister and they treated me that way. Though they admitted that I had many qualities they wanted in a wife, none of them felt "led by God" to date or marry me. That played off my fears of always being ugly—of the words spoken in junior high, "Stick a bag over Ruth's head because her face is so ugly—but she's got a knock-out body."

Their obvious delight and attraction towards Alicia and other girls only served to reinforce that fear and anxiety. I found myself asking once again, *God, why am I never good enough? What am I… chopped liver?*

One time I walked into my dorm room and Ted and Alicia stood ready to kiss. I was stunned. He looked embarrassed when he saw me. Alicia was thrilled that Ted was dating her. I walked out of the room. They broke up after a short while but remained good friends.

There were mixed signals about Ted's feelings towards me. One time he drove me to his house a few hours away from my old hometown. I spent an afternoon with his family and the weekend with a female friend from his church. I was extremely awkward and realized how far out of my social and financial league Ted's family was. In addition, I met some of his church friends and I told one girl how much I liked Ted and that I thought I would marry him someday. She listened but said, "Ted likes Jenny. He's praying about a future with her and is just waiting on God's timing."

That was an embarrassment and a shock to me. Ted couldn't wait to introduce me to Jenny. She was sweet, beautiful and godly. I couldn't deny his attraction towards her. I had thoroughly misunderstood his intentions. I had manipulated my way down to his hometown since I needed a ride. John had also come with us since he lived only a county away from Ted. All of us were within about forty miles of each other and Ted, being gracious, offered to drive us where we needed to go. It resulted in a strange weekend.

I was visiting with one of my girlfriends and she was telling me about a relationship that appeared to be headed for marriage. She commented about how God was putting it all together. We sat at her table eating spaghetti. In my heart, I spoke to the Lord in a simple, honest way. *Lord, I release You to choose whoever You want me to marry. I surrender.*

That night we went to church and a speaker preached and prayed over various people. I was excited to get to know God in this way as well. This same man had come to the church before and called me, as well as several others, to listen to specific things that he felt that God was showing him. I had an unusual pain in my arm and he came over to minister to me. He said, "I smell Italian. I smell spaghetti."

I was embarrassed and immediately clapped my hand over my mouth. I assumed he smelled my breath, since I hadn't brushed my teeth because I was visiting with my friend. I had stayed and joined her for church instead of returning to my dorm. I responded, "That's what I had for lunch."

The congregation laughed as he continued, "Lord, I thank You that You know all things. I thank You that I see her walking beside one whom she loves, one who loves her, one whom the Lord has chosen, and that she will say of You, "Lord, You do all things well.""

I let the tears course down my cheeks as this man spoke to the depths of my soul. I knew that God had heard my heart's cry of surrender. This man didn't smell my breath; he spoke the heart of God to me. Never had I been given such a precious promise from Jesus. He knew all of my past and He still promised me that I would have someone who would love me and that I would really love. I could trust God in this most intimate area of my heart and life. I pondered that word in my heart many times. I had the word "twenty-five" come into my mind and I wondered if I would get married then. There were still some challenges ahead.

One Valentine's Day, it snowed so much that classes were cancelled. Pete called Alicia and me and asked if we wanted to go play in the snow. He wanted to come and pick us up. I was excited and I somehow strongly communicated to Alicia that I didn't want her to come. I wanted a "date" with Pete. After all, he always talked to me. She reluctantly consented and I had a blast with Pete.

We played in the snow and one time we fell and the scene was perfect for a kiss. But we both wanted to wait on God. So, we got up and laughed together. By the end of the day, in my dorm room, my heart raced from pure joy. Whether it was from the pizza or the caffeine all I knew was that I "heard" in my head, "Pray for Pete." Well, I did pray but in my flesh I became deceived and thought those three words had a greater meaning. I convinced myself that "God" promised me that I would marry Pete.

From that point on, for the next year, I saw Pete and my inter-actions with him through the clouded view of "God's will." These "words" were all my mind and my flesh but I wanted to marry Pete so badly that I refused to listen to the truth.

After Bible study one time, Pete called me aside and confessed in tears. "I struggle with lusting over you." I forgave him and prayed that he would see me as holy, godly and as his sister in the Lord. I was a mixture of emotions. I didn't want him to "lust" over me but I did want him to be attracted to me. It saddened me that all he felt was "lust." Those were his words. He didn't indicate that he wanted to date me.

Later on, Pete invited me to a Christian concert and then on the way, he let me know that he had also invited Kimberly. She was gorgeous, sophisticated, godly and his age. I felt like a kid sister being dragged around. It was terribly awkward. They started dating after that.

One night Pete called our room and talked to Alicia. She was thrilled for him because he called to tell us that he and Kimberly were getting married. I tried to make small talk with him but I struggled with my own emotions.

I realized once again, that I had totally misread the intentions of Pete towards me. He saw me as a friend, a "little sister" in the Lord. Alone in the quietness of my room, I wept. I poured out my heart to God. It was then that I was able to finally hear what He had tried to impress upon me. I had refused to listen but now I was ready to hear God and not my own desires. I clutched a small teddy bear, pressed it against my chest and allowed the Lord's soothing Voice to bring healing to my heart and soul.

"You want that cookie and you can't understand why I won't give it to you. What you don't realize is that I have already given you five cookies and if I give you that cookie, you will vomit the others up."

He was referring to John, Ted, Alan, Stan and Craig. The Lord taught me how to have pure relationships with my spiritual brothers and certainly I "couldn't marry them all." With each friendship, God taught me more about Himself and developed areas in my life that needed to mature.

From John, I saw rich perseverance and loyalty to friendships. He was refreshingly honest and loved to understand "why" and he wanted deep conversations and sincere closeness. He was faithful through hard times, misunderstandings and various challenges.

In Ted, I saw tremendous humility and a passion for the lost. Ted loved people and he didn't judge them. He accepted them where they were and let them know how much God loved them and how much he did, too. He was an amazing Christian who welcomed people into his life.

In Alan, I saw such a sweetness and joy towards life. He saw the simple pleasures of obeying Jesus and caring about people. He was a good, hard worker and he allowed his light for Jesus to shine in every circumstance. He had a gentle heart for prayer and that was a primary focus for him.

With Craig, he was radical for God. He wanted to think, understand and be actively involved in seeing people's lives change. He loved to laugh, was great at humor and was a tremendously philosophical young man. He hated boredom and couldn't figure out how some of the "Christians" he had met could be so dry, dead and lifeless. He was powerfully saved and his zeal left most of us in shock at times.

Stan was so kind, sensitive and caring. He and I often talked with each other more "one-on-one" and I loved his vulnerability, his passion for God and his commitment to truth. He struggled in deep ways in his life but he was willing to be accountable and to be teachable. I loved encouraging him.

I loved these brothers in Christ because they were family to me. There was such a richness of sharing, love, laughter and mutual caring that we had towards one another. I had never had such pure relationships with guys before and there was never anything ungodly or sexual in any of our interactions. It was beautiful to me and I learned to love for the sake of the friendship, not for my own selfishness.

At the same time, God continued to heal my relationship with my parents. For my twenty-first birthday, I asked them for only one gift. They gave me a few presents but the gift they gave at my request was what I cherished most. I asked them to each write a letter to me. On my birthday card, in their own handwriting, were the most precious words I had read about their love for me and how blessed they were to have me as their daughter. I loved that card and re-read it many times as I allowed their words to remove the pain of the past and restore me. That birthday card was a strong testimony to me that I was a different person and that God had touched my life. It felt wonderful to be affirmed, loved and admired by Dad and Mom.

Dear Ruth Mary,

"You have come a long way, baby" so goes the Virginia Slims ad. And you have. It is a long time since I waited on the 24th floor of the Nix Hospital while your mother labored on the 23rd floor and the announcement came to me of the birth of a baby girl, 21 years ago. Then you were a dark complexioned little child. Today you are a bronzed beauty. Then you could cry. Now you can sing, write poetry, express yourself on paper and with words.

As you launch out from your 21st birthday my hope and prayer for you is expressed best by Paul in the letter to the Ephesians Chapter 4:13-16. May you keep on growing in the knowledge of the Son of God and becoming more and more mature in Him and bearing more and more His likeness in manner, in thought and in action. Happy Birthday...21 year old!

With love, Dad.

———— ✳ ————

Dear Ruth Mary,

    Like your father, I too recollect your birth and childhood—those times when you had a string of beads or an aluminum foil crown atop your head and a smile that proclaimed you to be regal. Today you have a radiance of your own that needs no costume. There were those happy days of Scouting when I proudly served badges, knowing that you had to meet <u>my</u> standards to get them. Today you have still higher standards to reach from One Who demands perfection and yet Who generously awards you through your faith.

    I recall the thrill of your editing the yearbook and the tremendous change in your attitude once you had the experience of Girls' State. As you look toward adulthood there will continue to be thrilling events and ventures. Although you may not know what the future holds you may be assured Who holds the future!

    Love to our little girl grown up, Mom

God worked on me from the inside out. As my desires changed and I wanted to please Him more, my clothing, speech, choice of music, interests and goals, changed as well. One Saturday, I felt His prompting, "You need to get rid of your poetry." *Lord, You can't be serious. That's my identity.* "I know. I want to be your Identity." *God, if I get rid of my poetry, I'll be left with nothing of my own plans and desires.* I struggled and wept. But as I prayed, it became clear that most of those poems did not glorify God and they were spiritual ties to an old life. I kept a few but the majority of them were torn to shreds, bit by bit as I joyfully surrendered to Jesus. I honestly did not know if I would ever write poetry again. I remained an empty vessel for God to lead and fill. Now, my only "career" was eventually to go into missions. My dreams of becoming a famous writer lay in ashes on the altar of commitment and surrender.

Pete and Kimberly didn't get married after all. Close to my Graduation, Pete called me to spend the weekend at his house. I could study for my finals and swim in his pool. It thrilled me to be asked and I knew his house had two bedrooms so it wasn't like I would do anything wrong. I didn't tell any of the guys. I said, "Sure!"

Pete came and picked me up. That evening we attended a Bible study and when he introduced me, it was just as a friend. Someone questioned him about my being a "girlfriend" but that wasn't the title he gave me. I got to his house. The pool was empty which he apologized for. He had hoped to have it ready. In the evening, we were in his room, on his bed talking. I massaged his back and we ended up lying down. The moment came when it was perfect to kiss. I looked at him, "So, if you kiss me, does this mean I'm going to be your wife?"

He stopped abruptly and looked straight into my eyes. "Ruth, I can't ever marry you." There was no explanation and I didn't say anything. The pain in my heart was deep as the sword of his words penetrated. I pulled away from him and left to go to sleep in my own room. I was too numb to react or respond.

That night there was a thunderstorm. In the morning after breakfast, Pete told me, "I hoped you would've come to my room and I would've comforted you." I looked at him, with all the dashed hopes of two years of friendship, "Pete, I need you to take me back to my dorm. I need to finish my finals." He drove me back to campus. I was emotionally devastated.

By the time we got back to campus, I had missed supper and started to boil water for soup. Squatting on the floor near the small electric pot, I started to stand up and I bumped the pot, knocking it over. The boiling water spilled on my bare feet. I screamed in pain and hobbled as fast as I could to get to the bathroom. I turned on the spigot and blasted ice cold water over my burning skin as I prayed out loud, "Jesus, heal me. Oh, God, please heal my feet!"

The girls came into the bathroom and the next thing I knew, buckets of ice were being thrown into the tub, onto my feet. The funny thing was that I knew they had all stashed ice to go with their alcohol for Finals week. I was touched by their care and concern.

I was transported by ambulance to the hospital with second degree burns on both feet. It was only a few days until Graduation. I prayed out loud and the medical student beside me encouraged me. That night, back in my room, Pete called to check on me since the guys told him about my accident. He didn't tell them about my staying with him. I was cordial on the phone but our conversation was extremely short. That was the last time we spoke to each other until four months later.

Right afterwards, I got a phone call from one of my spiritual "mothers" saying that God had laid me on her heart. "Are you okay?"

"As a matter of fact, I just burned my feet."

"No, the Lord told me to call and ask you about your hurting heart." That was the first time she'd called me at college and I hadn't spoken to her in almost two years. God was aware of the deep pain in my heart. I now knew that I had deceived myself and that Pete wasn't going to be my husband.

My feet were bandaged and I had crutches. Three days later at my follow-up visit the doctor said, "You don't have anything more than what looks like a bad sunburn." I didn't need crutches anymore. The blisters and exposed skin were healed. God did a complete restorative miracle!

The last four years I had worked diligently to be the best student I could be. At the end of my first semester I made the Dean's List for my grades. I was so amazed and proud of that achievement that I made that my goal from then on. As a result, I sacrificed a lot of fun and extracurricular activities but I concluded my college career graduating with honors. Cum laude! That thrill was no small achievement for me.

I walked down the aisle at Graduation with perfectly normal feet and said good-bye to college. I now had a bachelor's degree in English and two minors, one in Psychology and the other in Counseling and Rehabilitation. I left with broken dreams of marrying Pete. I never seriously dated any Christian man and I didn't have a "Mrs." degree or any sign of getting close to marriage.

I wondered what direction my life would take. I still felt called to be involved in missions and I didn't find any of my godly brothers drawn in that same direction. I knew that I would compromise Jesus' plan for my life, if I settled for a man who wasn't called to missions.

After college, I lived by myself in a furnished garage apartment. I got a job in telemarketing and I was terrible at it. Within four months I was laid off permanently. During that time, Kyle wanted to date me. I kept trying to tell him that I just wanted to be friends but eventually we started dating. Kyle was cute, still in college, and he went to my church.

My old college friends planned a surprise birthday party for me. It was so good to see them all again. Pete came also but by then I was dating Kyle. During the party, Alicia flirted with Kyle and he flirted back. It was painful for me to watch especially because Pete pointed it out. I didn't go back with Pete. I knew I wanted marriage and he didn't want me for that.

That evening when Kyle and I returned to my apartment I confronted him. "You either choose Alicia or me but it's not both."

"Oh, Honey, I want you. I was just being friendly with her." I didn't exactly believe it but we stayed together. Alicia's ways reminded me too much of Vicky, from my high school days. Alicia was a believer but there were areas in her life that needed to mature.

Kyle was from a country background and raised chickens, pigs and other animals. He wanted to have a simple lifestyle with lots of children and animals. He wasn't much of a reader and didn't share my intellectual level or interests. Though he was in college, he didn't seem to have big dreams for his future.

One day he showed me a large black and white rabbit. I petted it. A few days later, I had lunch with his family.

"Kyle, where's the rabbit?"

"Oh, Honey, what do you think we're having for lunch?" I was shocked. I didn't get sick at my stomach but I felt sorry for the cute rabbit that I had played with and petted. I had never eaten rabbit before. It tasted greasy but other than that, it was okay.

Kyle had earlier dated a girl who he believed "God" told him he would marry. She broke up with him. While he dated me, he said, "If Cathy ever changes her mind, I will marry her." I felt like "second best" and it didn't make me happy. He was just as deceived about "God's" voice and "leading" as I had been about Pete. Kyle mentioned marriage to me. I didn't want to marry him but I began to wonder if anyone would ever want to marry me. I felt like my chances were slim. He was using "God" as if "God" were telling him, "*Now*, I want you to marry Ruth."

Mom's wisdom came over the phone, "Sweetheart, don't go off and marry the first man who asks you. You really haven't had that many good, healthy dating relationships. You need to be sure this is someone you want to spend the rest of your life with."

It comforted me. For some odd reason, I had it in my head that if "God" wanted me to marry Kyle, I had no choice. While visiting Kyle, he talked about wanting alligators as pets and I became more and more perturbed. Then he said he wanted snakes! I protested and said they were cursed and he continued to argue. We dropped the subject.

I went home and spent time telling God how I felt about Kyle. Then I heard His still, small voice, "I never told you that you had to marry Kyle." It was a tremendous relief. I broke off my relationship with him, left my apartment and headed home to live with my parents. All I knew was how to be a good student.

Chapter 12

Precious Promises
and Renewed Visions

I got a job as a counselor at a new church camp with an
extremely small staff. I began the summer on fire for God
but the spiritually of the staff was extremely low, and as the weeks
waned, I became desperate for a guy. I didn't have any strong godly
supports and I was ashamed at how sensual and compromised I
became. I didn't get involved with any guy sexually but the scary
thing is that I wanted to. Surely, God would have my husband here,
wouldn't He?

Towards the last week I had a dream. I was in a red convertible
with a female friend and we were speeding. We hit something and
I flew out of the car. I knew that I was going to die. I was aware
that I had fallen away from God and I had tears streaming down my
face, telling my mother I was sorry and remembering, "I never even
got married."

I woke up and there was a tremendous solemnity about the dream.
I kept having the words in my head, "though Esau wept bitterly, there
was found no repentance." I sensed strongly that God spoke to me but
I didn't realize how strongly until later that day. We took the campers
on a canoeing trip and the other girl counselor and I scouted out the
path by the waterfall and how we definitely needed to avoid the rocks.
We emptied out our canoe of supplies into the other canoes. We were

chosen to be the last to go down. All the campers made it safely as did the male counselors so we took off.

Somehow we got all messed up and went down exactly the wrong way. It was terrifying! In a split second, we hit the rock broadside and the impact threw her out into the water. She grabbed her head and went under—I thought she had died. I was helpless to do anything as I tried to guide the canoe away from the waterfall. For what seemed like an eternity, she re-surfaced, grabbed the canoe and we made it to shore. The other campers and staff helped her out of the water. Her leg was in great pain and they made a stretcher out of canoe paddles. We all hiked back to the main camp. Her leg was badly bruised but nothing was broken. I was physically fine but emotionally shaken. The summer had ended and I knew that once again, I was away from God.

My brother Walt, called and invited me to Maryland for a few days to visit. "I am like the Prodigal Daughter." He seemed to be okay with that and came and got me anyway.

The sad irony was that before I got the summer job, I had prayed that God would give me a job so that I could earn money so that I could go to a missionary school in Texas. By the time the summer ended, I would be grateful if I could just sit in the house of God for the rest of my life. I felt like I had disqualified myself from ever being able to serve God or be used by Him.

Walt's church had Revival services. I couldn't stand it in the sense that my heart broke over my sin and my feelings of failing God. Because He had changed my heart those last two years in college, I never went back into sexual sin. I got in one or two compromised situations, but I was so convicted, ashamed and guilt-ridden that I never wanted to go any farther. There was too much at stake with my love for Jesus and my desire to please Him as my Lover. I just couldn't cheat on God like that.

I cried as I sat outside the sanctuary. A lady asked if she could pray for me. I consented and as she prayed, she stopped and looked at me, "Have you ever thought about missions? I see you in a place with oxen and carts and I believe the Lord keeps giving me the word, 'Islands.'" I was ecstatic! God still wanted me in missions. I hadn't fallen so far away that He didn't want me anymore. Joyful tears coursed down my cheeks as I briefly shared with this stranger that I had wanted to be a missionary since I was a little girl.

The last night of Revival before I went home to my parent's house in West Virginia, I was at the altar praying fervently to make sure that God wanted me to go to a missionary training school in Texas. I sought His will and surrendered mine. It was a huge step for me and I wanted so much to make sure I heard correctly.

The Pastor leaned down and said to me, "The Lord says, 'this move you're about to make is His will and it will be years before you fully understand the significance of the step you are taking.'" Wow! Talk about another confirmation. I was amazed at how God met me in the most loving ways as I sought His guidance.

Chapter 13

Unraveling the Lies
and Binding Cords of Love

I prepared to move to Texas to attend Youth With A Mission (YWAM) for the next five months. YWAM was a thirty-year old missions organization that worked with many denominations whereas my parents' denomination had been doing missions for over a hundred years. YWAM required its students and staff to raise financial support to attend. That was difficult for my parents to accept. In Dad's words, "We raised you and educated you so that you wouldn't be in the position of siphoning money off of people." I wasn't getting a job; I was raising support for "someone else to take care of me." I wasn't investing my education to work for me and thus they felt that they couldn't support my choice.

It was a difficult time for me and yet, I couldn't blame them. They had paid for my college education and I never once had to work a job while in college. They wanted me to be able to concentrate fully on my studies and knew that an outside job might be too stressful for me.

While in college, I stopped attending the church of my Dad's denomination. Instead, I mainly went to charismatic, non-denominational churches. As I embarked on this move to Texas I sensed there would be pain related to the missionary call of God on my life and that it wasn't going to be easy. I sang prayers as I packed. Though my parents loved me and prayed for me, there were still many hurdles to overcome. I entrusted my parents to God. I moved in faith because even I didn't fully understand what He had planned for my life.

I boarded a Greyhound bus and rode it for thirty-eight hours straight. I arrived at two in the morning. On the way to the base, I began asking questions. "How do you know when you graduate? How are the grades determined? What kinds of courses are offered?" They were baffled and I was perplexed. The brochures I read all said this was a "Discipleship Training School." Having recently graduated from college, I expected a Bible School.

My room housed six girls with about sixty in the entire dorm. The atmosphere reminded me of a glorified church camp. My head reeled with the reality of what I stepped into. Most of the students were straight out of high school and the staff were only young people as well. The "deans" the staff had talked about were Deans in name only. There were two men on the teaching staff who were named Dean. With my college mindset, I had completely misunderstood.

After introductions the first night, the speaker started talking about "Relationships," —relationships with God and relationships with others. I was jolted. *Relationships! I don't have relationships. I have acquaintances. I don't even have a "relationship" with God. I love Him and I obey Him but "relationship"?* I had too many painful memories associated with that word.

This was crazy! I thought I had enrolled in a Bible college to get trained on how to become a missionary. I had graduated from a four year college. I knew how to study, to write papers, to research, to be godly—but this word, "relationships" quite frankly scared me. I really didn't want to get to know people. I wanted to be a missionary!

Staff members of different ministry departments stood to share aspects of what they did. The School of the Bible Director said, "Once you finish your two training sessions here, come to SOTB for a year. We'll study the Bible in-depth along with lots of other subjects and you'll receive an Associates' degree in Biblical Studies." Now, that was where I was supposed to be. It frustrated me that I had to wait a year but I saw it as a "necessary evil" or maybe a "prerequisite" until I could get to the major.

In class, we gave our testimonies. I was frightened to speak in front of all these strangers and furthermore, I had never given a testimony. I didn't know what to say. From what I gathered, people talked about their lives before Jesus. I was sure that all the students were strong in their walks with Jesus and that none of them had been recently backslidden. I felt like a hypocrite. I became extremely nervous. I shook, sweated and stumbled over my words.

The shock rate skyrocketed. I managed a few words about my childhood as a preacher's kid, being molested and that I looked for love in all the wrong places. I broke and cried and couldn't believe that I was so stupid to tell everybody my secrets and shame. I heard my mother's voice reminding me, "Ruth Mary, nobody needs to know what you've done. In essence, sweep it under the rug, and move on." I replayed my words to the class, over and over again and kicked myself many times. *How could I have been so stupid? Why did I open up and tell everybody? What was I thinking? What does any of this have to do with becoming a missionary?*

I sat down and avoided all the eyes. I was mortified at my vulnerability. No one else came near to a testimony like mine. At lunch, different people quietly shared with me that God was going to bless me. I just wanted to crawl under a rock. I knew without a shadow of a doubt that I had just blown it for any man to consider me as marriage potential.

As I prayed and asked God to help me now that I had so vulnerably shared my heart's secrets, I felt like He said, "Your husband isn't here." I was disappointed but at the same time, it freed me to just be myself without any concern as to crushes, infatuation, boyfriends, or anything else. It didn't stop those feelings but I didn't think it would be so easy to become deceived as I had in the past.

The teachings in class were deeply personal and I discovered my emotions again. It frustrated me that I seemed to have so little control over my feelings. I wiped tears away and during breaks, I went to the bathroom and cried. These concepts penetrated years of closed off places in my heart. I felt like everybody thought I was a basket-case. I disliked my emotional instability.

Tears gushed as more lies about God were exposed and the truth seeped into the dry and dusty cracks of the walls in my heart. I felt lonely as I watched the students hang out and occasionally flirt. It tore at me. I tried to apply the principles of building relationships with both guys and girls but they seemed to avoid me. I had some friends but we were less popular. It was clear to me that Christian or not, there were still distinct differences between those who "had it" and those who didn't. The pretty girls and the cute guys—but I was here to get an education.

When I left home, I had cashed in my bank account and waited for the money to arrive to pay my tuition. Consequently, I didn't have any other money to spend. I didn't engage in a lot of social activities. Instead, I focused on the books and homework. Most of the other students studied less than I did or they pursued relationships more. I went to bed by nine o'clock regardless of what was going on around me.

We had a teaching on Restitution—making things right with people that we had sinned against in our past. I thought once everything was "under the blood of Jesus" I could move on and forget about the past. But God showed me what my sin did to His heart and to those He created for relationship with Him. I saw a path behind me strewn with broken, shattered hearts that stretched across the canvas of my life. It hurt to see my own sin and to weep over hurting God's heart. I spent that week writing several letters. I confessed my sins, took responsibility for my choices instead of blaming other people, and I asked to be forgiven.

Living a life without God in some ways seemed easier. In the past, I focused on my own selfishness and didn't care about who I hurt in the process. By contrast as a Christian, Jesus called me to love my enemies, to bless those who had hurt me, to forgive far more than I had ever imagined. This heart surgery went deep and lasted a long time. The rewards of obedience far outweighed the emotional tearing that I went through. To have a clean and clear conscience before God was something that was so precious to me.

There was a teaching about sexuality. I sat with great anticipation as the speaker began to reveal the definition of a "real woman" and a "real man." I wrestled with these ambivalent feelings, *Was I really a man in a woman's body? Were the kids in school, right?* I sat upright with my pen poised. "A real woman is— a female one." And "A real man is— a male one." That wasn't profound, but it settled the accusations of the enemy once and for all. I shed many tears as I forgave my peers and asked God to break the power of their words over me.

Chapter 14

Victorious Victim

I went to a seminar for girls held in the gym. It was on Rape. I listened intently and I finally got the courage to go to the speaker at the end. "Is it possible to be so paralyzed with fear that you can't do anything, even if there's no gun, no knife, and no sign of physical abuse or being taken advantage?"

I was shocked when I heard the answer. "Absolutely yes! It was against your will. God grieved over the pain other people were inflicting upon you. It wasn't something you wanted; it was forced; it was playing on your weakness. God saw your heart, even long before you did."

I felt like another layer of a peeled onion with accompanying tears that burned. The things that happened in my childhood produced a pattern of fear, lack of control and weakness. I was terrified of rape because I knew the emotional torture and shame. For years I had denied that I had been raped in my high school years. This seminar made me face the truth of my own deception.

It was a beautiful night of transformation. I dug deep to the places where I had refused the label of "rape victim." In high school, I sarcastically quipped, "You can't rape the willing." I spouted that lie as a defense. I knew that being treated in such a disrespectful manner could never equate to "love"— not even in my own distorted fantasy world.

God became even more intimate with me. Godly men and women spoke into the depths of my soul, fragmented personality and wounded heart. These experiences and words penetrated and saturated every part of me. The painful, infected places became cleansed as the deep love of Jesus poured into me. He healed a vessel that had been violently abused.

In college, no one knew my past and it didn't matter. I kept my personal life to myself and the friendships I had with the "guys" were all based on my present life with Jesus. In contrast, at this missions' school, I dealt daily with unresolved issues in my past. As a result, I felt alienated from many of my fellow classmates who appeared to have much healthier and godly lives and didn't seem to struggle with the teachings like I did.

In a devotional time, I felt like God spoke to me. "*I want you to take all your affections and emotions and give them to Me for a year. Every morning we'll have a date because I love you and I want to shower you in My love. I am your Lover and I want to kiss away the tears, caress you in My arms and touch your lips. I want to hold your hands, flatter you, bless you, and tell you how beautiful you are to Me. I am with you always. I want to run through the fields with you, take walks in the evening with you, and spend time with you. Come away My beloved.*

You can stand tall because I am beside you, holding your hand, and telling you how much I love you. I want a year of showering you in My love because you are My bride. You don't have to stifle all those feelings, I want you to open your heart and give them to Me.

I will be the Leader in this relationship. I will pursue you, and I will woo you to My heart. When there is an empty chair beside you, it's not there because people don't like you; it's there because I am sitting beside you." < Is this what intimacy is? >

"*Pour your desire for a husband into Me. Give me one year of your love. You need to learn to receive love from Me, so that when I bring a man into your life for you to marry, you will receive his love and not blow him off.*"

"*I am not ashamed to be your Husband. I have redeemed you. I will give you a man with the same convictions you have. He will be the head of your household and your love for him will be magnified and multiplied as you fall in love with Me."*

The emotional rawness of being passionately loved in purity from the Almighty God was incredible and burned into my feminine heart. It satisfied and delighted me. The inexpressible joy knowing I was forgiven was wonderful. Many nights I sang outside to Jesus as I ran in the fields with Him and danced. I imagined I was a little girl with a garland of flowers on my head.

My heart burst with love—something I had never felt before. There was no lust or violence and I didn't fake my emotions; this was real. I was enraptured with Jesus as my Lover and no one was that special or significant in my life. This wasn't a stuffy religious exercise or a relationship of a Master to a slave. This love relationship with Jesus, the Holy Spirit and my Father God was that of deepest friendship and as profound as a bride and groom. There was a mystery to it all and I thrived in my life. Laughter was restored to my soul and my mouth was filled with song.

Chapter 15

A New Identity

What God began in college, He now reinforced and strengthened. I felt vibrant and joy radiated from me. I learned to embrace the truth of my identity in Christ and that was powerful enough to silence the lies of satan. God continued to send more confirmations of the work that He was doing in my heart. He spoke through other people to let me know that I did indeed, hear His voice.

We had a specific time of ministry and I was one of many students called out. That meant that as the staff had prayed earlier, they felt that I was to be ministered to in specific ways during the gathering. Evie shared John 4 and said I was like the woman at the well. She felt like an outcast and Jesus met and ministered to her. Evie said, "I feel like you have had that identity as an outcast and you come into the Throne room with your head bowed down and your countenance down like, 'Who am I to even talk to You?' I see Jesus just reaching out and lifting your head." She lifted my chin and made me look into her eyes. "God doesn't want you to identify with the past anymore. He has forgotten your sins as far as the east is from the west. I believe He wants you to receive the new identity in Christ and He wants us to pray for you."

So, the staff prayed and severed the cords of my past. She saw me covered in a white robe of righteousness, running through the fields of flowers in a white flowing dress with a flower garland in my hair, running to the Lord. "God is your Dad and you can call Him that. You're as pure and white as a lily of the valley. You're a rose. God will restore innocence and all those things satan stole from you. You're the daughter of your Father God. You're precious. Meditate on Ps. 45 as the King's daughter of the royal priesthood, adorned in purple, which you are wearing."

After the ministry session, I told everybody how I literally ran in the fields and imagined myself dancing with Jesus just a few nights before. "As I let the Lord be my Lover, then He'll bring the man in my life to be my husband, because then I won't worship the man, I'll worship the Lord because I'll see in this man the characteristics of Jesus."

This prayer time came after obedience to God to repent and write letters of restitution. He promised to restore but this was way beyond any of my hopes or expectations. This marvelous and miraculous restoration fascinated and amazed me. The love of God was so much richer and deeper than I had ever experienced or even imagined.

As God poured these deep truths into me, He revealed deep-seated humanistic, anti-Christ philosophies. He exposed my ugly heart attitudes of selfishness, perversion and sin. We listened to a teaching on abortion. It was difficult and it challenged me. God pricked my heart and reminded me of the few times I counseled my friends to get abortions. I shared in their sin because of my heart attitude as a murderer. If I had gotten pregnant, I wouldn't have hesitated to end the life of the baby. I shudder now to write those words but I had believed for so long that "a baby was nothing more than a piece of flesh."

I wept over my selfishness, hatred of God's creation and the intent of my heart. I rocked back and forth in my brokenness as I confessed and renounced the spirit of murder, abortion and hatred. There was a tremendous spiritual release and then I felt God's sweet, gentle voice.

"I will give you a strong stomach. You'll be able to handle it."

I had such a hard time whenever anyone vomited and all I could think about babies was spit up and snotty noses. I couldn't imagine the responsibility of life and death in taking care of a baby. I feared the thought of children whether that was giving birth or raising them. There were so many unknowns and what if I did something wrong? What if a child died and I was responsible? What if I had a daughter and she was abused? But God continued to speak to me about His desires for my future.

"The children of my husband were to be blessed of the Lord—to share love with them and for God to pour out His Spirit on both sons and daughters. I will restore your maternal desires and your innocence. I will give you a son and you will name him Samuel. Like his namesake, he will influence the changing of a nation."

In class, we watched slides of abortion and then slides of a baby developing. I felt love and such tenderness towards little ones! I desired to have children. God changed my emotions so rapidly.

In prayer one time I felt, "You will give your life to Me. You will lose your life for Me." I wasn't sure if that was literally as in physically losing my life or whether it was spiritually. But I responded, *Father, may my life be worthy for You that You will be pleased with me.*

God did many other key things that transformed me from a broken, timid, fearful person into one who was confident in His love, identity and power. I experienced a greater awareness of the truth of Who He is.

After our lecture phase of about three months of intense teachings, we were required to go on an outreach and apply all that up until that point was more of "head knowledge" than heart application. My team went on Outreach to rural Mexico. The last words my mother spoke on the phone to me, "Don't forget your make-up."

Because our team was backpacking, we were told to lighten our load. I went to extremes, as usual for my personality. I only took cover up and no blush or lipstick. I walked with one other girl on our team in the village and I saw some little Mexican girls pointing and overheard them saying in Spanish "very pretty." I thought they were talking about Sherry but she let me know that I was wrong. "Ruth, they're pointing at you." It made me feel special.

One time as our team members spent several hours picking up trash, I thought about my life. I finally understood the big fat lie of "get a good education, get a good job, a nice house and things" and all that ticket to "success" merely resulted in emptiness and grasping for more. I thought about the irony of the situation—me, a college graduate—picking up trash in a foreign country, feeling like a no-body. How contradictory to all that I had been trained to become. This was beneath even the lowest job in Mexico. I served for nothing—no money, recognition, title, award or tangible honor. The accolades that I received came from God alone. What foolishness to have given up "all my life" for the sake of the souls of men, women and children.

Later, as I shared my thoughts and struggles with Sherry, she commented to me. "Ruth, one day you'll be picking up broken lives not broken trash."

Once I broke from the disillusionment of "success" I discovered the joy of the simple life in a rural village. I played with orphans and shared the love of Jesus. This was my calling and it brought fulfillment and satisfaction. I obeyed God and He changed my life. All the teaching sessions and classes were applied in real life settings as we worked for six weeks in Mexico. We did physical labor, performed various skits, street witnessed, sang, prayed and served in whatever tasks we were assigned.

Chapter 16

Giving Up Fantasy
to Embrace Reality

The second phase of our training began in March. We learned a drama called "Toymaker and Son," an allegory of the Gospel that was narrated as we acted it out. I was chosen to be three different parts— the tree of the knowledge of good and evil, a demon, and part of the barrier separating the "toys" from "Toymaker." The barrier became the Cross. Every day from April through June, we worked our bodies, minds and hearts for God's glory. This drama was the highlight of our upcoming summer outreach.

God continued to break forth in my life. I developed wonderful, caring friendships with both guys and girls. I loved to encourage, bless, laugh with and pray for my friends. It was evident to all who knew me that Jesus had done a deep work and changed my life. The teachings were focused more towards theology and evangelism.

Because I was focused on God as my Husband, I felt free to invest my life into other guys' lives without any hidden agendas. I was still capable of infatuation, just like in college. I was surprised at how fickle I seemed to be. There were many young godly men whom I found quite attractive. However, I still saw myself as inferior to the other girls so I wasn't aware of the growing admiration and friendships.

There was Art. He was drop-dead gorgeous with sandy brown hair, mustache, beard and a beautiful smile. He was a perfect gentleman with a sweetness and charm that was captivating. I was very aware of him but so were almost all the other girls in my school. I convinced myself that I would never be anything special to him, precisely because he was so handsome. I couldn't pronounce his name the way he did. He never mentioned it, but other students were able to imitate his Australian accent. He befriended me along with other guys and girls. Art and I were on a worship team together during our Mexico outreach. He and I had a wonderful friendship. I really appreciated him. He was so neat! He was a missionary kid with his parents being Wycliffe missionaries. We often swapped stories. He was polite and sincere, intelligent, humorous and so special. So, call me an "unnatural blonde" but I was oblivious to any interest in me other than a friendship.

Art was in my prayer group. One day he told me, "I look at this picture of shoes and I think of your feet as the readiness of peace but also to jump right in and serve. You're a servant. You're also an encourager. You've encouraged me a lot. I also see shoes as going forward and you've opened up so much in the last eight months. You're just willing to share your life."

There was Charlie, an eighteen year old, straight out of high school. He was fun, kind and like a little brother. He also went on the Mexico outreach. During that time, I admitted having a crush on him and he confessed that he had a crush on Sherry. I got over my feelings quickly once I realized they were not reciprocal.

I flitted in my heart from one young man to another. On some of the guys, I let my thoughts linger longer. I interacted freely with my brothers in Christ and I enjoyed them as people. It was a delight to have so many friends— both guys and girls. As the same guys seemed to spend more time with me, I began to question their feelings.

One day, after many such encounters, it struck me that Ryan spent many days with me. He was twenty-three with dark hair and dark eyes, a friendly and flirtatious young man—a naturally likeable guy. Girls swarmed around him like bees to honey. I was shocked when he began to single me out for conversations. I certainly didn't fit his "type." He liked a variety of cute girls and he treated me like his big sister.

I was in an empty classroom singing hymns and having a private time with the Lord. I didn't know that Ryan was in an adjoining room. I came out and we met. "You have a beautiful voice, Ruth."

I was surprised that he had heard me but we sat down and got to know each other. I enjoyed his friendship and his humor. We were both preachers' kids so we had that in common. Ryan wanted help in writing newsletters and he came to me. I tweaked his words and our friendship grew. He sat beside me in class a lot and I wondered, *"Does he like me?"*

With Ryan, Art and many of the guys, I gave hugs freely. It just felt nice to be loved in a safe, caring way. I also hugged many of my girl-friends too. God restored the joy of physical affection and we were all a big family.

Ryan kidded me about not sitting by him, so I did. He told me all about his life, dreams, plans and hopes. He shared his crushes with me and asked for my advice. We were constantly sitting with each other, laughing, joking, talking and just being together. I was comfortable with him and it was nice being together. Even at meals he chose to sit beside me. At one point he commented, "This is getting to be a habit." The thrill in my heart was that he pursued me!

At the end of June, right before I left on outreach, my parents came to see me for a brief visit. We only had a few hours together. They wanted to see the mission organization for themselves. I was glad to see them and everyone was so gracious and kind to make them feel welcome. They commented, "We feel so much better now that we have come here and met all these fine people, both students and staff. We are pleasantly reassured that this is a good place for you to be." Mom then asked, "Ruth Mary, is there anyone in particular you would like us to meet?"

"No, Mom, I don't think so."

Within a few minutes, the door to the restaurant opened and Art walked in. He immediately walked over to our table and introduced himself to my parents. He was the perfect gentleman and made me glad that he was my friend. He spoke kindly to them and he highly praised me. I didn't expect it but I certainly was flattered.

Ryan made sure that I met his parents when they came for a few hours on the base. A few days later, Ryan was sitting beside me and he rested his head on my shoulder! By this time, I definitely acknowledged to God and a few friends that I liked Ryan. I didn't tell him how I felt. I merely waited and watched to see how our friendship might progress. He opened up his life to me and I cared enough to listen, encourage and pray for him. I wasn't his only friend. He laughed a lot with other girls but he didn't open up to them to the same extent as he did to me. As I saw him spend time with other girls, I spent time with other guys and then I'd pour my heart out to God.

God, I just want to kick myself—and I'm frustrated. I honestly don't know how to deal with this and I need You. What is the answer? A friendship. Sometimes I want to run. Oh, Jesus, teach me, help me and hold me. I wish that none of my girlfriends ever knew how I felt about Ryan. I wish I knew where I stood with him. It is so frustrating because what do I do now?

The outreach lasted six weeks and we went to Chicago, Michigan and Washington, D.C. We performed in various settings; even at Cabrini Green, a notorious project in Chicago. Life happened all around me with real people and real pain. A little girl was there with burn marks on her legs and arms and she was so skinny. It looked evident that she had been physically abused. I don't think I had ever seen anyone who had been physically abused before. But it thrilled me to pick her up, place her on my lap and sing simple songs over her. I hugged her and told her about Jesus.

One day we were on our bus driving through D.C., and a fight was taking place. I saw a man slam a hammer into another's man's head and he crumpled to the ground. That vivid act of violence jolted me as this was no actor on a movie screen.

I was so angry that we didn't stop and intervene but I had no idea the seriousness of what that might mean if we had. It was a memory I never forgot. On the television, actors portrayed violence but to see it with my own eyes broke my heart. This outreach made me aware of the injustices in the world and that God's heart grieved over these little children and the lost, confused people who had never heard of Jesus' love for them.

We went to Michigan and had a few days off from performing and ministering. I went for a walk in the woods among the blue spruce, the tall pine trees and the quaking aspen. I recalled when I was sixteen how I had pretended that I sang and spoke to large crowds of people and told them about Jesus. Here I was years later and I still lived in that same fantasy world. I broke in tears before God and poured my heart out to Him.

"God, I'm sorry of being so afraid. I'm tired of always living in a dream world instead of the truth. I want to stop pretending that "someday" I'll minister to people—pray over them, sing, and even preach. I see these things in my mind but all my fears crowd out my desires. I don't want to look back on my life years down the road and see only missed opportunities to be used by You. Please break through all my fears — fear of man, fear of failure, fear of attention, fear of pride, fear of being foolish, fear of competition, fear of rejection. I want to cease singing to the walls and prophesying to the wind. I want eyes to see real faces with real hurts, real needs—real people."

Each member of the team was encouraged to speak after the dramatic performances. I kept avoiding that. I cringed when I recalled my "testimony" and I was afraid to speak in front of crowds of strangers. I knew that my time was nearing. My school leader assigned me to speak about the five loaves and the two fish.

Many of my team prayed for me because I was so nervous. I walked back and forth, but once I started speaking, I wasn't nervous. My words just seemed to flow. It thrilled me because I saw the fulfillment of what God had shown me many years prior but I was always so afraid. He took me seriously when I prayed out in the woods and I surrendered my fears. I had such a special time being used by God because my knees didn't knock, my voice didn't quiver, my body didn't shake and I had no fear!

Ryan and I went on two different outreaches. He left for Washington, D.C. and I went to Chicago. In saying good-byes, he kissed me on the cheek and told me that he'd see me in four weeks. I was deeply touched. God used me to continually pray for him and he was a great friend and encourager to me.

Art and I spent time talking on the bus as we sat together and rode from Texas to Chicago. He shared all about his life and I drank it in eagerly. "Ruth, I don't make friends easily. I'm a loner. I think the best way to get close to a person is to pray with them. Do you like being alone? Do you have a friend that you're always around?"

"I like being alone. No, I don't have one friend that I'm with all the time."

I shared my college experiences of walking with God. It was neat, even though I blushed at times. I realized that I liked Art and Ryan but I didn't honestly know if either of them liked me for more than a friend. They didn't talk exclusively to me and I wasn't foolish enough to think that I would capture either of their hearts.

Ellen and I untied Art's shoes for fun and he ended up wrestling her. Later he told me, "I wasn't sure how you would react if I wrestled you, Ruth so I didn't. I knew how Ellen would react." I just listened because I didn't know how I would've reacted either. I found his statement interesting, though.

We continued to sit on the bus together as we traveled and shared more about our lives. He fascinated me and I so delighted in his friendship. He was easy to talk to and the more time we spent together, the more I enjoyed getting to know him.

We got to Washington, D.C. and Ryan and I hugged. From that point on we tried to catch up on the last four weeks of being apart. He grew so much in his spiritual maturity and the staff members all noticed and commented. It thrilled me to know that I had prayed for him and now I saw the fruit of those prayers.

"Cheryl and I have gotten super-close. I'm amazed at the depth of the relationship—it's just a friendship though—even though I talk to Cheryl – it wasn't the same as talking to you. I just wanted to talk."

"Ryan, I missed you so much. I kept thinking while we were apart, "Where is Ryan? I want to talk to him."

Over the next few days as we interacted, we expressed lots of affection. We hugged freely, smiled and laughed together and we even held hands!

As we were saying, Good-night, Ryan said, "Every time I talk with you I leave encouraged."

He enjoyed the encouragement and I received fulfillment from a friend. It was a nice touch to end the evening.

A group of us were cleaning the house where we stayed. I cleaned the stove and Art did the chandelier after me. We had individual meetings to attend. Bruce said, "I'm after Ruth."

Art responded, "Oh, isn't that sweet." He was teasing and the three of us chuckled.

On our day off, in D.C., Ryan spent it with Crystal, a girlfriend and the sister of Charlie. Charlie and Ryan were best friends and Charlie was the guy I first had a crush on in the beginning of my missions training. I joked around with various guys but I stayed at the town-house, rested and read books. I teased and laughed with Art.

As we left D.C., I was on the bus with Ryan. We sat together and talked almost the entire time for thirty-five hours! There were so many things we shared. I just reveled in our friendship and my genuine love and concern for him as a person.

The outreach finished and I felt led to return to West Virginia long enough to raise financial support to come back and join the logistical staff in the accounting department. God did such a major overhaul of my character and these were impressions of His voice.

'This has been My year and as you have given this year to Me, I will give manifold years of ministry to you. This has been a year of planting seeds and I will feed and nourish you and cause you to grow into a beautiful woman of God. I will cause you to blossom and flourish like the vine.'"

When we returned to Texas, a friend cut my hair. I received many compliments.

Charlie saw me, "Ruth— yeah, it looks great!" Ryan was behind him wearing sunglasses. Charlie said, "Here, let's take these off so you can see...."

Ryan looked at me, "Wow!" *I think he likes the haircut.* It was the last night of our year-long training. Ryan and I were talking about saying "good-byes."

"Ruth, this may not sound like it but it's coming from my heart. You've been there. You've slapped me in the face (not literally) and made me face facts and you've always just been there—you're a good friend. I was talking to someone and saying, 'Yeah Ruth and I talked about that.'

They said, "Oh, I didn't know you were so close to Ruth.' "Yeah, she and I are close like this." He placed two fingers side by side.'

I responded, "Like what? Not like this?" I crossed my two fingers.

Ryan said, "This is close. (the fingers side by side). This (the crossed fingers) is like God or (as both of us smiled) – a wife."

We continued to talk and be light-hearted. He had his arm around my shoulders. "Ryan, I don't think we should try to have a meaningful conversation tonight."

"Why? Why not? We talked thirty-five hours on the bus."

"Oh, you're saying we never need to talk anymore. Are you implying that I'm boring?"

"No, Ruth, you're reading stuff into this. We talked twenty-nine hours."

"No, we didn't. You were asleep and for two hours you weren't even on the bus. It's hard to communicate on two buses."

"Didn't you hear me yelling at you?"

"Oh, you were, huh, Ryan? I saw you smiling when you passed us but for all I know you could've been smiling at the landscape."

"I was smiling at the bus — at the people on the bus."

Later we went and watched a movie with some other students.

"Well, Ruth, I really enjoyed tonight."

We hugged each other and went our separate ways. *Wow! He does care. I was flying inside.*

The next day as we said our final good-byes, Ryan looked at me, "Okay, Ruth, you've been an awesome friend, helped me walk through a lot, God's really used you to speak into my life." We hugged each other. He said, "We'll have to write each other." It was neat.

Our Worship team gathered for a picture. Carol, Charlie, Art and I posed for a shot. Art decided to be crazy and he jumped and reclined on our arms as the three of us held him and we all smiled. I talked to Charlie as he decided to return to his hometown and work with the youth of his church. I kissed him on the cheek two times and we hugged. He was a special young man.

Ryan talked about Crystal and he teased me that maybe a few years down the road, he and Crystal would be married. "You never know."

As we talked I commented, "All my crushes are over, thankfully."(I don't know why I said that. It must be my defense mechanism.)

"Yay."

Being that blunt with his feelings, I felt it safer to tell him that I had no more crushes.

I made it a point to say good-bye to Art. I knew that he was coming back on base to join a traveling ministry team but I didn't know how often I would see him. As I hugged Ryan for the final time, I kissed him on the cheek. "This is for Cheryl."

He laughed and said, "I would give you one too….but maybe a few years down the road."

I laughed and said, "You never know."

I wrote in my journal, *So Lord, I'm waiting and God I really wonder about Ryan but Lord I need to close this chapter and know that Your will is the highest priority of my life. Lead and guide him.*

Chapter 17

The Cost of Discipleship

I arrived at my parent's house that summer and they listened to me effervesce about what God had done in my life. They were genuinely moved at my transformation. I didn't realize what a deep chord it touched in their hearts. Dad approached me, "Honey, your mother and I are thrilled at what God is doing in your life. We've decided that if you really want to continue to pursue this missionary calling, we will pay for you to go to our denominational school and get further training."

Wow! That was against all their philosophy of "fairness" among the siblings. They were willing to pay for two to four more years of higher education just for me. I knew what my heart said and it wasn't my intention to hurt them, but I turned them down. We had begun the tiniest buds of a beautiful, mended relationship and this decision brought opportunity for rejection and hurt.

Over the next year, there were many phone calls fraught with much misunderstanding. Several times I hung up the phone, wept and cried to God to heal the fissures in their hearts and mine.

In Dad's eyes, I still "siphoned" as I sought financial help to return to Texas. All during my first year, I gravitated towards some of the Accounting staff and at the end of my training I understood what God had prepared me for. I am not a "numbers" person so it didn't make sense why He would call me to serve in that department.

After a few weeks of being with my folks in West Virginia, I wrote Ryan a letter. I got a letter from him within a few days! I laughed so hard because we probably wrote each other around the same time. In his letter he said, "You've been on my mind. Radically, your friend." Of course, I was so excited.

Two days later, the phone rang and Ryan called me! He had gotten my letter that day. We talked for a good while and I was concerned about the cost of the call. He assured me that, "God will provide." Towards the end of the conversation, Ryan said, "Well, let me get off here so I can go and write you a letter."

I told him, "I love you," and I don't know what he mumbled. Naturally, I flipped out again. I just talked with God and prayed. *(Lord, help me not jump to conclusions. I contained myself—only God knows what's happened in the last two days— it's too special to me to see it trampled on or misunderstood.)*

A guy from high school contacted me and came to see me. It was the first real "date" I'd had since college. We talked about our lives and where God had brought us. He was divorced and planned to become a minister. "Ruth, some people's feelings I trampled on— you were one of them. I trampled on you royally. Will you forgive me?" I did forgive him. He talked about us from the past." It should have been serious."

We returned to my parents' house and prayed for each other. We had never prayed together before. As we hugged, he kissed me on the cheek. It was a bittersweet reunion as we realized there was no future for us together but we would be friends in eternity.

I spent time one day laying all my feelings about Ryan before God. I gave up and surrendered the relationship to Jesus. Later that day, I got another letter from Ryan!

For my birthday, I received a card from Walt. It came with a number of prayers, "that God would provide you with a companion, that you would seek first the kingdom of God and His righteousness, that God would bring a close, loving relationship with Mom and Dad this year." As I sat at the table, Mom prayed a birthday prayer over me."Thank You for the good and the bad, grant her desires, hopes and even her dreams that she may continue to serve Thee."

I tried diligently to raise support. I became more discouraged as the monies didn't come. I still felt that I was to take the right step to join the Accounting department. I approached my Dad on the topic of asking for financial support at a different church in town that I attended, and in a nutshell, I had his permission to ask for money, but he didn't feel that I was using my education in the best way.

The night I shared in my church about God's calling on my life, an older man came up to me and shook my hand, "We're so proud of you. God bless you. Only one in a million would do what you're doing. God bless you—His blessings and riches upon you."

Really, only one in a million would do this? Why so few?

They voted to send me twenty dollars a month. That was my only pledged support. I had sent all kinds of letters, prayed diligently and served anyway I could find. There was just enough financial giving to buy a one way ticket on the bus to Texas. My mother thought I gave up going and was surprised to hear that I was leaving. It was a severe test of my faith. As much as my parents loved me, they did not agree with this direction and consequently did not financially support it.

I awoke with such an expectation of the manifestation of a miracle. I read the promises in the Bible on prosperity and I was even jittery about checking the mail. Finally I did and there was nothing. I was so quiet just seeking to hear what God was saying to me. After a while, *'It wasn't money that kept you there, it isn't money that's going to bring you back—it is only the mercy and grace of God.'"*

So, I called the base and spoke with the head of the Accounting Department. "We'd like you to have some monthly support—so you can live—we believe it's the Lord's will for you to be here. If you keep pursuing to take care of your tuition, doing what you can each month over the next six to eight months, we feel it'll be okay for you to come back. You pray and we'll keep praying."

Wow! I hung up the phone and praised God. I scheduled the bus ride for the next day. With the promised commitment, prayer and support of my church, I was sent out under their covering. My mother rejoiced with me, "I know you're glad to be going back." Dad wondered, "What will you be doing a year from now?"

"Dad, that's too far ahead, too much growth, leading and guidance to begin to answer that. Sufficient for the day is the evil thereof." It was my typical "rely on Scripture" to answer tough questions. Dad prayed his blessing on me, "May the Lord be with you. May He lift up His countenance upon you and give you peace." I set off on a new adventure with joy inexpressible and a heart full of gratefulness. I had experienced a miracle and God confirmed His call on my life. I took a new step in the journey of walking with Jesus.

Part Three

Romanced

~ Metamorphosis ~

Like a butterfly
Set free
To know life
Outside and apart from
A dead cocoon
That's how are you are
Since Jesus
Broke the casing
Split the coffin
And set you free
To fly.

Chapter 18

We Need More Men...

I was back in beautiful East Texas and I felt like I'd come home. My heart filled with expectation and I wondered if this would be the year that God would bring a husband to me since I was twenty-five. It was wonderful to be among my friends and to know that I had obeyed the call of God on my life.

For the first time since fourth grade, I didn't wear glasses. I had contacts and I loved them! I felt so assured, confident and pretty. The lies that had been so much a part of my life were broken and replaced with the truth that God had changed me from the inside out. I no longer hid subconsciously behind those dark lenses that doubled as sunglasses. God had healed my heart and I joyfully and trustingly embraced and loved people. I was free to focus on others and not be so self-absorbed.

I easily related to being "just one of the guys," as in my college days but now I also developed close friendships with girls. I related to them in freedom and acceptance. I wore flattering colorful clothes, pretty make-up, stylish jewelry and a short, fashionable hairstyle. I dressed femininely and attractively as I celebrated the joy I found as a Christian woman.

I began working in the accounting department and loved my job. I wrote personal letters on behalf of the ministry to the donors. I made the monthly updates come alive for the readers and as a result of those letters, the financial giving to the ministry increased steadily and rapidly. It took me awhile to realize the connection that I helped play in that change. I was both thrilled and humbled. Back in college, I had asked one of my favorite professors, Dr. L., "What kind of a job can I get with an English degree, if I don't get a teaching certificate?" "Ruth, you can work for any major organization with your command of the English language. There are always newsletters and other correspondence that has to be written."

I had a "job" and I used the gifts God gave me. I found great joy in serving. Later, I voluntarily worked on the weekends and I secretly filed a backlog of receipts. I enjoyed the office work and eventually they convinced me to enter donations on the computer. I finally relented. God brought healing in this area, too, and I discovered that I *could* understand finances.

I got back a few days before Art's team left so I was able to hug and say "Hi" and "Bye" to him. One of my roommates opened up and told me that she was attracted to him. In my typical fashion, I encouraged her and then I let my own feelings towards him diminish. It was only right since I had wrapped more strings around my heart towards Ryan.

Ryan called me the next day at my office. He wasn't on the base and he needed some encouragement. He hadn't sent me another letter because, "I didn't know where you'd be." After I listened to him, he said, "Thank you, Ruth." I blushed as I hung up.

A few days later, one of Ryan's good friends on base asked me, "Have you heard from Ryan?"

I smiled, blushed and defensively asked, "Why?"

He quietly answered, "You *are* friends."

I got a letter from Ryan, "I'm feeling like you're already praying for me. Thanks."

Another staff person said, "Did you hear that Ryan is coming back? I'm going to call him today. Is there anything you want me to tell him?"

"No." I blushed and then said, "Tell him I said 'Hi,' and I'm praying for him."

Cindy and I walked from the cafeteria and I scanned the parking lot. The bright red car caught my attention as I read the license plate,

South Carolina. A guy scrunched in the front seat as his legs dangled out the door while he tinkered with his head under the steering wheel.

I thought, *"I'll introduce myself and maybe we'll become friends and then I can get a ride to West Virginia without having to travel the whole 38 hours on the bus."*

I left Cindy and walked over to his car.

"Hi, I'm Ruth. "

He sat up and looked at me. He was skinny with light blond hair and a friendly smile.

"Hi, I'm Ross, from Rock Hill, South Carolina."

"Where's that?"

"It's up near Charlotte, North Carolina. You ever heard of PTL? I used to work there."

(In my college days, there was a huge scandal in which Jim Bakker, the founder of Praise the Lord (PTL) ministries was accused of sexual misconduct and mismanagement of funds. It had been in the early days of television evangelists and the ministry was also a vacation spot for Christians. It consisted of a water park, music shop, ice cream parlor, camping facilities in addition to many buildings that offered various teaching seminars, workshops and church services. The scandal had left a bitter taste in the mouths of many people and had rocked the nation.)

Ross talked about how he used to work there and the sadness that this fall-out brought in the Body of Christ. It was clear that it was a tender spot for him. His family had benefitted greatly from the ministry before all the negative publicity. I turned the conversation. "Are you here for DTS? (Discipleship Training School?)"

"Yeah. Are you?"

"No. I did my training last year. I work in the Accounting Department."

Cindy waited for me impatiently at a distance. "Come on! Ruth."

"Okay, I'm coming." I called to her.

"Uh, nice to meet you, Ross."

"Yeah. What's your name, again?"

"Ruth."

He is a very intense person. Was he angry? (It would take a long time before I would be able to discern that intensity doesn't equal anger.) But suffice it to say, I honestly thought that would be the end of any great friendship. In a way, it put me in my place since I mainly wanted him for a ride home.

Ryan arrived on the base and it was wonderful to see him again! We hugged and laughed and caught up on the latest news of what God was doing in our lives. It was absolutely thrilling to have my best friend on the base with me. My heart was filled with joy. Even some of my girlfriends noticed my changed countenance.

One of them said, "When you talk about Ryan, your ears turn red."

It was true. I was beyond just simple friendship even though Ryan had told me more than once that was all he felt towards me. I found my own blushing to be both embarrassing and revealing at the same time. I couldn't and didn't want to deny how I felt about Ryan.

Because of my friendship with Ryan, I was free to be friends with several guys and I was. I genuinely cared about my new Christian brothers but I was oblivious to their potential interest in me.

So, as I made friends with these various guys, somehow Ross joined the group. I had already "walked the loop," with Mike, a new 18-year-old student. "Walking the loop," for a guy and a girl often meant a "romantic stroll" but in this case, I just desired the walk. Mike and I laughed at the heat lightning as he said, "God was taking pictures-that's His flash." I chuckled and enjoyed the fellowship but I was 25 and saw myself as a "big sister" in the Lord.

Then there was James. He was 29 and though I didn't know much about him, I still hung around with his group. One day he asked me, "Would you like to come with me to get gas?" I thought the request strange, but I went anyway.

He asked personal questions about my family, hopes and dreams. I was perfectly able to blend in with a group of guys but this one-on-one stuff left me bewildered. I didn't know how to answer him. Once we returned to the base, that was our last "dating" experience.

Though other guys invited me out and bought me dessert, I believed it was only a matter of time before Ryan's eyes would be opened to see me as the love of his life. I expected him to fall madly in love with me so I didn't have eyes for anyone else. I was comfortable as I talked with other guys because my heart waited only for Ryan.

I continued to get to know Ross, along with other students in his class. He was 18 and had just graduated from high school. He had played trumpet in his school and church band for a number of years. He could hear a song one time and play it. He had also taken up the flute, learning to play it by ear. He loved a wide variety of music ranging from classical to rap, from reggae to Western, cowboy songs and several styles in between. I had that same love for a variety of music.

One evening a group of guys were looking through the "Lost and Found" closet and Ross pulled out a skirt and made some comment about girding up his loins. He then pretended to wrap the skirt in a fashion to demonstrate how it would've been done in Bible times.

I was the only girl in the group and I couldn't believe his seeming naiveté. I was blushing and everyone was laughing. Then Ryan grabbed a blue cloth and threw it over his shoulders and we all started walking towards the Guys' Dorm. As we strolled across the lawn, Ryan tossed the material over my head and shoulders and began narrating,

"And it came to pass in those days that a decree went out from Caesar Augustus..." *I couldn't believe it. Was Ryan pretending we were married?*

Ross casually asked, "Can I join you two?"

Ryan immediately replied, "Sure, 3's company, 2's a crowd." That's how it became Ross, Ruth and Ryan. How it evolved from there, I'm not exactly sure. During that time I was "just friends" with Ryan. That's how it was explained to Ross who had naturally assumed that Ryan and I were "a couple." In reality, we weren't. (However, it would take some time before I would be able to admit that to myself.)

A few days later, in preparation for the Harvest party, Ross was setting up the sound system in the gym. I walked in and we casually chatted. As we talked about missions, I passionately declared, "We need more *men* in YWAM!"

"What am I... chopped liver?" Ross retorted. *How wild! I had always thought of myself as "chopped liver" and not anybody else. Gosh, he's blunt! And no, he's not chopped liver...but do I tell him that?*

"Uh, no. I mean, uh, older men." I stammered.

"Oh, you mean, like James?" *Nice guy but older than I'd like*.

"No," I replied awkwardly.

"Oh, like Phil?" *Cute but too young. He's 18, just like you!*

"No, I mean *my* age!" I flustered.

Ross just laughed.

We talked for a long time, seemingly about everything.

"Ross, how did you hear about YWAM?"

"Well, when I was sixteen, I was praying about what I should do after high school. 'God, I don't really know how to hear Your voice so will You please make it clear for me what You want me to do?' A team came to our church and performed, "Toymaker and Son." It was really interesting and I began wondering about what YWAM was like. The next day, my Pastor mentioned, 'Ross, if you want to go to YWAM, the church will pay for your training.'

"I was offered a science scholarship to Duke University, but I felt that God was calling me into missions. So, after I graduated, I came here. All I knew before I came was that YWAMers smuggle Bibles into foreign countries and they perform dramas."

"What do you see yourself doing?"

"I think that YWAM is a "stepping stone" to the ministry that God has for me. I think that I'll join the staff after I finish my schools." *So, he's thinking of hanging around here*.

"How long have you walked with the Lord?"

"I got saved while listening to Jimmy Swaggart on the radio when I was four. I started crying. My Mom says that I asked, "What is that man talking about?" She led me in the sinners' prayer. Later, I gave my testimony in Sunday school, 'Before I came to the Lord, I was just a sinnin', and a sinnin' and a sinnin'.""

I burst out laughing. "Gosh, you can remember that? You were so young!"

"Because the Sunday school teacher was so tickled by my testimony, she went and told my mom."

Ross and I talked about musicians and Christian artists like Keith Green and his influence in both of our lives. Even though Keith died in 1982, Ross' life with God was already established and mine was in that topsy-turvy time right after high school. I was amazed at how many songs, bands and other interests that Ross and I shared in common, in spite of our age differences.

I was surprised at how easy it was to talk to him. He freely gave his views, opinions, feelings and his family background. We began to form a friendship and yet, there was such depth of maturity that I witnessed in just one afternoon of conversation. I now knew far more about him than I did about most of the people I had known for the last year. Even though Ross shared many aspects of his life, in the midst of it all, there was also the exchange of bantering laughter. I admitted to myself that he was physically attractive, but so were the majority of my male friends.

I ended up beside Ross for most of the Harvest Party instead of square dancing like the rest of the people. As he ran sound we just talked and laughed. I kept my eyes on the dance floor and watched Ryan. I was too shy to join the crowd but I enjoyed listening to Ross. I reminded myself how many hours that Ryan and I spent together and what good friends we were. Surely the day would come when he would realize that he wanted to be "friends" for life. Though I listened to Ross, I still longed for Ryan's company.

At the end of the evening, I hugged Ross as we laughed together.

He asked, "How old are you?"

"How old do you think I am?"

"I would guess 24, with no grey hairs to prove it."

I laughed as I definitely had a silver streak in my hair but I said, "I'm 25."

The next day, I went to church and Ross sat beside me as we listened to Winkie Pratney, one of my all-time favorite youth evangelists. Back at the base, my folks called and we decided that I wouldn't be going home for Christmas but I had no idea where I would celebrate the holiday. Later that night I talked with Ross about Barbados since that was his upcoming outreach destination. I teased him.

"Ross, I could easily live in Barbados — it would be ideal for me. I could enjoy the flair of the tropics with the beach, the gorgeous sunsets, the waves on the ocean and the opportunity to tan. I'm sure I could 'suffer' and 'have a beach ministry' there."

Chapter 19

Budding Friendship
and a Shotgun Sermon

I walked into the dining room for breakfast and passed by a table where Ross was seated. All of a sudden he stood in the midst of the room and loudly declared, "Well, fine, just be anti-social and don't speak to me!"

I couldn't believe it. What was I supposed to do? I felt strangely flattered and embarrassed at the same time. So I regained my composure and spoke to him from several tables away.

"Well, uh, Hi, Ross." *Does he like me?*

Then Ryan smiled and patted the empty chair. "Hey, Ruth, I saved this just for you." *Yes! Ryan wants me to sit by him. He saved a seat just for me. Can you believe it?*

I smiled at Ryan and joined him. My insides whirled with joy. It was sweet to be noticed by Ross but Ryan wanted me to sit beside him.

Often I visited the Guys' Dorm, mainly to visit with Ryan. Ross was in Ryan's room and looked at me.

He enthusiastically declared, "Hey, Ruth, I'm listening to a teaching series on Christian marriage. It's really good. You should listen to this with me!"

I was surprised and then I teased him, "Oh, *I* should, huh?" I placed the emphasis on the "I" so that he would see that his request could easily be misconstrued.

He bantered back laughing with me and then Ryan walked into the room and all three of us sat and listened to the series together. After that, the topic of marriage seemed to creep into Ross's and my conversations on a regular basis and it provided a chance to laugh with each other.

I listened to some of the teaching and it really was good. It was a reinforcement of God's design and plan for His desires to give us the best, if we're willing to wait on His perfect timing. We listened together and I saw even more the maturity that Ross exhibited. I also wondered if Ryan was thinking about me like I was thinking about him when I listened.

All three of us wanted to wait for God's best, to not rush into a relationship for ego or fleshly purposes and all of us wanted to honor God with our thoughts, actions and attitudes. I listened to these two godly gentlemen and realized that God had given me some special friendships.

Ross told Ryan and me about a time when a bunch of guys held a pornographic magazine in his face and taunted him to look at it. "I kept my eyes closed and they finally gave up. They teased me about being a virgin. I just looked at them and said, 'I can be like you any day but you can never be like me again.'"

That was a dagger through me and I stifled a gasp. Immediately, my mind echoed my mother's words, "You can never wear white at your wedding."

I quickly brushed aside the fleeting thoughts of being attracted to Ross, because I knew my past. Even though Jesus had forgiven me, I wasn't so foolish as to believe I ever deserved someone as pure as Ross. "Deserved" probably isn't quite the right word—but the idea that he would want someone who had never been with anyone else was obvious to me.

He raised bees and had started his own honey business when he was twelve. In addition, he had spoken at several museums, schools, and lecture halls on bees and beekeeping when he was sixteen. He wanted to become a millionaire by the time he was thirty.

I was shocked and asked, "What would you do with all that money and all those years without a job?"

"I want to travel and spend time with my children. I want to be able to give a lot of the money away."

This guy's going to make something of his life. He's on his way to becoming a millionaire and he already has the business mind. Surely, this will happen in his future. (I didn't realize for a long time that he chose to give up the dream of becoming a millionaire when he joined YWAM.)

He had a heart for kids and though there were only a few on the base, he was child-like among them. The playfulness and the tenderness as he played "peek-a-boo" or delighted over some simple gesture of a toddler's smile or hug warmed my heart. He had such a sensitive nature and yet his passion for God with his zeal for holiness along with his bluntness was such an adjustment for me. In so many ways I saw a mature man, yet my mind constantly reminded me, *He's only a teenager; he's only eighteen.*

Ross thrived on debating—not just arguing but thinking through deep philosophies and searching the Scriptures. He fascinated me as I had never met anyone quite like him. I just couldn't fathom that someone could possibly be this wide-ranged and wide-scoped in his talents, abilities, interests and desires. He was like a "Jack of all trades." He knew how to do electrical, plumbing and construction. He could work mechanics on a car. He loved to worship, study, sing, play his flute and talk.

He served people anyway that he could. He dared to be different than his peers. He had his own car in Texas and a motorcycle back in South Carolina. He loved to learn and had a wealth of knowledge on just about any subject. He had an extensive vocabulary and a great sense of humor. We were always laughing and using puns together. I hadn't had that much word play camaraderie in years.

He was excellent in drama and in photography. He made his dreams and desires happen with all the details and planning, instead of just waiting for the "great someday." That was evident by his bee-keeping business.

He loved nature, hiking, camping and the simplest things in creation brought about in him a sense of wonder and delight. He was drawn to flowers with their intricacies and beauty. Many times I found him with his nose to the ground, examining a wildflower blossom no larger than a quarter of an inch. I couldn't believe that this one young man could have such a diversity of experiences.

Ryan needed some teeth pulled and Ross took him to the dentist. Ryan couldn't talk for a few hours with gauze pads in his mouth so he wrote me a note, "Will you take care of me for awhile?"

It was so sweet and Ross and I stayed to visit with him. Ross was more help than I was. He went to make Ryan some fried eggs and as I watched him, I felt even more intimidated. Through my mind, like a flash, went this thought, *This guy doesn't need me for anything….he can cook, sew, etc. All he would ever need me for is to have his babies…*My mind jolted with even the thought and I immediately began an argument within myself. *Where in the world did that thought come from? Ross— marry me? Are you kidding? There is no way; he is a virgin and I am not. He is so much more than I could ever be. Sure, he's attractive, but seriously, Ruth? Have you lost your mind?*

I deliberately shoved those thoughts way down somewhere and went to tend Ryan. Ross came to check on Ryan while I was there and then he left. Every few hours Ross returned to see if we needed anything. He was a gentleman and I liked how nice and caring he was.

Once the gauze was gone and the numbness wore off, Ryan talked about his thoughts on marriage and of course, I eagerly listened. I hung on to his every word and I loved Ryan's company. It was easy to serve him, to take care of him, to encourage him and to be his friend. There was nowhere else I would rather be than with him.

"Sometimes I get this feeling that it'll be like I'm friends with her and I'll be saying, 'No way—no way—no way' and I won't hear God. He'll be saying—'Look, she's beautiful, you get along great, you encourage each other—she's everything you've ever wanted.'"

(Wow! That was weird. Did he realize what he just said?) I mean, isn't that what I had watched for months? I was almost too afraid to believe what my heart wanted.

Ross came by later that evening. He brought supper for Ryan and me on plates from the dining hall. He shared about the night he took a lot of his fellow classmates to the Mall. Because he had his own car, which few students did, they asked him for a ride. Everyone went with him. However, at the Mall, they all met up with other friends and everybody left Ross to drive back to the base by himself. In the midst of his hurt, loneliness and frustration, he blurted out to Ryan and me, "I need a girlfriend."

In Ross' words, I pulled out my double-barreled shotgun and blew him away.

"*How* old are you?"

"Eighteen."

"The last thing you need in your life right now is a girlfriend. You came here to find the call of God on your life and you need to get right with Him. This is His time. You're only eighteen. You have your whole life ahead of you. I'm twenty-five years old and He hasn't brought a husband to me, yet. You need to focus on the Lord and not on *some girl*."

I was firm and strong and I wasn't going to back down. I had seen too many people get distracted by wanting some boyfriend or girlfriend. I wasn't about to let that happen to Ross. God had far too much in mind for this young man to be derailed by a girl.

Ross started to say something to defend himself. Ryan shot him a look that said, "She knows what she's talking about."

I was on my soapbox and I continued. "You need to put God first in your life and develop that relationship. Then the friendships will follow." I finally calmed down, even though I wasn't angry. I was just convinced that this young eighteen year old amazing Christian man had several years before God was going to bring a wife to him. For heaven sakes, I had been waiting for five years myself and God hadn't brought my husband, yet. Ross still had his whole life ahead of him.

I don't know exactly how it transitioned but once I had my outburst, I quietly retreated to my shell again. Ross had not seen me impassioned like that before, though Ryan knew my personality a lot better. Somehow, Ryan and Ross started talking about their past dates and girlfriends.

Ross said, "You know I dated several different girls. I often got flowers or planned a dinner date. But in the back of my mind I was always evaluating, 'Is she the woman I want to be my wife? Is this the kind of woman I want to be the mother of my children?'"

I was shocked and thought, *Boy! That would be intimidating*. Then I listened and realized that Ross wasn't like what I had assumed.

He didn't date a lot of girls for his ego or to be a flirt. He was serious. I couldn't imagine any sixteen year old guy that I had ever known who would have seriously been asking God, "Is this the woman for me?" That concept of marriage, especially from God's perspective, had not been on guys' minds when they were with me.

Once again, I fought the remorse and the jealousy as I heard how polite, godly and romantic Ross was towards the girls he took on dates. I thought of how incredibly special it would have been to have a young man lavish me with tenderness, respect, affection and honor. What a contrast to a past that I could never erase. I could choose to forget it but I could never change or re-write it.

He was honest and open and shared that he had his own faults and failures and didn't always do everything right, but in the end, what stuck out the most in my mind was that he was still a virgin. I was extremely quiet and withdrawn as they talked.

In the awkward silence, the next thing I knew Ross spoke to me. "So, Ruth, what's your story?"

Even though Ryan and I were close, I didn't talk about my past. I had only referred to it at the beginning of my training, in my slaughtered "testimony" and even then, I had barely said much of anything. I hadn't talked about it for years and I hadn't planned on saying anything. But by that time in the conversation, I felt lousy.

"I didn't date guys. They only found me acceptable in parked cars and in the woods. Just stick a bag over her head but we love her body."

How I wanted to take the words back! There was no verbal response to anything that I said. I certainly didn't mean to tell Ross any of my history, but there weren't any roses and special dinners to remember.

Great...I just let him know about my tainted past. Stupid Ruth, just stupid. Why did he have to ask? Why didn't I see it coming? I wanted to crawl under a rock once again. Instead, I mumbled something about it being late and I left.

None of what I said was something I was proud of or had any desire to reflect upon. The next day I met Ryan and asked his forgiveness for my sarcasm and then I said I didn't want to remember the past because it was under the blood of Jesus. I think he was relieved as well. I think Ross might have been there for that conversation, too.

However, due to the "shotgun" sermon, Ross and I then struck out on a friendship with no worries or anxieties. From my perspective, there were no hidden expectations. I certainly wasn't the pure woman he was looking for and besides he was far too young for me.

Ross was only eighteen and straight out of high school. Ryan, though younger than me, was twenty-three. Ross was just a teenager, so I didn't allow myself to dwell on the fleeting thoughts. It made us able to be ourselves.

Chapter 20

How Old Did You Say You Were?

*R*yan, Ross and I went to the store together in Ross' car. As I sat in the back, Ross looked into the mirror and asked me bluntly, "Ruth, what would your parents' reaction be if you were to develop a dating relationship?"

The question wasn't anything I anticipated. Then again, I never knew what Ross might ask me. At the mention of my parents, there was a sense of loss in my heart. I loved them and they loved me but after years of not having a close relationship, it was hard to build one. So I answered as truthfully and non-emotionally as I could.

"Probably none. They don't ask me about marriage or that part of my life." It was true. Our conversations were still sometimes tense as I was bolder in my faith and at times it became a point of contention. Then again, there wasn't anyone pursuing me for a dating relationship, even though I longed for the young man with dark hair and dark eyes to see me as more than a friend.

The conversation didn't continue. Daily, I spent time talking with Ross. I can't begin to remember all that we shared but I begin to develop the same closeness I had with Ryan. Ross wasn't a flirt or someone who was just surface. He didn't fit in to the crowd of older teens who had just recently graduated from high school.

Ross looked the part of the typical cool teenage guy with spiked hair, a red hot-rod car, leather jacket and sunglasses. However, as soon as he opened his mouth, he revealed someone of much greater depth, intelligence, wisdom, sensitivity and commitment to God than what a casual glance might have indicated.

His maturity astounded me so many times. I felt such a connection with him and I loved how I felt when I was with him. I didn't feel any need to impress him, so I was simply myself—carefree, humorous, joking and at other times serious and contemplative in my discussions. There was no striving inside of me in hopes that he would like me for more than a friend so I was comfortable around him.

There was never a feeling that he was too immature to be my close friend. I related to him as if he were my age. But I knew that he was not even in his twenties yet and so the more I found myself drawn to him, the more I had to bring myself back to reality. I did this by reminding myself of the truth.

Frequently I would stop him in the middle of a conversation and ask, "How old did you say you were?"

"Eighteen."

Then I would pick right back up in the conversation where we had left off. I desperately tried to rationalize my feelings. *Get a grip. He is a **teenager**. It doesn't matter that he is intelligent, mature and serious about God…..you are twenty-five. You are nowhere close to being his age. No way, no way, no way…..this is not God. This is the devil. This is the flesh. This is a distraction.*

At the same time, Ryan constantly confused me. He wanted to hang around with me almost every day. However, whenever I mentioned anything beyond a friendship, he strongly denied having special feelings for me. It was like playing a ping pong game with my emotions being swatted back and forth. I thought that he fought his feelings because he was trying to deny his emotions towards me. Why else would he choose to spend hours with me? What was I supposed to think when he'd look at Ross after a while and say, "Hey Ruth, should we pay Ross a quarter to go away?"

No one had ever said that to me before but I knew that phrase meant that the guy wanted to be with the girl exclusively. That phrase was reserved for boyfriend/girlfriend relationships. When Ryan said these words, Ross did leave but it almost seemed at times that he was sad to go. I brushed those thoughts aside and concentrated on Ryan.

Ryan often asked me for advice about his various crushes. It was hard to hear how thrilled he was over the girl he liked, but I figured the day would come when his eyes would be opened and he would awaken from his sleep to see that the woman he wanted wasn't a dream—she was sitting right beside him.

There had already been several stories of girls and guys just like that who the girl kept befriending the guy and eventually God woke him up to realize for the rest of your life, this is the one. I encouraged Ryan as best as I could.

Ryan's crushes were my friends and they wanted my advice about life and especially about Ryan. It was hard to hear them tell me about their hopes and dreams to someday be more to him than "just a friend." I was sincere as much as I could be because I genuinely wanted God's best for Ryan and for me. It's just that I thought that God's best for me *was* Ryan. It was an exercise many times in patience, love and loyalty.

I was caught in the middle of all these emotions so I turned to my friendship with Ross to find comfort from the churning of pain as Ryan wanted a girlfriend, and it wasn't me. My friendship with Ross was a place of joy, peace and safety as I wasn't going to hurt over my liking him and it not being mutual. Ross and I were friends and I knew that he was a sweet brother in the Lord. I couldn't think of him as my "little" brother in the Lord, because his maturity continued to astound me.

Christmas season came and it was the first time ever that I spent it without any family members. Instead, I stayed on the base and house- and dog-sat for a family. One of my girl friends put together a special "devotional" book for me to study during that time. It was on various topics from the book of "Ruth" and marriage. I was seeking God fervently as I knew that He had been preparing me for marriage for a number of years but these past two had become far more intentional.

Journal entry — Dec. 1988

Even thinking now, in the quietness and peace of the gentle strokes of the Holy Spirit and how He has tenderly and delicately wooed me—such softness, so gentle. My body designed to be used to glorify God. Amazing how I blush now, how cautious I am, how shy, and yet, how charming! I flit around issues with the smallest hint of

163

a smile playing about my lips. My dancing eyes speak volumes in pure intensity and passion. To know another's heart and the depth of shared emotion—that will be intimacy.

Is the time nearing when I will have a husband? Is it too soon to ask or is it God stirring in me? Even as I've read more on marriage tonight—I find myself desiring it—really wanting to pour my love on one man—not necessarily soon—but in a few years. Seems like I want to give, to encourage, build up one man and see him fulfill his potential in Christ. I want to give up my independence, to lay down visions of grandeur and to willingly submit to being a wife, to merge into a ministry.

No greater vision—no Africa, no Europe, no singing, no life on my own—alone—Many thoughts unspoken but shed through tears. The deepest desire as I realized I am longing for someone to love more than wanting to be loved.

One night Ryan came over to watch a movie and he gave me a Christmas present. He gave me a small box of chocolates. It was so sweet of him. I was touched. Ross had just arrived back on base and Ryan invited him over to join us. To my surprise, Ross had also brought me a gift of tea and a jar of his own "homemade" honey. I was so blessed that he gave me a present too, and this was from his own business.

The three of us sat to watch the movie. Ross sat beside me on the couch. He seemed to be quite happy to be physically close to me and I noted that because Ryan was almost always uncomfortable with me if I tried to get too affectionate. In fact, I realized that Ryan was in a chair away from me while Ross easily sat close to me.

A tiny spark flickered in my mind. *Does Ross like me?*

After the movie, Ross hugged me goodnight and left. Ryan stayed for a short while. I hugged him goodnight as well. I was a jumble of emotions. I liked spending time with these guys but my interactions with Ryan were becoming more awkward as he continued to insist that we were just "friends." Ross was easier to be with as I didn't feel "kept at a distance," and I didn't hear about his crushes or girlfriends because he didn't have any.

Ross left a few days later, in January for the outreach portion of his missionary training. He returned from Barbados, West Indies two months later. During that time, I wrote him two lengthy letters to be hand-delivered. He never wrote back.

During the time Ross was away, Ryan had to have a heart-felt talk with me. I had sensed it was coming but it didn't make it any easier to hear it. Before he started talking with me, he prayed out loud for God to be there with us and help him say the right words so he wouldn't hurt me. I wasn't exactly sure what was going to happen.

He breathed deeply and cut to the chase. "Why are you jealous? My intentions towards you have always been friendship and yours...." His tone was tender, sad and broken. They were words that were spoken with the deepest kindness that he could offer.

I tried to slowly share my heart and the pain that it was to communicate what I felt. "You've spent all this time with me. There have been so many things you've said and you've given me so many mixed signals."

He was soft and sweet. "I did a lot of things that weren't wise. I said things I shouldn't have and I am truly sorry."

The realization of all my dashed hopes, prayers and dreams came to surface and I couldn't deny the painful reality of truth. I quietly looked at him as I fought back the tears.

"So, are you going to be the *sixth* guy that says, 'Uh, Ruth you're a good friend but...?"

"Ruth, you have a lot of qualities I deeply respect. If it weren't for God using you to pray for me and having someone to talk to...I probably would've gone nuts. God has good things in store for you. It'll take a much better man than a young, fickle guy like me. I don't want to do anything to destroy this friendship. My question for you is, are you going to be a faithful friend to the seventh, the tenth or even the fifteenth guy or are you going to close your heart and put up walls?"

He waited for my answer and from the place of resolve, I responded,

"No, I'll still be committed and faithful."

Ryan continued speaking. "...and somewhere down the line *my* wife will be happy for what *you* did in my life."

We chuckled together, stood and hugged one another and both of us said that there was a point in which we thought we would've cried, but we didn't.

It was good to be alone so I could express my feelings. I went back to my room and cried. God reminded me once again of being back in college, when I held my teddy bear. He had used my friendship with Ryan and other brothers to work on areas in my life that needed more polishing. Mistakenly again, I had allowed my emotions to develop further than they should have. Ryan, though special, like many before, was never physically attracted to me. *So, here I am God—walking it through with tears in my eyes. You know best how to help me and once again—I'm falling into Your arms....when I feel I can't go on—please hold me.*

I felt a myriad of emotions and then I felt numb. It would be "so easy" to just don the all independent woman façade but God had torn down those walls of my heart and I didn't understand why He would do that if He didn't intend for me to be married.

For years I had held the view that I would be a single missionary for God, live in Africa, minister to twenty thousand people and be a great evangelist and healer for Jesus. Marriage was seen as compromise and children weren't seen. This "vision" was set up in college as a defense against all the pain of my past—a modified version of a broken, wounded, abused girl who prior to that trauma wanted simply to be a missionary and to be married.

Chapter 21

Walking the Loop

$\mathcal{B}$y the time Ross returned from Barbados, my emotions towards Ryan had faded and I accepted the reality that I would never be anything more to him than a friend. The day the team came back, I was in the gym and another couple, who were engaged, embraced after not seeing each other for two months.

Ross walked in and teased them. "Aww, look at all that mush!" I saw him and I was thrilled and smiling but then he turned and saw me. His face lit up and he grabbed me, hugged me, picked me up and twirled me around. By the time he set my feet on the floor, I was dizzy. I felt so shocked at his affection but I enjoyed being missed. No guy had ever picked me up and twirled me at the joy of seeing me. *He likes me…I think?*

Ross had tentative plans to come back to Texas for the next training session but that was a month away. He walked me to one of my staff meetings and later in the evening, he was just coming to find me.

"Ruth, will you walk the loop with me?"

Having recently recovered from my misunderstandings of Ryan's feelings towards me, I was not about to get sucked into that deception again. In the past, Ryan had asked me to walk the loop with him, and now I knew that his intention had only ever been friendship.

I quickly responded to Ross, "No…. but I'll walk around the gym with you."

We began walking as we carried on our conversation. At one point, I looked up at the sky. It was a breathtakingly beautiful full moon on a black velvet background with a twinkling of stars. I was caught up in the wonder of the sky and I wasn't thinking when the words came pouring out of my mouth.

I gasped, "Oh, look at the moon! How romantic!"

Immediately we both started laughing and I tried to recover myself. "Uh, I mean, ignore the moon! Just ignore the moon."

Ross asked, "So, have you had a lot of "ro—-tic" nights?"

I had never heard that word before and I didn't know what he meant. So I said, "What's "Ro—-tic?"

"Romantic....without the man."

I laughed, "Yeah, I sure have had a lot of those."

I was very aware of Ross but I knew that there was no guarantee of his return to Texas and I didn't want my heart to deceive me again. I knew all too well that for Ryan, I was just a big sister and that was all I was ever meant to be. Although Ross spent lots of time with me, he was only eighteen and he had never told me that he liked me. So, I wasn't going to take any chances.

The Texas night air grew nippy, it being the end of February. After we had walked twelve times around the gym, we retreated to one of the classrooms where it would be warmer. I sat across from him at a table. He asked me, "So, what do you like to do?"

"I like to eat and I like to sleep."

"I'm being serious."

"So am I. That's what I like to do."

I honestly can't tell you where the conversation went from there. We exchanged addresses and I encouraged him to write me. The next few days we spent time together and laughed a lot. I hugged Ross good-bye. He asked me to hold onto a package for him until he returned in three weeks. Though Ryan and I were still friends, there was no more attraction to him and my heart found this budding relationship with Ross to be "strange and almost silly."

Ross left and my life went on. I did write to him and this time he did write back. I realized that his letter was a "form" letter and only at the end was anything "personal." That was a joke, too, because all he did was send me two names of some people who wanted more information about our mission organization, and would I be willing to send it? Ryan asked me about Ross and I said, "I think Ross might be number seven." I only put snippets in my journals about Ross but I did write, "It's a different comfortable—I share more with him." After having written detailed pages of my relationship with Ryan for the last few years, it seemed foolish of me to start detailing things about Ross. I didn't want to look back later and see how deceived I had been, again.

The day Ross returned to the base for his second missionary training phase, I was working in the front office. The receptionist called me on the telephone from the front desk. "Ruth, Ross is here to see you." I shrieked into the phone with utter delight and then I realized my "unprofessional" response.

Certainly, I didn't want *him* to know how thrilled I was to see him! So, I tried to compose myself and slowly walked to the front, and was generally quite formal with him. I only gave him a half-hug, but my actions in no way reflected what my emotions were at seeing him again. It seemed that from that point on, we just kept "running into each other".

One time, I saw Ross in the passenger seat of his car and I jumped into the driver's seat. The next thing I knew, he turned the key and said, "That's it. You're driving." I panicked, but he was insistent. I managed to back the car out of the lot and drove briefly with my heart racing and my palms sweating. Ross had no idea of my paralyzing fear of driving.

Immediately after my high school graduation, my father had insisted that I get a drivers' license. He knew that I needed to face my fear and within a week, I passed the test. Other than a handful of times, I had never driven.

I parked Ross' car within a few minutes and then I told him all about my fears of driving and the responsibility of life and death if I ever caused an accident. I further let him know that I didn't feel confident about a car because I didn't understand how it worked.

Later in the evening, Ross took me for a drive and we just talked some more. I told him that I am no longer greatly attracted to Ryan. Ross and I talked seriously and then we laughed. I could not believe how hc could only be eighteen.

Ross caught me off-guard again. "Ruth, I wonder about when I'll get married. I think it will be soon, maybe when I'm twenty-one. I want to be good friends with her first though." He abruptly turned and looked at me, "I think we're a lot alike."

"You do?"

"Yes, you're like me and I'm like you."

We were outside in the dark, illuminated by the boardwalk and street lights. I was sitting on a wall and he was below me. Since we were sharing our hearts, I felt vulnerable enough to let him see mine. "I don't know when God will ever send my husband. I'm already twenty-five and I've been waiting for over five years."

Ross looked straight into my eyes and quietly said, "How do you know that he isn't right under your nose?"

(Flabbergasted, I thought, **You** *are right under my nose. I held my breath and didn't say a word.)* My heart leapt as I considered. You mean Ross might like me? This whole atmosphere is serious. He has never once told me that he is attracted to me. Is he? The silence lasted until he broke it.

"Yeah, I still wonder about Karla." *He's still thinking about his ex-girlfriend.* I kicked myself for thinking that Ross felt anything else towards me but the "little brother-big sister" syndrome. *How grateful I am that he can't see my heart.* I thought he was implying that he liked me, but he was just making conversation.

Consistently I saw Ross and we chatted and laughed together but I reined in my emotions. I was grateful that he didn't know how I had started to feel about him. I was the only girl that showed up to celebrate his birthday. There were just a few guys there and we watched movies— "Princess Bride" was one of his favorites.

One evening I was scheduled to babysit. Ross told me to come and find him once I returned to the base. Our curfew on the weekends wasn't until 1:00 in the morning and he wanted to talk to me from 11:00 on. Though we had not said we liked one another, I began to give greater consideration to my former fleeting thoughts. *That's really late. It's odd that he would want to visit with me.* I was too tired once I returned from babysitting so I only briefly chatted as he had plans to see me in the morning and drive me to church.

I walked toward his car and I saw him as he started to back up. I assumed he saw me but I was wrong. I had my hands on the car as it moved and my heels slid on the asphalt as I banged on the window to get his attention. For a few brief seconds I was scared and then he saw me and stopped. I had been in his blind spot.

I was dressed in a modern style and he was in an old fashioned suit with a hat that belonged to his grandfather. The hat was from the 1930's and Ross was confident enough to wear it and not care that he was different. I teased him about being a man from the 1800's and he teased me about being a woman from the 1980's. As we sat together at church talking and chuckling before the service, someone in the congregation asked,

"Are you two together?"

We chuckled and said, "No." As he drove us back to the base, he challenged me with my fear of driving. "How do you know that God won't have me join staff—so you'll learn how to drive?"

"What would you do if I totaled your car?"

"I'd trust God….but I don't think you will. I have more trust in you than you have in yourself."

"Are you serious?" I was incredulous that he would think of trusting me with such an expensive thing as a car.

"Yes, I have a real peace about it—I don't with other people. The car is just a mode of transportation. If it gets damaged, it can be replaced."

Later, I was out with him and I teased him, "There you go again. I think you're flirting." He surprised me because he said, "Funny, I watch you do the same thing." We didn't comment anymore on that topic. It seemed that we spent time with each other every day and I knew how much I was drawn to want to be with him.

One night there was a spectacular heat lightning "show" as is so common in the spring in East Texas. Paul and Sandy, newly engaged, kissed and watched the display. They were several yards away from us and lost in their own world. *What could you expect? I'd do the same if I were with one I loved.* At times it was awkward and at other times I just laughed. It was another "Ro—-tic scene" –without the man, in context, of course.

171

Ross sat beside me, taking pictures. I was acutely aware of him physically and as I sat near him I could feel his body heat. I was so comfortable with him. The thought drifted into my mind, *I wonder what he kisses like?* That thought really shocked me because even in my feelings towards Ryan, I never thought about kissing. That was to be reserved for my husband. Somehow, once again, the conversation turned towards marriage.

"You know, Ruth, I am still so young. I don't know what I want in marriage. Sometimes, I wonder, what do I have to offer?"

"Ross, I have a question for you. Is flirting the same as teasing?"

"Well, in my opinion, I think they are two different words." I listened as he continued. "But is it flirting if you care, if it is more than surface—if it's more than self-gratifying or an ego-boost? Is that flirting or is it just a way of relating to the opposite sex?"

"I don't know. I had several Christian brothers in college. We were all close. I was attracted to some of them but they were never attracted to me."

"I'm glad that God blinded them."

I was shocked and mortified. *Oh my gosh! Ross thinks I'm a dog. He is glad that God blinded those guys because I am so ugly. How horrible. All along I thought this was going somewhere...he doesn't even find me attractive. How grateful I am that he can't read my mind. I was 'falling in love' with him....Oh, how devastating. I am just a big sister.* I didn't understand the guessing games but our time together abruptly ended. I firmly resolved to remind myself that nineteen was too young, regardless. So I began to wonder if this "thing" with Ross was just my flesh toying with me and nothing else?

Earlier in the fall, I had prayed about going to Barbados and possibly joining a team to help pioneer a base there. So, one evening as Ross walked me to my dorm, I teased about being called to the tropics...He said, "Barbados?" He went there for his outreach. He believed that he would return some day. So we laughed and he said that for him, it wouldn't be for vanity reasons.

"I don't tan. I get as red as a lobster and then I peel and go back to being white." *Well, I guess he'll just have to slather on lots of lotion to stay out on the beach. Then he won't burn and he'll tan.* (I didn't understand that Ross didn't have the pigment in his body to tan.)

We spent time in worship together as he played his flute and I listened and talked with God. Neither Ross nor I spoke that night; we just enjoyed one another's company. Later as he walked me to the dorm, the next thing I knew, he was down on one knee, as if he was proposing. I reacted quite firmly, "Do you have the word of the Lord on that?" He got up and the teasing on both sides stopped.

A few nights later, a group of guys and girls were watching a movie, a teenage romance. I don't remember what it was but at the end all of us were talking about what we wanted. One of the girls naturally wanted the date, another the flowers and I said "I want the romantic dinner." We were all crammed in a car, driving back to the base. Ross was smashed beside me and I was against the car door. Out of nowhere, with the barest of whispers, I heard him say, "What kind of wine?" I was so shocked, I wasn't even sure I heard correctly so I didn't respond.

Within a few weeks of Ross returning for his second phase of training, a first phase student latched onto him. Katie was eighteen with long black hair and she was gorgeous in face and figure. She was also emotionally needy. A group of us were at the Substation, a restaurant on base, sitting together talking and laughing. I was there with a bunch of my girlfriends. Ross came and talked to me for a while and then he left to talk with Katie.

The next day, Ross wanted to tell me all about how he'd "passed a test" from God as it related to guy/girl relationships. I didn't want to hear about his victory. Whatever the test was, he passed. As he tried to relate the night's events, I snapped at him, "No, I don't want to hear it. You were flirting."

"I was not flirting."

"Yes, you were."

He tried to be serious with me. "I mentioned you to Katie because she has a troubled background and I think you could help her. "

I walked away. Once again the thought jolted through my mind. *He's just number seven!* The reality of that hurt. It made sense, though. I was jealous and grateful that Ross had no clue how I really felt.

Here we go again. I have to minister to a girl who I am jealous of. I knew as the day wore on, I would have to ask Ross for forgiveness for treating him in that manner. Only at the moment, I didn't want to think about it. The situation reminded me of Ryan and my fiasco of misinterpreting his feelings towards me. As evening came, I couldn't find Ross. Instead, I saw Katie in his leather jacket.

I turned to my safest place and poured out my heart to Jesus. I could be transparent with Him. *"Lord, I'm jealous of this eighteen year old girl. She is wearing his jacket. I feel like a high-school kid all over again. I am twenty-five and I don't know what Ross even feels about me. I am a woman and I really don't want to minister to her. But if You'll give me Your heart for her and the words to speak, then I'll do it."*

I did minister to her about the love of Jesus, power to forgive and more. I even shared some of my testimony. She talked about how sweet I was and how much Ross admired me. Then, she asked me if I would return his jacket to him! So, God uses a willing vessel in His strength and not in my own.

Later that night, Ross returned from Dallas. He was outside and I made my apology and gave him his jacket. It was cold so he asked if I wanted to sit in his car and get out of the chilling wind. I did. The rest of the conversation was the most profound and life-changing one I have ever had.

In a manner uncharacteristic of Ross, he spoke solemnly for the rest of the time. It was a quiet atmosphere in the front seat of his car. "Ruth, I want to say some things to you but I don't know how it will affect our friendship."

I sighed resignedly and prepared myself. Here we go again...the proverbial, "I like you as a sister in the Lord..., but..."

Ross continued speaking, "Last night, Katie and I were sitting outside and she was opening up about her struggles and she was crying. She looked at me and said, 'Throw your arms around me and kiss me!'

Ouch! As I felt the sharp pang of jealousy in the pit of my stomach.

Ross continued, "I just looked at her and said, 'Is that really going to help the situation?'

I had a hard time stifling a giggle as I thought about how I would feel if a guy said that to me after such a request and a desire. I saw how serious Ross was. I honestly couldn't fathom a guy turning down a gorgeous, needy female who wanted to receive his kiss. That caught my attention.

"Ruth, I passed my test from God, not to enter into a special relationship. I made a commitment to the Lord not to date anyone and I felt like this was a test to see if I would honor my commitment or give in to the flesh."

That surprised me as well. *I thought I was the only one who had this commitment to God. He made the same one I did? Odd and interesting.*

"Ruth, I really value our friendship. I like how we can talk about so many different things and I enjoy spending time with you. I'm attracted to you...but I don't know how you feel about me. I don't have a release to date and I don't want to do anything to damage our friendship." (*So, he's not number 7!*)

He was attracted to me. He liked me. He hadn't been playing my emotions or just teasing me. He was serious. This was almost like being in a dream and any moment I was going to wake up. But the conversation was real and I wasn't imagining this. I was caught totally off-guard and sat in stillness as the dawning of reality crept across my heart.

I finally found my voice. "Ross, I am attracted to you, too. You sure did your best to keep me guessing. I wasn't sure if you were flirting or being truthful with some of the questions you would ask. There was that time when you were on your knee as if you were proposing."

Ross smiled, "I was flirting the truth."

"I'm concerned about the difference in our ages and the fact that you are a student and I am staff. I have a call on my life and I can't compromise that."

"Down the road, age doesn't really matter. My school leadership has seen us together at times and if they were to ask me, I'd have to slur it together, 'I like her. We're friends. We're friends, but I like her.' I talked with Paul. He cautioned me about our spending so much time together. 'Either you two are going to get serious or you're going to get hurt. Would you marry her?' Ross said, "You probably won't want to hear this answer."

"You're right. It'll probably be negative."

"Gee, you're awfully hard on yourself."

"No, I just face reality."

"Well, you're wrong. The answer was positive."

"What? You said yes?"

"Ruth, if God told me I could, I would marry you."

Deep in my spirit, I knew Ross well enough to know that he was too serious to be playing with my emotions. Again, I could say nothing. After an eternity of silence he asked, "So, like I said before, how is this going to affect our friendship?"

I finally found my voice again and quietly spoke. "Ross, I don't just blow people off.... I am attracted to you too.... But I don't have a release from God to date, either..... So, I guess we just stay friends."

We got out of the car. He asked for a hug goodnight and he said that he'd pray for both of us. Though we had hugged many times before, the significance of the conversation made the hug feel totally different.

As I walked to my dorm, I stopped and I looked up at the sky. I normally didn't address the Lord with such intimacy, but that night something different was happening to me. I spoke with a catch in my throat as the tears formed in my eyes, "Daddy, do You realize that if You tell him he can, he would marry me?" I walked into my dorm as if I were in a daze. Something so amazing was happening and I couldn't even voice it. I went to my room and picked up my Bible. *"I'm not going to play Scripture roulette, but I am going to see if You're going to speak through Your Word."*

I opened to the New Testament selections for that day. There was nothing significant. Then, I turned to the Old Testament. It was as if the verses were highlighted. I Samuel 16: *"Do not look on the outward appearance.....for the Lord sees the heart."* God told me, "Don't look at Ross' age anymore." I continued reading, *"And they brought forth the youngest and he was ruddy, and good-looking and the Lord said, Arise, anoint him, for this is the one."* Never had God spoken so clearly to me about marriage. I shut my Bible and said, *"God, You've got two weeks."* I meant that during that time one way or another He would confirm if Ross was to become my husband, or if I was completely nuts.

After reading those passages, I went into the bathroom and stared into the mirror. I must've been there a long time because girls kept going in and out. Katie came in. I was startled out of my reverie because I told her that Ross asked me to marry him.

She threw her arms around me as we hugged and she kept gushing about how happy she was for both of us. "You guys are amazing. I have such respect for both of you. God is awesome!"

Honestly, even when I said the words, "Ross asked me to marry him," it just didn't seem real. I couldn't grasp the significance of it. I had never been speechless with joy in my life and that's all I could do was be dumbfounded. It was too good to be true. This incredible, godly man wanted to marry me!

She was exuberant enough for both of us. She hugged me but I was still in a stupor. There was a deep sacredness that I didn't want intrusion. It seemed if I acknowledged Ross' love for me, there would be some inner sanctum that would be disturbed. It was a delicious secret that I wasn't sure if I even trusted myself to believe.

As always, I pulled myself into my relationship with God and I poured my heart out to Him in my journal. *Never in my life have I felt like this — so in shock! but it was good –full of joy and not some great emotional frenzy. I believe he's serious enough not to say something he doesn't feel. He isn't some fly-by-night flirt and all I know is I've never felt like this before. Beyond a doubt, I need God's direction and I keep committing myself, my heart and this whole thing to Him. All I could think of was that Ross said YES—the incredible impact and the wonder for truly—God did it!* I was awake most of the night and I dreamed that Ross met my brother Walt and my mother and that they all got along well. I have so much whirling through and yet, *O Jesus, — I'm committed to You.*

Chapter 22

A Night of Painful Transparency

I awoke the next morning—singing, joyful, happy and thrilled—and still inside was this joy inexpressible. Gee I wonder—the fleeting thoughts I've had even before last night. *So Jesus—what incredible thoughts and Lord! (is this it? Is Ross the man You've chosen for me?) I want to hear when my emotions are calm. In the next two weeks I will know. If I sat down and wrote all the things that line up—God—will You give Your blessing? Is this the one I've waited for? Jesus, I need You!*

Although, Ross has dated many—he hasn't settled down with one. *I wonder if God will have him fall so deeply in love with me and it will be that love that keeps me loving him back— isn't that being wooed?*

I struggled with feelings of pride and inferiority–I didn't know how to "be" a couple. We left the crowd of people and found a quiet place to talk. I told Ross about my choosing not to date, being faithful and waiting. "I hope my husband-to-be is suffering…without a girlfriend. I hope he appreciates that I haven't been involved with a guy for five years."

"I hope she appreciates it—that I've kept my virginity."

Teary-eyed, I looked at him and spoke softly, "Whether I ever marry you or not, I greatly appreciate that you are a virgin. Ross, I had a friend back in my college days who told me, 'I think you'll get someone pure—who hasn't gone through what you have—but will be really sensitive.'"

I knew that he had to hear the truth of what my life had been. It was a heart-wrenching conversation as I related to him pieces of my past. It hurt to tell him of all my experiences and I couldn't look at him; I only stared at the wall. The words came slowly and with much regret and sorrow. This beautiful, pure man sat and listened to me with such tenderness, compassion and love. It tore me apart to relate to him all my unfaithfulness. Though I knew that God had changed me from that identity, I also knew that Ross had every right to change his mind about the woman he wanted to marry.

There was so much about me that up until that night he had never heard. I think it was the most agonizing conversation I had ever had. My entire future was at stake and deep in my heart I knew it. I told him that I would be so blessed if God gave me someone who'd never been with anyone else. I related the events of my life—daycare and being abused and every guy I'd ever had sex with—how I never wanted it but they played on my weakness. Sex was always a way to get acceptance and affection but when there wasn't sex—there was rejection.

I shared how I had a heart to minister to young people and I know that God is faithful and He can restore—"I'm my own best testimony." Then I shared my fears of having children and the hope for God to physically restore my virginity. "I feel like a virgin—I blush when a guy has his shirt off. I stand amazed at what God has done in my life." Finally it was over and the silence was deafening. All that I shared just permeated the quietness and sacredness of the prayer chapel. After a long time, I ventured a question as I looked into Ross' eyes. "What are you thinking?" I sat with the deepest pain of knowing how much I loved this man, this virgin, and how my world could change as my heart trembled and waited for his answer.

Ross looked into my eyes and his glazed with tears, too. Ever so gently and tenderly, with no bitterness or condemnation, he stated, "The past is the past. She's dead…What you've shared with me tonight shows me that you really trust me and I appreciate and admire that you told me. If you never share anything else about your past than you have tonight, and we do get married, and somewhere down the road something comes up—condemnation won't because you've been open. The foundation of any solid relationship is based on openness and honesty."

Relief and joy flooded my heart. He still wanted to marry me. I wasn't "used goods" in his eyes. He could see the transformation that God had done and it didn't change his feelings towards me; in fact, it made them even stronger to know what God had done in my life.

We talked about the lightning evening and my being so aware of him. "I was afraid that you weren't attracted to me, that you thought I was ugly and like a dog and that you were glad that God blinded those guys so that they couldn't see how ugly I was."

Ross broke out in great laughter. "What? Are you kidding? I was glad that God blinded them; otherwise I wouldn't have had a chance. Ruth, you are beautiful. It was their loss, not mine."

I leaned against him and he ran his fingers through my hair. "You like my hair?"

"Uh-huh."

"It's just dead skin cells." I hadn't heard many compliments and I often quipped to diminish the effect of them.

"They're yours."

At the beginning of our friendship, a friendly hug from Ross was normal and it didn't make me feel much of anything but a brother/sister relationship in the Lord. But now when he hugged me, there were all kinds of deep emotions that went with that affection. I hoped that if God was putting us together for life, that He would release things slowly. First, it was okay to date but that our relationship would develop in a gradual process—that I would be wooed by Ross to learn to love him—(even the words sounded so strange) How funny! When I was twenty-one, he was fourteen. What a sense of humor God had. I cried out at that time, *"Lord, where in the world is my husband?"* God was probably saying, "Give Me time. He has to at least turn eighteen first."

Ross shared that the other night he was bombarded with fear. "How would you support a wife? You don't even have a job. What would you do?" Then he realized these fears weren't from God. At the same time I felt so inadequate to be a wife and I was discouraged. Then I realized that God never asked me to walk it out alone.

Marriage was His idea and I'm sure those fears were common but I would trust God to help me overcome them.

We planned our first date for the next day. I hadn't gone on a date in several years. The thought of all that was happening, was overwhelming. It was so much better than a Hollywood script and I was amazed at what God was doing in my heart and life.

Chapter 23

Our First Date and Beyond

$\mathcal{L}$ate the next morning, I got in Ross' car and as we drove away from the base, he asked me, "So, where do you want to go?"

"It doesn't matter. Where do you want to go?"

"No, I asked you."

I was flustered. I wasn't sure what this date would be like. I mean, he didn't even know where we were going—he wanted to take me where I wanted to go. What if I chose some place he didn't really like? What if I chose wrong? What if I regretted my choice? This whole scenario reminded me of too many wrong choices. I didn't want to be "in charge."

The next thing I knew, Ross pulled the car over on the side of a country road and turned off the engine. "This looks like a great spot to me. When you decide where you want to go, let me know."

He was serious. I would have to make some decision. "Well, at least give me some choices."

"Okay. Do you want to eat Mexican, Chinese or American?"

I decided on American and we stopped at a fast food restaurant and picked up fried chicken, biscuits and corn on the cob, along with two soft drinks. We went to the Tyler Rose Garden. Tyler, Texas, is known as the "rose capital of the world." The roses were spectacular and the garden was filled with fountains and an immense variety of roses. We prayed and then we ate. There weren't any napkins in the bag so we had to lick our sticky fingers. I wasn't all that hungry.

Ross ate both pieces of corn because I feared the threat of corn getting stuck in my teeth. I re-read my letters to him along with my journal and we laughed because even though I flirted with him then, he never saw it.

As Ross quietly processed what he'd heard, he spoke. "You don't talk the way you write—you write creatively. I'm learning about your intelligence by hearing you write—because you don't talk about it." He held my hand in the car on the way home!

It was such a simple gesture but his hand in mine sent thrills to my heart. It was as if I was experiencing love for the first time and the innocence and purity of holding hands was like fireworks exploding. None of my past mattered. God had restored me.

Later that night, Ross came to find me. I didn't have to pursue him, another answer to my prayers. "Ross, it's so awkward for me to pray with you and I struggle with being a couple in a public setting. It's hard for me not to want to withdraw."

"God is faithful. He'll help you in praying and it will get easier."

"What did you want in a woman, a wife?"

"I didn't want someone fat, or an air-head and she didn't have to be the most beautiful. She didn't have to be Miss America because I'm no Mr. Universe."

"So, what do you like?'

"You. Ruth, you're beautiful."

We talked about Barbados. The information blew me away because it reminded me of the vision the lady had seen of me, "being in a place with cows and carts, islands….have you ever thought of missions?" Ross said, "Ruth, in one of our prayer times, one of our team felt that five people will pioneer the base in Barbados but at the time only four of us felt called there."

Both of us had told God that we didn't want a relationship until it was "the one"—no need to date anyone else—we laughed so much together with so much wonder and amazement at the ways God prepared us for one another—missions calling, simplistic, love to worship, study, learn, disciple—enjoy creation, outdoors. "Ruth I long for the day when you will be, 'Ruth McElwee.'" My prayer, *As usual and again Lord Jesus, please fulfill Your will—NOT anyone else's—if this is Your will—keep releasing and if not God then please halt it—(Even now though you'd think if it wasn't God's will that He would've stopped it—or we wouldn't have this great, tremendous peace.)*

As I went to church with Ross on April 16, I felt like God said, "I'm going to confirm My will in this service." I laughed with Ross about how he accidentally almost ran over me the prior week. I reminded him of how I had been in his blind spot and I banged on the window as my heels slid on the pavement. I teased him about almost "running over your destiny".

During the praise and worship time, I wanted to hold Ross' hand....but I didn't. Then out of nowhere, the pastor encouraged the congregation, "Take the hand of the person next to you and sing, "He Who Began a Good Work." During the sermon, I thought about Barbados and I imagined my Dad with a smile on his face. There was a powerful presence of God and peace. At the end of the service, the Pastor quipped to the flock, "Oh, Thank the Lord for wives...."

Ross and I were quiet as we got into the car. He didn't even start to drive. We just sat together and then he broke the silence. "The service was on Barbados." There was a song during the service and Ross felt "we should've held hands" when we sang, "called out from darkness and set apart." I had felt that same prompting to hold his hand, but I chose not to follow it. He reminded me I'd heard "islands" and felt like Barbados is 'home base' for the fire of God for revival to spread to the other islands. He drove back to the base as we silently contemplated the significance of what God confirmed to us. We parked at the base and Ross took both my hands, looked deeply into my eyes, "I have no doubt as to where God is leading this relationship." He kissed my hand.

The solemnity and beauty of the moment left me silent once again. There was no need for words. As I left to go change into more casual clothing, I nearly burst with joy.

In my dorm room, I was overwhelmed with tears of joy and the reality of what was happening. I hurriedly wrote in my journal and went to meet Ross. We both hummed and were happy. Finally I showed him, "Arise, anoint him for this is the one." Like David, he wanted to be best friends and to have a heart that seeks after God. *So neat! So close –so much peace—(dare I say it? So much love?)*

Ross again told me I'm beautiful. "The glory of Lebanon has come to me." He referred to me more than once in that way because of my Lebanese background. Later that afternoon, once I returned to the dorm, I wrote in my journal: *Lord Jesus—I just want a good, joyful cry.* Then I sensed, "Your 7th cookie has been given to you." I had a thought, "Today Ross will kiss you."

Later that evening, we walked the loop, arms around each other's waists. He stopped in the road and pulled me close and I felt that he wanted to kiss me. We were out in the public view but I wanted some place more private. I don't know why I said it, but I said, "Not here."

We continued our walk until we reached the little prayer chapel. It was away from the main base, quiet and secluded, overlooking the lake. We were outside in the dusk of the evening with the warm April breeze. The scene was peaceful and rich with meaning. In one week, God had confirmed His will for our lives and my heart was filled with joy and anticipation. Ross sat below me and his voice was tender with emotion.

"Ruth, will you marry me?"

My eyes filled with tears and my heart burst with joy. I gladly said, "Yes!" Then we kissed for the first time! It was so beautiful! So tender! So God! The tears gently rolled down my cheeks as I sensed God's voice, "I am pleased with both of you." Then Ross told me that when we stopped on the other side of the loop, he felt God say to him, "Kiss her." How funny since I didn't know what he sensed but I said, "Not here." God told him to kiss me. What a confirmation!

I smiled into his Ross' eyes and said, "I am going to marry a virgin. I am going to, in God's timing, share my whole body with you." Ross just kept looking at me. "Do you know how beautiful you look in the moonlight? I love you."

"Goodnight Ruth McElwee." *Well, Lord, in seven days You've confirmed and sealed commitment with a kiss and Jesus I love You because truly Lord –You do all things well.*

GOD IS A GOD OF ROMANCE!

Chapter 24

Why Can't I Say, 'I Love You'?

A week later, we went on another date, again to the Rose Garden. We held hands almost the whole time while Ross drove. We talked about dates, finances and how God will have to provide. After we ate, we watched the squirrels; we lay down beside one another and just relaxed—it was so peaceful, so gentle—just watching the clouds and being close.

My emotions were so content—I was so satisfied. I didn't feel shame, conviction, lust or anything negative. Time could've stopped—it was so unreal and yet it was real. Ross spoke, "God, promise me when we're married that we'll be able to do this once a month—just be together and talk." We got up and walked around to look at the roses. Ross took pictures.

I teased him, "So, I guess you're looking at the scenery?" It was such a delight to be the focus of his attention. I loved seeing his face as he gazed at me. I never knew what he would say next.

"Yes. I'm looking at you. You are a rose—just as subtle, soft and delicate." What a romantic man! He whispered in my ear, "I love you."

"I know."

It amazed me that God knew us so well both intimately and physically. It blessed me that I was being wooed. At the same time, it was hard for me to express my own emotions. Ross, does it bother you that I can't say, 'I love you,'?

"No, because when you do, you'll mean it. Love and courtship and being wooed are a process. If I send you a dozen red roses—will you understand what I'm saying?"

The next day Ross got a letter from Karla and I got a letter from Kyle. It was uncanny and odd as neither of us had heard from our respective "old flames" for over a year. Both of them wanted to revive a dating relationship. (I wondered if even through these letters and circumstances that this was another confirmation that God's will was Ross and Ruth.) I felt intensely possessive of him in relationship to other girls — I didn't want to be jealous but I desired only me for him and him for me.

"Ross, I don't want you to kiss anyone else again."

"I don't ever want to kiss anyone else again. You are mine and I am yours."

It was so neat to see these feelings were reciprocal; he was defensive about me, too. We walked the loop and talked more about how we finally got together. When he said he watched me flirt—he meant with him, and not with other guys. I had totally misunderstood him months prior. In spite of not letting the other person know how we felt— God brought it all together. In the natural, we fought it so much— you wonder how much God laughed at us? We both so desperately wanted only Jesus and nothing with the opposite sex until there would be marriage.

We talked about the physical part of our relationship with God, I said, "Lord, we probably won't kiss much......"

Ross answered, "Why? It's an expression of the way you feel. As long as we don't put each other before God or we don't do something we shouldn't, it's okay."

Ross explained to me that when he was with a girlfriend and the temptation came to move beyond what was appropriate, there was always a red light that would go off in his mind and heart. He would sense, "You don't want to continue this. You should stop." Most of the time he would listen to his conscience because he knew that God was speaking to him. "With you it's different. I don't feel those alarms or sense the boundaries, which is even scarier. Instead, I have to choose to control myself and not step past the line, because the reality is that I am truly going to marry you and at that time, I will fully give myself to you."

I kissed Ross and sat quietly. I waited to feel conviction, condemnation, anything negative— but all I felt was tremendous peace. I did not feel lust, perversion, selfishness or sin. It was mind-blowing that God approved! *(Still in my heart was fear— just waiting, timid and shy. I wanted this to be God's will. I wanted to love Ross— and I needed Jesus to show me how.)*

A few days later, I met with my small group leader, "Do you love Ross?"

"To the understanding I have of love, I think I do."

"Do you love Ross for who he is? his character? his walk with the Lord? Not what he does but who he is? Love is selfless—giving, pouring out, blessing, and expecting nothing in return. It is a commitment to choose the highest good—and be honest with one another. It is not feelings—love is a choice."

I prayed silently for God to help me to love Ross the way I knew he loved me. She continued, "As you see God's love for you, from that relationship love flows naturally. Don't condemn yourself and don't compare yourself to Ross or anyone else. Let God examine your heart and teach you how to love. Encourage Ross. Express appreciation. Go ahead and take little steps— if there's peace, then it's God."

Ross and I went walking. "Ross, I've held back. I've been so cautious because I don't want it all to end. I've been like a sponge—soaking it all in but not squeezing any out. I've wanted to love you but I don't know how. Ross, I appreciate your waiting for me – even though you didn't know me."

"It was worth it. You're so much fun. I love being with you. I love your laugh—I enjoy your company –I love you."

"Ditto."

"You smell good."

I quipped, "Is that a combination of perfume, soap or me?"

"It's you."

"Get used to it."

"I'll have all my life."

Chapter 25

Leaving to Cleave

For a few days, I wanted not to kiss. We talked about developing our spiritual relationship. It was so neat because God had already spoken to Ross about the same thing. We prayed about my financial struggles and the misunderstanding of some of my family about the call of God on my life. He looked into my eyes, "If you never get their acceptance or approval—they might not accept me, ...or your going to Barbados—how will that affect you?"

"Only God can change their hearts. It will hurt but I'm committed to Jesus."

Ross prayed and then he inserted my name instead of Abram's, as he read, "The Lord said to Ruth, Gen. 12:1-9, 'You will leave your country, your kindred; your father's house and go to a land that I will show you.' "

I took Ross' hands and looked straight into his eyes as I knew the significance of the words I said. It was my answer to living in Barbados and whatever acceptance or rejection I would receive from my family. I looked into Ross' eyes and quoted from memory a life verse from the book of Ruth. It was significant to me, not just because of my name, but because, like my namesake, I was committing to leave my own country to go live somewhere else for the rest of my life.

I recited Ruth 1:16: "Then Ruth said, Entreat me not to leave you or to forsake from following you, for where you go, I will go; your people will be my people, and your God will be my God." We held hands and hugged. Ross told me his heart fluttered like it did when we first kissed. He walked me to my dorm and we held hands and were so thankful to God for our special prayer time. We did connect spiritually and it was such a wonderful experience. We didn't need to kiss in order to feel close.

I struggled to tell Ross "I love you." The struggle over declaring those words made me feel immature and insecure and I didn't like the hurt I inflicted on Ross. It seemed I needed time to process all that was happening and those words held a weight to them that I just couldn't say. There would be no turning back for me when I finally admitted those feelings, both to myself and to him and I just didn't know how to overcome the fears.

Ross assured me that his love for me wouldn't change and we talked freely about my struggles. He had insight that helped me. "You can't tell me you love me because of the rejection in the past and there's still fear there." *I believed that after Ross's outreach I would be able to say, "I love you," and that I would mean it with everything in me—but I thought that God would use the separation at outreach to bring me to that place. It's also why I looked forward to Ross's outreach and continued to mention it.*

"Ruth, I love you. I never want you to doubt it."

I let him know that I did love him but the words I used were simple phrases like, "Ditto." "I know." "Thank you," or later, "Olive juice." It discouraged me not to be able to break free from those fears and verbally declare my love for him. "Ross, are you willing to wait?"

"Yes, I am. Ruth, you're like a dam and God is pulling out the sticks. One day it's all going to gush forth and I don't pity the fool who's standing under it either. The dam is made of sticks and stones—words. You're walking beside one who loves you very much. I'm committed to you."

We walked to the Prayer Chapel and had a Bible study together on the Potter and the clay and the process of God preparing us for ministry. We talked about how our relationship happened and how so many things were miscommunicated. He had been determined not to tell me that he liked me unless it was God and I had been just as determined not to tell Ross that I liked him until he told me how he felt about me. He was comfortable interacting with me in a group but then he clammed up when we were one-on-one. With me, I could treat him like everyone else in a crowd in a joking, fun-loving, playful manner but one-on-one I'd get more serious.

As we reflected on the night we walked around the gym twelve times, Ross told me that first he thought I must not have liked him because I declined walking the loop with him. Then, we just talked about how we spent hours together. All the remembering helped me be more assured of God's will and it also freed me to "love" Ross more. *(There were times tonight I could've said the three words.... how exciting for me.)*

Chapter 26

A 30 Day Commitment

*O*ur pastor always encouraged us as a congregation, "Give a holy hug or a holy kiss", "Bless the person beside you, and put your arm around the person." It was funny because often I wanted to be more affectionate with Ross but I needed a "nudge." Even though the pastor knew nothing about us as a couple, as it was a fairly large church, God often used him to prompt me to express my feelings to Ross.

I was deeply concerned that if we had no physical expression, maybe we wouldn't have that much of a relationship. (Though this may sound off the wall, or crazy, I had never had a relationship that stayed a pure friendship, once a kiss had taken place.) I remembered a challenge by Josh McDowell years before, and I wanted to follow this "simple" test. Ross was willing because "it was my choice." So, for the next thirty days we made a commitment to only hold hands, hug and kiss on the cheek.

We got into some small arguments that led to my hurting Ross' feelings. I kept rejecting his expressions of love and tenderness. He was deeply hurt, bewildered and confused. Then he looked at me, "I love you but it's your choice—it takes two to have a relationship."

Ross was concerned that I would let my fears control me and that I would choose to reject him rather than staying committed to our relationship. The fears that Ross would leave me or change his feelings about me were also my own. He shared that hurt is in proportion to value and apart from his relationship with God he valued me most in his life. Deep in my heart I struggled with my emotions and silently talked with God. As I did, tears came into my eyes and I didn't stop them. I shared my heart with Ross when I prayed out loud, "God, please break down my defenses and teach me how to love Ross." We spent a long time in quiet as we just looked at each other and it was so tender. The words went from my head to my heart to the depth of my being—like they used to. "Ross, I wanted you to hurry up and go on outreach so I could fall in love with you."

"I think you already have—you've said it through your actions and through your eyes—and when you do form the words—you won't say them flippantly."

(Inside of me, I said the words—*I love you, I love you, Ross!* but they never found voice.) When I returned to my dorm that night, the realization came, "*Wow. I am in love and I love Ross.*" I was amazed at how passionate I felt when we kissed on the cheek. We were committed to God's grace. We freely talked about the Lord and to Him when we were together. Ross shared, "God, You've given me someone who loves me for who I am—not for what I'm not. I don't have to pretend to be someone else. She just loves me." Then he turned to me and said, "Promise me one thing, Ruth—that if we ever disagree, that we'll be open and honest with one another and talk it out."

I smiled warmly at him and chuckled, "You know me well enough by now that I couldn't keep it in long."

"I love you very much, Ruth. I don't want you to ever doubt that. I don't want you to ever forget it. Look into my eyes. Look into my heart. I love you. I will never reject you; I will never intentionally hurt you. I love you." Those same words were in his eyes.

We had decided to attend the upcoming School of the Bible together. He encouraged me that our training wasn't supposed to be a time to just "get through" individually, but a time for us to grow together. At the end of that beautiful evening he told me, "I love you," and once again all I said was, "Ditto."

In many ways I felt so angry at myself when I didn't say, "I love you," and when I sought God for answers as to why these words were so difficult to voice He revealed something I had forgotten.

God showed me that often as I was growing up when I said, "I love you," I was answered with, "I know," from certain guys or "Thank you," from my Dad.

My father grew up in an orphanage and he had heard very little positive affirmation in his own life. He struggled with self-esteem and often felt unworthy of being loved. He did love me but he had a hard time expressing his feelings with words. I never realized that until I struggled in my own relationship with Ross.

Ross and I had wanted our parents to know about what God was doing in our lives and we didn't want to overwhelm them so in our letters to each set of parents, we only mentioned our special friend. I had never written my parents about "a special young man" so I assumed that they would see what I was sharing and that they would understand how much this young man meant to me. There was no direct mention of marriage.

Ross' parents were a source of confirmation to us as we sought God's will for our future. Ross' Dad told him, "Your Mom and I have a real peace about Ruth....but don't run off and get married really soon." Those words blessed me because Ross' dad was happy for us and he mentioned marriage even before we did.

Weeks of emotions, feelings, prayers, interactions with Ross had gone by and I knew that all of my jumbled thoughts were fast approaching a final conclusion. Normally I would have gone to the office and started my work for the day. But there was a torrential thunderstorm and there was no pressing need to come in to work so I was told to stay home. I used that time to seriously focus on all the emotions that had been building in my heart and I wrote in my journal. The storm outside seemed to reflect my inner struggles as I poured out my heart to the Lord.

Lord, let it keep thundering until You're finished doing with me what You want done—until I cry. As I sang and trickled tears, I thought of how much I wanted approval and acceptance. There was deep weeping of fears that God would take Ross away or that He would change His mind; my own fears of being deceived—being afraid I would pour all into Ross only to find out "No" —and I just wept before God.

I kept thinking of various verses of the goodness of God, "delighting myself in the Lord and He will give us the desire of our hearts", that "no good thing will He withhold from those who walk uprightly." I kept remembering that, "My sheep hear My voice and a stranger they will not follow." Then He spoke, *"Go get your teddy bear."* I wanted God to break the dam of my emotions and to me it was significant that it was raining and I was crying. Then I inclined my ear to the sweet voice of Jesus, *"Ruth, I remember that night in your room at college where you wept before Me and you were like Hannah as you cried. You were wanting the barrenness and broken-ness healed, wanting to pour your love onto one man and not under-standing that it wasn't My time—that you couldn't have the cookie yet. Those prayers didn't bounce off the walls. I didn't ignore them and go read a newspaper—I heard them all."*

"Many were the nights that I held you like a husband would while you cried. Many were the nights that you weren't even aware that I held you. I was the One who spoke 25 to you—then you gave Me the year in your training schools and every time you sang, "Lord, You Are More Precious Than Silver,"–you were re-committing yourself to be single for Me if that was My will. Many were the nights that Ross too cried and said to Me, "Lord, where is the woman who will love me for me?" Receive from Me that Ross is to be your husband. Hear the "Yes," in your heart, even as you did the night I showed you the verses in I Samuel. Then, the Lord said, *"Arise, anoint him, for this is the one."*

Later, I shared with Ross what God did and I hugged him like God told me to, but I didn't tell him, "I love you," even though I knew God told me to say it. Ross thought it was neat that he had to remind me of our physical commitment. He said, "I've watched God pull out the rocks and let the roots grow deep and I'm watching the plant begin to bud—I'm watching your love for me grow and I'm looking forward to the day when you can tell me you love me." My heart's cry was not voiced, "Marry me. Marry me Ross and teach me to love you." It was so passionate and so real. Instead, I said, "The greatest of these is love. I can love you with the love God has given me and I can love you with that love." I felt his heart beat faster and I commented on it.

Ross responded, "That's from looking at you." We teased about how I wouldn't always sleep with a teddy bear. Even though our wedding was over a year away, it was still my reality.

We often prayed and ministered together as we encouraged fellow students, staff and mutual friends. We blended well and drew from one another's strengths. It was a joy to see how well God fitted us for each other. More than anything in our relationship, we wanted God to be glorified.

As the time neared for Ross to leave I became more concerned. "Ross, promise me your love won't change while you're away."

"No, it won't. Why would you think it would?"

"It's a long time — like the final test."

"God will give us the grace. I love you, Ruth— nothing will ever change that. All the money in the world wouldn't buy what I've found." He stated that the evidence of his love for me had been in his continued commitment to me. It was hard to believe that I had only met Ross in September. To consider God had done all that match-making in seven months was amazing.

During this 30-day commitment, God taught us patience, endur-ance and self-control. Even though God had done a work in me, I still had not yielded to speaking those three profound words and we only had a few days left of the self-imposed restrictions. I kept teasing and flirting with him and then I asked him, "What would you do if I kissed you?"

"I know that I wouldn't kiss you back. I made a commitment to you and to God and I won't break it. Ever kissed a dead fish?"

It went all through me. First, rejection and then I saw the depth of his love for me. He was so incredibly quiet and I couldn't figure out what was wrong. I heard him whisper, "In time," and I knew what was wrong. Ross implored me, "Just say it. What do you want me to say, Ruth? You've said it a hundred times with your eyes—but you've never told me that you love me."

"It's not that I haven't said it a hundred times with my eyes…."

"Just say it."

So, I looked at him, took his face in my hands and "To the depth of understanding that I have—I love you, Ross."

"That's all I ever wanted to hear."

We held each other and he broke into tears. I told him that I almost said it. "Ruth, it's only bothered me in the last few weeks because I've known, you've known."

I wasn't going to tell him until after outreach—or until our 30 days were over. I knew that God had made a great spiritual breakthrough in my heart. I kept telling Ross, "I love you," and he kept saying it back. I felt like a little girl. We were smiling and laughing and commenting on waiting for each other. I teased Ross, "Have you been waiting for me a life-time?"

He smiled and said, "Yep!" Then I caught him off-guard, threw my arms around him as I spun him to face me and I passionately kissed his cheek. "Ross, I want to spend as much time as possible with you tomorrow."

The next day Ross taught me about the basic mechanics of how a car worked to try to ease my fears of driving. I didn't thoroughly understand all that was second nature to him, but I came away not being so afraid. We talked about our future and I told him that I had felt God promised me a son named Samuel, some day. We went to the zoo together and had a wonderful date as we laughed and just enjoyed God's creation. I was publicly affectionate and we acted and looked like a couple "in love." It was great fun.

We went to the Rose Garden and talked about our wedding night and how we were going to laugh, when suddenly Ross looked up as a bird flew overhead and "blessed" his shirt." It was funny and temporarily ruined our romantic moment. After I helped him clean his shirt, he resumed talking seriously. He told me how he would talk to the Lord. "Lord, why am I keeping myself as a virgin?" The Lord told him, "Because I am going to give you a virgin."

I bolted upright, "God said what?" Ross reiterated, "God said, 'I am going to give you someone pure—you are going to marry a virgin." As those words penetrated my mind and heart, I realized what God said about me. What a tremendous confirmation of the healing and transformation that God did in my life, even prior to giving me to Ross!

God promised me my virginity again. He saw me as pure, white, clean and untainted and my soul thrilled to hear the words that Ross shared. All my past was forgiven and I was as white as snow. My ability to blush, to be naïve and to not think impure thoughts was restored and had been for several years. But the reality of God's approval and blessing was much richer than I would have ever imagined. Regardless of a past of being sexually abused or of making wrong choices or even in having lustful dreams and fantasies, God's holiness had cleansed me and made me new. There was a depth of gratitude that I could not express in words but oh, how my heart soared in adoration to Jesus for His resurrection power in my life.

Although I had known all these deep healings in God for several years, to see them come to fruition in a man/woman relationship was almost too much to believe. The joy in my heart overflowed and I was free to love Ross and to receive his love for me.

We prayed together and Ross gently spoke, "I commit to be holy in our relationship. I promise that I will do nothing that would intentionally hurt you or God. After we are married, then like the Word of God says, I will rejoice in the wife of my youth and always be satisfied with her." It was so beautiful expressing our love together and it felt like I just fit into his arms.

We were overcome with emotions throughout the day and at one point, Ross looked at me and tenderly said, "I can wait a year for you." Then he gently kissed me on the lips. I was too shocked to respond. He was so upset with himself for breaking our commitment. I kept trying to talk to him, to assure him that kissing me was okay but I knew that he was a man who took keeping his word seriously and that he was upset with himself. So I prayed silently and then I said, "Ross, I forgive you and I release you. I trust God in you to hear His voice and to believe your word."

"Thank you, I love you, very much." He hugged me. We held each other and he joked about the ocean. As he kissed my left ear, "This is the Pacific and this is the Atlantic," as he kissed my right ear.

Then I teased him, "Where's the Caribbean?"

We laughed and said it was in the middle. I told him, "I'll remind you next week when you can do something about it."

Ross asked, "Will you marry me?"

"Ask me that again when it's public, permanent and I can kiss you." Our date was absolutely wonderful with my being publically affectionate all day. We weren't going to make a habit of this physical closeness but God showed me that I did passionately love Ross. As I spent time with God alone, I wept over the truth that He revealed to me. *"I am a virgin— no fear of AIDS. In the intimacy and privacy and ecstasy of our honeymoon, I will give my virginity to the man I love. Lord, no one condemns me and no one's accusations stand. You do not condemn me, either. I hope someday to share this beautiful restoration with my mother. God, You said I can wear white at my wedding. You have restored me!"*

It was a joy for me to be used by God to pray and minister to Ross as well. As he shared some of the places of his own life where he had been hurt by words, teasing, rejection and insults, I was able to listen and pray for him. God used me to minister by breaking the power of negative words over him and releasing him into the ministry that God has for him. I prayed out that God was giving him His heart of compassion. We both felt that God was setting us up as an example of what He wanted a godly couple to look like. Ross felt an impression, "We are fast approaching a time of testing where we can respond in humility with a heart of David"— and the challenge was how we would respond. Our separation of Ross' two months of outreach was coming and another time of testing and proving our love and commitment to one another. We needed to depend on God.

One time, I asked Ross, "This might be a dumb question, but do you ever get bored with me?"

He cracked up laughing. "No. You're too much fun. I've never known a girl who likes the zoo for a date, who likes nature and flowers and who enjoys just sitting on the grass talking." We spent time just laughing, joking and trying to tickle one another.

We were out one evening and there was another couple off in the distance who had just begun liking each other and they were kissing. We passed them and my heart began to hurt deeper and deeper. I kept asking, 'What do I want, God?' and I thought, 'to be held and consoled.' Though I didn't tell Ross verbally what was going on, he said to me, "I just want to hold you and be close to you."

We continued talking quietly and I shared with him some of my struggles. "We have this commitment for three more days and they are kissing. They have only started a dating relationship but we are assured that God has called us to be married. We aren't kissing." I was concerned that I was compromising our commitment by wanting to kiss. I told Ross that I wanted him to know whether our kissing would be wrong. I struggled because I didn't want to kiss out of self-ishness and I was honest, "I keep thinking, 'I need to be kissed', but that is a lie because I won't die without a kiss."

Ross took my hand, turned me to face him and gently kissed me—a long time. I almost cried as I responded back to him, expressing our love for one another. Afterwards, I quietly asked, "Why did you kiss me?"

"Because I kept hearing, 'Kiss her,' and I was looking for some-thing to confirm it. I had a real peace—a release to kiss you. I love you, Ruth. This commitment hasn't been broken—it's been com-pleted." We spent a wonderful evening together in worship, Bible study, prayer, singing and just celebrating God's goodness in bringing us together. Ross loved God more because of his love for me and he saw the love of Christ for His church because of his love for me. My love for God developed as my love for Ross deepened in seeing God's faithfulness and goodness through our relationship.

Chapter 27

Preparing for School of the Bible

*W*e attended a meeting for the students interested in pursuing an Associate's degree in Biblical studies. From the beginning of my training I felt that one day I would be at School of the Bible (SOTB). Ross felt led to go to the school as well. The more the instructor talked about what the year would require, the more overwhelmed I became. I didn't want to assume that just because Ross was going at this time that I was also to attend. Furthermore, I was still trying to get out of debt from my former missionary training and this new school was going to add another $4000 to that debt-load.

I spoke with the director about my hesitation based on the financial commitment. He assured me that if it's God's will, then He will provide. As he spoke, my heart's desire was to study under this man who had such an anointing of wisdom. We left and Ross said, "I really believe that God has drawn our relationship together and I sincerely believe that you'll be at the School of the Bible. I believe that God is going to show you clearly His direction and that He's going to do some mighty things while I'm on outreach. When I return, I believe there will be no doubt in your mind about your destiny."

We went to the prayer chapel and prayed over the finances and asked for God's will to be done in my life. After we praised and worshiped for a while, we got into a massive tickle fight. We were laughing and rolling around and being silly—it was so much fun! Then we kissed and I almost "froze."

"Ross, is it right to feel this much passion for you?"

"Only God can tell you that."

There were tears in my eyes.

"Ruth, I love you. I would never want to do anything that would harm you or cause there to be a hot coal waiting to be burned. I would never want to cause you to stumble."

I was depressed about SOTB and this part of our relationship changing. School of the Bible shared a campus with a K-12 private Christian school and Ross and I were told that we needed to conduct ourselves "with no public display of affection." This was due to the rules that the high school students were not allowed to be couples on campus and even though Ross and I would be engaged, it seemed that for the leadership, it was easier if we just acted as a platonic relationship. That was a place of pain for me. It seemed to make no sense especially as I thought, our godly relationship would be a great example for those high school kids to see and eventually emulate. However, that was not to be.

Ross said that passion isn't good or bad—it's what we do with it that makes it good or bad. I realized that I didn't have to fake my emotions for Ross. There was no conviction, only peace.

We went to the Rose Garden, our favorite "date" spot. Ross said we'll probably be engaged before we go to SOTB. He believed that before I ever saw Barbados, we'd be married. That reminded me of Sarah in the Bible and what a woman of faith she was to follow Abram to a country she had never seen. It seemed like I would have a similar opportunity. The more we talked about our future, the more relaxed I became in thinking of going to SOTB. It was evident that God was making His plans something I could trust Him to accomplish. *I wonder if we'll get married on September 16? Will we get engaged on my birthday?* I had a connection with numbers and anniversaries and since April 16 was the first time Ross ever proposed to me, I wondered if we would get engaged on September 16 or on my birthday, September 6?

As for the physical aspect of our relationship, we recognized that we needed to use wisdom. Once we enrolled in SOTB, there wouldn't be that much time as the classes were a college level and the nine months of intense study equated to eighteen months and a completed

Associates of Arts in Biblical Studies. Having already gone through four years of college, I knew that this training required a lot of time for reading, writing, and studying.

Ross teased me, "Sometime in the future at SOTB, over a stack of papers, I'll reach over and kiss you….on the nose." How much we enjoyed laughing together!

Chapter 28

Hearing from My Parents

My parents called me almost every weekend and I waited to hear from them with their response to the letter I had sent regarding "my special friend." I assumed that they had made the connection with the seriousness of my emotions about Ross and I looked forward with great hopes and expectations of the joyful rejoicing over the phone that we would share. My expectations didn't prepare me for reality.

I finally got the call from my parents but it didn't turn out the way that I had hoped. First, I made sure they had gotten my letter about my friend Ross. I talked about my coming home.

"Ross is bringing me home—first we're going to South Carolina and will be there a few days—then we'll come to West Virginia." My voice was bubbly and excited. I was so thrilled that I had finally found the man who I would spend the rest of my life with. I was twenty-five and by now I should certainly have someone who wanted to marry me.

Dad: "Why is he coming to West Virginia?" His voice was awkward and puzzled as if he were in a fog.

I was caught off-guard.

"You guys *did* get the letter I sent, didn't you?"

Dad, "Yes, we got your letter. South Carolina is his home."

I told them that I had been trying to communicate to them about Ross through the letters I sent to them…"Well, he's bringing me home so that you can meet him." By this point my emotions and delightful feelings took a nosedive and I reined in all the exuberance that I had had only a few minutes before.

Dad: "What are you saying? ....Oh, I didn't get that." I was deflated. I couldn't believe this was happening. Never in all of my life had I written a letter home to tell my parents about any "special young man."

My mother's lilting voice came to the rescue.

Mom: "Yes, Ruth Mary, I got it a long time ago—I can read between the lines. Your Father doesn't get things like that—I've even told him things but he doesn't get it."

By this point all of my hopeful "once in a lifetime" expectations weren't just dashed, they were shattered. My heart churned within me.

Dad: "Well, have you proposed to him, yet?" That hurt so deeply. It was bad enough that Dad hadn't "gotten" the meaning of the letter but now to make me feel as if I had to propose to Ross....I just tried to make the conversation something that could be salvaged.

I managed to choke out, "No."

Dad: "Has he proposed to you?" (His tone sounded so sharp and I already stung from his seeming accusation that I needed to propose to Ross.)

"No, but it's leading in that direction. His parents have a real peace about our relationship—those were their words." I knew I was not totally truthful and justified my words with thoughts like . . .But I wasn't wearing a diamond ring and I wanted Ross to ask my father for my hand. In addition, my Dad's tone of voice seemed so cutting that I didn't answer correctly.

Dad: "Is it the leading of the Lord?"

"Yes, very much so. We feel like we won't be married for at least a year."

Dad: "A year!"

"Yes, we feel like we'll be going to School of the Bible and we'll get married sometime next fall. Ross asked his parents yesterday if I could come home with him and they said, yes."

Dad: "Would you be going back with him?"

I mentioned that Ross had an aunt in Ohio and I didn't know if I would be coming back with him in his car or if I would catch the bus to South Carolina. I tried to be lighthearted and laugh to diffuse the tense communication.

Mom: "Yes, you're quite welcome to bring Ross home with you. This is your home in a sense. I know it hasn't been your residence."

Dad: "This is where your dog is."

"It's where the two people I love very dearly are. Thank you for letting me bring Ross home."

Mom: "Ruth Mary, I've known ever since he had a name."

We changed the subject and they planned on sending me some money. We exchanged "I love you's." I was happy Mom understood but the waters were bittersweet. I couldn't wait to tell Ross but then again the reaction from Dad hurt deeply and I was only consoled by Mom's soothing voice. *Oh, God, please minister to Dad. Help him receive peace from You and oh, Shepherd, heal my heart.*

Later I broke down with emotion and Ross held me while I cried. A friend had told me earlier that my Dad was in denial. She said that my life was a source of conviction and I shouldn't take the rejection personally. "Your Dad hasn't had the benefit of knowing Ross, or what Ross has done for you. To your Dad, he's probably a pimply-faced, immature 19 year old who doesn't know one end from the other—You are his youngest and it's hard to let go."

Those words were comforting and shocking at the same time. I felt that I had been "on my own" ever since I had graduated high school. It was strange to think that Dad was having a hard time "letting me go." From my perspective, I wasn't getting any younger and marriage wasn't something that was all that strange or unusual. Yet, in many ways, I guess I still wasn't very grown up and in his eyes, I was still not using my education and I wasn't at a healthy financial place, either. Nevertheless, my friend's words gave me a tender place of prayer for Dad so that God would comfort him and help him to let me go.

Chapter 29

Seeking Confirmation

We went on a date to the library to research Barbados. All along as I fell in love with Ross, I wanted to know and understand what God meant when He gave me the vision of Africa as a child. We sat across from one another looking at a map of Barbados.

Ross asked, "What does that look like to you?"

I answered, "It looks somewhat like the Middle East."

Ross picked up the book, turned it upside-down, and set it down in front of me with the map upside down. "Now, what does it look like?"

"Africa!" I almost shouted. This was the same image I had seen as a little girl. The coastline had no Horn of Madagascar— and neither did my vision. We were thoroughly delighted as we continued to study. I was thrilled as God continued to confirm that I was called to marry Ross and to live in Barbados. It was so real and amazing that no man could ever have manufactured such an extraordinary story. During our four hours at the library that day we learned that Barbados was also known as, "Little Africa."

We went to eat at a steak restaurant. After the meal, I went to get ice cream and when I returned, wrapped in a napkin was a small box. I was silent and still. Then I opened it. Inside was a ring that Ross' Dad had made in shop class out of titanium and had given it to Ross' Mom as a promise ring. Later, Ross's Dad gave the ring to Ross, as a symbol of keeping his purity.

Ross gave me his ring as a promise of his love for me. I kept looking at it and finally out in the car I put it on my right hand and had tears in my eyes. We went to the Rose Garden. Then, he took the ring from my right hand and put it on my left. As far as Ross was concerned, this promise ring symbolized that we were engaged. I dreamed about the future and wrote my thoughts to God. *Will we get married in the Rose Garden? That would be so beautiful Lord Jesus and so significant a place. I wonder if Ross will propose to me in the Rose Garden?*

Though the promise ring was a symbol of a betrothal, Ross mentioned getting me a "real" engagement ring. I laughed out loud and told him, "I bet it will be on September 16th!" The first time Ross ever proposed to me was April 16 and if we did get engaged on September 16, it would mark six months from the first time he declared his love for me. Call it woman's intuition or God's leading, but often I "knew" what he was planning or thinking.

A few nights later, our last night before Ross left, we prayed for one another. Then Ross was almost poetic in his prayer about me. "Thank You, Lord, for this holy woman of God. The most beautiful woman in the world and You've given her to me. Her beautiful hair and how it feels to run my fingers through it. Her soft skin and how I love to touch it. Her eyes— the eyes of a deer. Her beauty—both inside and out. I could go on—I love Ruth, I love you very much."

He took me in his arms, "I just want to hold you, Ruth."

I hugged him.

"Ruth, you're shaking—what's wrong?"

I couldn't look at him. The pain was so real.

"You're crying."

I didn't think I could love Ross so much. "Ross, you're really leaving."

"For two months and, Ruth, I'm coming back."

"I already know the answer but why are you coming back?"

"I'm coming back to take you home with me to meet my parents, to meet your parents, to come back for SOTB, to marry you and then to spend the rest of my life with you." We embraced and kissed. We prayed over each other and committed one another to God's care and protection.

We were outside together. The moon was almost full with a beautiful starry sky. Ross said, "God did this just for us. When it is full, I'll look at it and think of you and of all God's done in this relationship and all He's going to do." It was solemn and real. *This is love.* I kept looking at Ross as if I wanted to memorize him.

"I'm going to miss you, Ruth. You're my best friend."

I kissed him. I didn't gently peck his lips as we often did, instead, I kissed him passionately.

"I love you."

"I love you, too."

As I walked away, I kept turning around to see him—this was the last night for a long time and it was beautiful—*Thanks, God!*

The next morning, as he boarded the bus, Ross cried. I encouraged him that the time would go quickly and that I loved him. As he rode away, I didn't have any tears but was overwhelmed with an incredible sense of peace.

A few days later I was in the dorm and my mother called me. She reassured me that in the last phone call, "Your Father wasn't angry. He's just extremely naïve and it was a peculiar tone. You couldn't see his face but he wasn't angry. " It was good to know Dad wasn't angry but I wished the conversation would've been different.

Chapter 30

Challenges While Apart and Together

I went to visit my small group leader who was always such an encouragement to me. She reminded me that love is a choice, not something that you "fall" into. Then she said, "If there's anything I can do...."

"Well, I do need a wedding dress..."

She got all excited and responded, "It must've been the Lord because right when I said that, I thought of your dress and Yes, I would love to make your dress!" I shared with her my hopes to be married in the Rose Garden. She encouraged me that God would make our wedding such fun.

"I believe He's going to bless your socks off. I believe that God is going to use you two as a testimony. When God does things in our lives, it's not just for us—but to be able in Divine appointments to say, 'I know what you've been through, what you're going through—I understand because I've been there.'"

After Ross called me during his outreach, from Chicago, I was so happy. One of my friends asked, "Where did your ears go?" because my smile spread all across my face. I eagerly shared with my friends and fellow workers on base what God had done in my life and about my upcoming future with Ross. The fears of what people might think about us as it pertained to the differences in our ages and that we were a student/logistical staff couple didn't seem to be so important to me anymore. I had on a promise ring and I had been assured of God's leading and Ross' commitment to marry me.

My small group leader visited me a few days later and gave me this Scripture. "Hebrews 12:13. "…and make straight paths for your feet, so that what is lame may not be dislocated, but rather be healed." She felt that God was going to make our paths straight and that where we were individually weak by bringing us together as one we would be healed!

Throughout my budding relationship with Ross, I periodically had nightmares about my past. The intensity of them seemed to increase and finally I told my small group leader because my sleep patterns were so off that I needed some reprieve.

I often dreamed of Anthony or of other guys and though the dreams weren't sexual in nature, they were demonic. The fear and shame in the dreams made me feel exhausted when I awoke. They were vivid and accusatory and when I awoke I felt cheap and dirty and that no matter how much I had changed, I wasn't "worthy" of Ross.

It was a ministry time similar to those given to me in the early stages of my missions training. She prayed over me, "No more ghosts from the past. I am going to be Ross's virgin bride. The fears are broken. I am to have spiritual eyes to see innocence and purity. I am a child of the Light. Perfect love casts out fear. All anxiety was broken and the feelings of inadequacy as a wife. I will have the grace of God for each day. Thank You, God, that Ruth is all that Ross will need and that he'll only have eyes for her." She reminded me of God's promise for sweet sleep and that He would fill my cup so that I wouldn't be running on empty.

That night I slept peacefully until the next morning with no disturbing dreams and I awoke fully rested. I loved how God was so faithful to answer prayer. *Thank You, God that these strongholds are out of my life! The ghosts of the past have been exposed and Jesus has kicked them out— showing no mercy to them. In His jealous anger He has made them leave and they are gone!*

Ross and I sent letters back and forth and a few times during his outreach, he called me. God continued to work on me and develop my faith to believe Him for financial provision for School of the Bible and to trust Him as I began to plan the details for our wedding.

In addition, I added more marriage books to my reading. I wanted to avoid the pitfalls as much as possible. I spent my devotional times with God and He revealed His heart for a married couple to me. As I read Song of Solomon, I became aware that God, Himself, was the One Who declared, "Drink deeply my friends," on the wedding night. These verses indicate that Love is a progression and my fears were alleviated. *It's okay to feel passion for Ross. My love will only continue to develop and progress. Oh God, that You would grant two people to love each other in a marriage.*

I had a quiet prayer time as I was greatly concerned about my financial situation. I had an image of me. *I am not before the Wizard of Oz but I am before the King of Kings. I am in a white robe, bowing before Him. Then the King rises and walks to me, extends His hand and says, "Arise My daughter." He lifts me up to His level and places both hands on my shoulders. I look into the sea of His eyes as He cups my chin to look up at Him. Then He takes my hand and He walks me to my Prince—Ross—and places my hand in his.*

The revelation comes that I am a princess because my Father is the King of Kings. I am of royal birth and not a peasant or a pauper but one with dignity—robed in purple. My prayer, *"Oh God how long have You sought to reveal to me that I am in a Royal Family— broaden my understanding and grant me revelation of You that I might comprehend Your purpose in my life."*

About that time I attended a staff meeting and there was a mock debate on pro-choice vs. pro-life. I chose to merely observe and not ask anything in a public format. At the end privately, I asked some deep questions to the women leaders. I realized only God can restore a woman who has had an abortion. I left with semi-heavy feelings as I remembered my own story of my twin being called, "just a piece of flesh." Those words were used in the debate and they triggered some deeper pain yet to be uncovered and healed.

I got alone with God and cried. I rebuked the lies of the enemy and the power of words as curses. Though I already had teaching on this subject, God made a deeper application. It was as if yet another layer of the onion of my heart was peeled away. It was the first time I grieved for my twin and the realization of all those years of feeling like, "a part of me was missing" and the joy of someday knowing I would see my twin face to face. It was a mind-boggling thought. Prior to coming to this mission's school, I never consciously thought of my twin as even being human. Now I felt that he was a brother and I called him, "Reuben" and cried for him. It freed me as I realized that God has a name for him—he is and was a real person. Once again, I asked God for a deeper restoration of maternal desires and that I could feel love towards a baby. *Thank You, Lord for helping me.*

On another night, in a large group setting, the speaker shared about the cost of discipleship and the choice to follow the Lord. He related our sacrifices in the light of eternity and the desire of God's destiny on our lives, as contrasted with our own plans. It was a convicting message for me.

I had often struggled with God in prayer and my own thoughts of a life lived in Barbados, another country. What would it look like? Who would I have as friends? What would I teach my children about America? How lonely would it be to live so far away from family? What would a life for over twenty years in another country look like? What if Ross and I were full-time, life-time missionaries? Could I love Jesus enough to leave everything that gave me security? Finances? Friends? My own culture? Did I love God that much? Would I be willing to live for eternal purposes?

Slowly and surrendered, I walked forwards for prayer. I cried and fully committed to our lifetime call of ministry.

~ Barbados ~

Come precious daughter
To My altar
Come let Me bind
You there with love
Where all of the tearings
Deep inside you
Will find peace
And rest from above.

I know you are weary
And anguished
And tears never ceasing
Seem flow
But I'm calling
You to a place
In Barbados
And like Ruth
Of long ages
You must go.

I've not called you
To walk solely
But I've chosen
A man with My heart
He'll hold you
And lead
Where I guide you
And nothing shall break you apart.

Come precious daughter
And trust Me
I've a plan and vision
For you
The youth are crying
For answers

And the truth I will send
Is through you.

Set your eyes in faith
To the future
To a place that you've
Never seen
Save in the vision
I gave you
Which I birthed forth through
Your heart's dream.

Barbados is a place
That needs My message
And the people are seeking My face
They're crying for the fire of revival
To sweep through the church
And the place
Will you go where I've called you
And trust Me
And see My glory on each person's face?

Yes, you'll go
Where I've called
You
And you'll trust Me
And you'll
See My glory
And the
Power of My grace.

Chapter 31

Reunited and Vulnerable

As Ross's team was returning from Outreach, the bus broke down and they were late getting back. I talked with Ross on the phone, "If I don't see you tonight…"

He immediately responded, "You will."

We both said, "I love you," and I was so excited. It was late at night and cold as I stayed in his car. I fell asleep until midnight. I got out of the car to wait for Ross and I was chatting with a friend when Ross tapped me on the shoulder. I turned around and he grabbed me in a strong bear hug and delightedly swung me around and around as we laughed and embraced. Once again, I was dizzy by the time he set me down. His heart beat so fast and we just continued to hold each other.

One of Ross's friends, Paul, told him later that he almost cried as he watched us embrace one another. People could easily see God's Hand in our relationship and many of our friends were deeply blessed by the joy that they saw in our faces. It encouraged and blessed me that we were accepted and that God was glorified in our lives.

Then Ross shared what God had told him, "My son the test is over. As you have honored Me, I will honor you. School of the Bible (SOTB) will be a year when you will grow closer to Me and closer to each other. I will richly bless you. You will both comprehend and understand things in SOTB that you've heard before but it will be a greater revelation."

I hugged lots of the team members. Then Ross and I walked to the Prayer Chapel. He showed me the picture he had taken of me in the Rose Garden and that he carried with him. (It's one of the best pictures ever taken of me.) Then, he showed me the verses in the book of Ruth, "Entreat me not to leave thee, or to forsake from following you. Wherever you go, I will go. Wherever you lodge, I will lodge. Your people will be my people and your God will be my God."

Ross seemed and looked older—he'd grown spiritually stronger. He carried me to the chapel and outside of it, we kissed! It was so wonderful to be with him again. Inside the chapel I read his last letter and we talked! He was so handsome and good-looking. Oh, I loved him so much! He'd thought of getting married in the Rose Garden and purple was one of his favorite colors. (Those were the same thoughts I'd had weeks ago: get married in the Rose Garden and purple and silver for my colors.) Up until my relationship with Ross, I had never given any thought to planning a wedding and I was thrilled to see how God helped us to figure it all out. We talked about a possible cruise to Alaska for our honeymoon since we would live in the Caribbean for the rest of our lives.

A day later, I listened to, "Imagine," an instrumental song by Keith Thomas. I thought that would be the right music for a wedding. We talked for a long time about marriage and being real. Ross said, "There's no fantasy marriage. Any potential conflicts can be worked out through open and honest communication." Ross said that there are many ways to say, "I love you."

We sat in a dimly lit room, across from one another and talked about the call of God on Ross' life. He shared how he didn't know where we would live, how he would provide, or whether we would ever own a house. He was committed to a missionary calling to Barbados but also anywhere else God would send him. After all his openness, he asked me,

"What really says, 'I love you,' to you?"

I made myself extremely vulnerable and shared my deepest fear and desire. "Financial security."

"Ruth, I can never promise you that. I can't deliver that— I can only trust God."

Instantly, Ross's expression turned into what appeared to be deep, deep anger and he swiped his hand across the direction of my face.

Fearing that he was going to hit me, I recoiled and screamed, "Jesus!" and then in a few seconds I burst into uncontrollable tears. I shook with such fear that for over twenty minutes I couldn't even speak. Ross held me.

"Ruth, I would never hit you. It's all right. It's all right."

He held me as I wept and my body shook uncontrollably.

Finally, I told him that I thought because I'd been honest about wanting money, that he was angry and ready to hit me. Though I had not been slapped much before, having someone angry at me often overwhelmed me and it was as if I could feel fear wash over me and paralyze me. In that instant, I thought that Ross was furious with me for wanting something that he couldn't promise to provide for me.

How far from the truth that was! It turned out that what I couldn't see was that a small mosquito had flown between us and he tried to end its pesky life. The look on his face was intensity in destroying a critter— not the beautiful, precious woman he was going to marry.

Never had I been more terrified and emotionally vulnerable at the same time. He held me and reassured me that he would never hit me, hurt me or abuse me. It was a special time for both of us. He was so gentle and tender and so protective over me.

I quietly related that I had been slapped before. Much later Ross asked me, "Ruth, do you think that I would hit you?"

I told him, "No," but he said that he could see the fear in my eyes. He felt so utterly helpless as he shared, "It's like the one I love is at the bottom of a mountain climbing up—it's hard and dangerous and I'm at the top looking down. Can't I even throw a rope?"

I had a scene from "Princess Bride" come into my mind, of Andre the Giant pulling the princess and her captors up a long rope along the rock face of a huge cliff. I thought about what that would mean in trusting God. As I shared these thoughts with Ross, he gently spoke, "The rope is the love of God and my love for you is that which keeps you going."

We finally left the room and went outside but I was jittery and still quite shaken. I queried Ross. "Will you still marry me?"

"Yes. Yes. One of the greatest joys of my life will be the day I say, 'I do.'"

"I need you, Ross."

"I need you. I'm here, Ruth."

Though I went back to my dorm, I stayed awake until 3:30 in the morning. I spent the time remembering my life and asking God to help me as this level of fear was something I had never experienced with Ross.

Growing up, I didn't cry in front of people; instead I got angry and yelled at them. I remembered many occasions outside when I cried alone or in the fur of a friendly dog. God revealed my fears but He also showed me the joy of being held by Ross and not crying alone.

Ross assured me that he doesn't ever want me to worry about finances. I let Ross know about what God showed me. Ross responded, "No one will ever slap you again— no one. I'm not possessive but I *am* protective."

The feeling of being protected and cherished was something so new and so foreign to me. I was astounded by how much God restored to me in blessing me with Ross. We were accepted to School of the Bible! On the last day of Ross' school, right before we left for South Carolina, a student came and gave me $100.00. Ross asked me what else I needed for the debt and he gave me about $20.00. That completed the debt that I had carried for the last two years. What was amazing was that the student had no idea how much I still owed. I had done all kinds of odd jobs from babysitting, house-cleaning, church nursery worker just so I could become debt-free. It was a glorious feeling to know that at God's perfect timing, He provided.

Chapter 32

Meeting the Relatives — Permission and Blessings

*R*oss and I made the trip from Texas to South Carolina all in one day. We left at 3:30 in the morning and drove non-stop for 16 hours. Amazingly, I drove a total of 400 of the nearly 1000 mile trip! I had never driven that far in my entire life. I felt confident and excited as I realized that with God's help, I could conquer this fear.

At one point, we ran out of gas. It was an opportunity for conflict but I chose to praise and pray. Within a short while, Ross returned from a brief walk with some gas. He said, "God, thank You for an understanding wife. It's important and a blessing."

I was so touched by his kindness towards me in calling me his wife, even before we were officially engaged. We spent hours listening to Christian music and talking. Ross even felt confident enough in my driving, that he dozed for a while.

Once we arrived in South Carolina, I met his parents. I had been prepared with fresh make-up and brushed hair about an hour before we got there. However, we ended up having to take a detour because of traffic and by the time we got to his parent's house, I was sweaty, frazzled and badly in need of a bathroom. I know that they were gracious and Ross' mom made some comment, "You don't look too bad for travelling sixteen hours."

I called my parents to let them know that we had gotten there safely. I was tired and as Ross and his parents talked late into the night, I excused myself, showered and crawled into bed.

When Ross and I talked with his parents, we shared our story of how God brought us together and how He confirmed His will. After we finished, Ross' Dad's eyes were full of joy! He said, "That's really sweet. You'll need to hang on to that later on down the road. I think Ruth's parents will be impressed with your story."

I met so many people from Ross's church, in addition to his family. It was awkward at the beginning because he didn't seem to be comfortable in expressing affection to me. I was introduced as "Ross's girlfriend," but there was a period of four days when he didn't even kiss me. I finally talked to him about that. He was awkward, wanting to introduce me as his fiancée, which officially, I wasn't, yet. He was still deeply in love with me but reconnecting with his church and his family was also challenging at times, for him. So many still saw him as "the twelve-year-old, blond-haired little boy with bangs," the way he first came to the church so many years before. His pastors were glad to meet me, though they expressed that they always thought once Ross finished his missions training, he would return to the church and become the youth leader. There were still girls that admired him for "more than a friend."

I had to work through so many different emotions and it was a whirlwind of telling our story, meeting new people and trying to get to know them. When Ross and I did have time for just the two of us, the stronger tendencies of expressing physical desires became more pronounced. The atmosphere was so different than our former times of only spending a few hours a day with each other and having other commitments to jobs, classes, work schedules and separation in different dorms.

He assured me of his love and it seemed that we became more physically expressive. We shared how God brought us together and we prayed and ministered to some of Ross's friends. As the time drew near for us to leave for West Virginia, God gently but firmly spoke to me. "I'm not angry with you but it's not wise. I will bless your marriage and it will be fun but please don't succumb to the wiles of the enemy to get you to fall. Be so filled and be so pumped up with

My Spirit that a kiss on the hand will satisfy. Love, being the highest good, would be not to stir someone's emotions. Those emotions only need to be fulfilled within the bonds of marriage."

I shared those impressions with Ross and he kissed my hand and agreed. It was a strange place to know that God spoke to me in a kind way as it pertained to my desires for Ross. God was not accusatory or condemning and I often was moved by how intimate He wanted to be with us. It often felt like the three of us were on a date together.

We said our good-byes to his parents and drove the five hours to West Virginia to meet my family. I washed dishes and talked with my Dad. It was all relatively surface because, in my mind, I wanted to give him time to adjust and get to know Ross. In the meantime, Ross spent time visiting with my Mom in another room. He shared with her all about his training and even our calling to go live in Barbados. She was so accepting of him that she said, "When the Lord leads in general is one thing but when the Lord leads in specifics....you should follow."

Later over dinner, I shared my vision as a little girl of "Africa," tropics and islands. My Mom shared that when she was in fifth grade she "saw" in her mind's eye, natives, and she knew she wanted to be a missionary. There were tears in her eyes as she related the story, one I had never heard. "If we had it to do all over again, we'd probably be in Africa."

She hoped when Dad retired that they would be able to become missions volunteers. Daddy had also desired to be on the foreign mission field, but neither of them could learn to speak another language—which was a requirement at that time. Though both of them studied diligently, neither of them could seem to gain adequate foreign language skills. Some of their best friends were able to go to Africa and other countries.

This sharing from my parents was the first time I ever knew their own desires, struggles and disappointments in not going to the foreign mission field. (It was not until several years later that I realized that my parents served in "home missions" by choosing to serve in the many small rural churches in Appalachia and South Texas.)

I was excited, surprised and saddened to hear their story. Listening to their hearts was a place of healing and compassion for me. I figured they would understand and bless our future life in missions.

Ross stood and we held hands. "I've never done this before... but we really believe that God has called us to Barbados... and I'd like to ask your blessing for Ruth's hand in marriage."

Inwardly I cringed and thought, "No, it wasn't supposed to be this fast. Dad needs time." But it was too late to say anything.

My dad said, "Ross, don't you think you should ask Ruth Mary first?"

That made things awkward and confirmed my fears that Dad hadn't adjusted to all the changes that would be taking place.

We explained about the promise ring but Ross was seeking for blessing, "as you are her authority, being her father."

I hadn't been prepared for everything to unfold so quickly but there it was. Mama's eyes were filled with tears. I had never felt so close to her in all my life. The joy and beauty that shone in her face made me beam inwardly and outwardly. She knew in a few brief hours how wonderful Ross was and she had seen the transformation of her daughter over the course of the last few years.

Mom came to the rescue and shared that we'd already made our commitment and she had heard of a promise ring before. As the awkwardness continued, Dad finally said, "Ross, since you believe this is the Lord's leading, it would be wrong of me to say no."

Mom started filling in the gaps. She took his hand and patted it. "Now Honey,"

"Not only would he give *his* blessing, *we* do."

My Dad slowly voiced, "Yes.....I do."

It seemed like forever and then he resumed speaking. "I'm scared— because I don't have the faith that you do...and I've trusted Him a lot longer than you."

I felt sad for Dad as if somewhere in his relationship with God, he hadn't found the intimacy that God longed for him to have. At the same time, I wasn't sure if Dad was challenging Ross.

Ross affirmed Dad. "You've been given wisdom."

Dad said, "Not enough."

Ross responded to my Dad. "Thank you for giving us your blessing."

I looked at my father and my heart swelled. "I love you, Daddy." I hugged and kissed him and he kissed me.

Then I hugged Mama.

She asked me, "Do you cry when you're happy?"

"Uh-huh."

"So do I. Where do you think you got it from?"

Then she asked Ross if he cried when he was happy.

"Yes," he said.

Daddy shared, "I hope you two have a close friend that you can share with when there are possible conflicts in your relationship. You both have different psychological backgrounds, friends, histories, and relationships with parents. You both have such a personal relationship with your Lord that you should be able to resolve possible conflicts in a meaningful way."

When Dad mentioned possible conflicts, my internal voice rationalized that Ross and I were different than other couples and we wouldn't have much conflict but I was also deeply blessed by his statement of each of us having a personal relationship with the Lord.

Ross and Dad went off to talk privately. They were gone for what seemed like a long time. Then they both came back to the table. Dad said, "Let's pray. God our Father, we thank You that You have brought Ross and Ruth Mary together—that You do work in mysterious ways—and we thank You that You will bless them in Christ's Name. Amen."

That prayer was simple but profound. The reality was that my parents gave their blessing and they saw God's Hand in our relationship. I was deeply moved at the beauty of the evening.

As we related our story of how God put us together and the vision of Barbados, my mother was especially fascinated and blessed. Dad had an upcoming Pastor's conference that he had to attend and as such, he needed someone to fill the pulpit while he was gone. Mom teasingly said, "Put Ross and Ruth Mary in the pulpit and let them tell their story of what God has done."

I was speechless and even more amazed when Dad considered the idea. Then when I realized that he was open to the possibility, I teased and said, "Gee, Dad, put us in both pulpits and you won't have to worry about being at the Retreat on time."

The atmosphere was lighthearted and the next thing I knew was that Dad made a decision and agreed to give us the Sunday morning services at two different churches that he simultaneously pastored. That was totally unheard of and he wouldn't even be there to hear what we said.

Mom commented, "We should call Walt and have him come here for Sunday to hear Ross and Ruth Mary." Dad whole-heartedly agreed.

Walt, age twenty-seven, lived in Maryland. He was the genius and the emotionally reserved big brother. I was nervous but Dad and Mom felt that "Walt will be pleased and pleasantly surprised with Ross."

Ross' age of nineteen, still a teenager, and my age of twenty-five, concerned my family. They all had wondered how mature a nineteen year old could possibly be and maybe I just wasn't thinking when I fell in love with a teenager. Mom called Walt and my parents talked with him.

Dad shared, "Ruth Mary and Ross are both close in praying together."

Walt said joyfully, "That's great!"

He was excited and made plans to come visit on Sunday to hear us speak. The phone call finished and Dad set his attention back on Ross. Daddy shook Ross' hand and smiled.

Ross and I went outside on the front porch and hugged. We sat on the redwood furniture together and snuggled. All that God had done in the course of one night overwhelmed me. It was like standing in a summer rain-shower of blessings as they cascaded down all over me, forming rivulets in my heart and soul. I had only dared to imagine that I could ever experience such pure joy.

We prayed for Dad and just thanked God! In one night Dad and Mom accepted Ross, our relationship, our call to Barbados and YWAM where I had been committed to for the last two years. Everything that had once been a place of confusion, pain, awkwardness and sorrow turned into joy, rejoicing and celebration.

The next morning I talked with Mom about Ross. She said, "I'm amazed at his experience."

"So am I and he's only 19!"

"Well, you would never know it. Ruth Mary, he has to be at least 24."

"I know, Mom, but he's not."

Ross came down and got ready to leave to visit his relatives in Ohio. He would return in three days. He hugged me and then he and Mom hugged.

"Ross, I so look forward to seeing you again."

He smiled, laughed and made a comment back to her that made her feel special. My mother greatly approved of Ross. It was a joy to see how incredibly happy she was with Ross and with me. I reveled in her acceptance and it made me feel that finally I had made the right choice.

I teased him before he left, "If you ever feel that you aren't loved, go stand by my mother."

He drew me into the circle of his arms to hug me and he looked at my mom because he was going to kiss me…and she laughed and smiled delightfully, "But, of course!"

I followed him out to the car. "Anything you need?"

"You."

He made me feel so special. I loved how romantic he was. I gently leaned in the open window and we kissed.

I went back inside. I was elated, thrilled and deeply in love.

"He's wonderful, Mom."

"Yes, he is. He is intelligent. Would you like for him to meet your grandmother and your uncle?"

Mom was thrilled with Ross and with the changes in me and she wanted her mother and youngest brother to meet Ross as well. The suggestion to introduce him to my grandmother and uncle was huge in my eyes. My grandmother was from Maine and I always thought of her as "prim and proper." I liked her but I was nervous about introducing Ross. In my estimation, my grandmother was even more formal and "perfect" than my mother. It had been less than twenty-four hours since I'd come home and the amazing acceptance and approval was like being in a lovely dream. For Ross to pass my grandmother's "inspection" would be about as miraculous as for him to pass my Dad's. We considered it for when Ross would return.

Later that afternoon, Mom and I went through my closet and found some clothes that had been there from years past. We decided what to keep and what to give away. I tried on a beautiful shimmery black and silver formal gown that had been Susie's from her high school days. Mom made a few adjustments to "modernize" it and then she said, "You can get dressed up, parade around, put on music and have dinner by candlelight when you're married to Ross." Mom was happy and it showed!

After Dad went to bed, Mom and I stayed up talking more. She was so surprised that I found someone so wonderful! "He's a delightful person." Mom and I were like two life-long friends staying up late, eating popcorn and talking about my love life. She squealed, laughed and giggled with me about all the wonderful ways that God brought Ross into my life. This interchange was beyond anything I would have ever imagined. The restoration of our relationship was rich and joyful for both of us. I knew that she was elated for me and that she was proud of me, for following God and letting Him change my heart and life.

In a moment of deep sharing she looked at me, "Ruth Mary, you are beautiful. You do have beauty. You are a beauty both inside and out." The words penetrated to the places in my heart where I once only felt her great rejection and I let them soothe and restore a little girl's heart and a broken teenage daughter. The love that we felt, shared and expressed towards one another could only be attributed to a miraculous intervention of God's Hand in my life. Several times as we talked, our eyes brimmed with tears of joy.

The next day, Ross returned. I called Susie and told her how wonderful Ross is. "That's great! You hang onto him." I was thrilled with her acceptance, excitement and joy that I had found someone who was wonderful and wanted to marry me. It felt delightful to be the center of positive attention and to be affirmed and encouraged. I was deeply blessed.

When Walt came, he heard us speak at both services and then he went back to Maryland. Mom said, "Walt really likes the new you. He enjoyed the service—said you had well thought out sentences, no quivering voice or shaking—and that your gestures were natural. I, too, noticed the beautiful way you gestured with your hands as you shared from your heart."

Ross, Mom and I all went to see my grandmother in another small town in West Virginia. My grandmother, in her seventies, with her coiffure of pure white short hair, wrinkled face and twinkling blue eyes sat attentively at the dining room table with her hands clasped together as she listened to Ross talk. My mother sat beside her and they exchanged pleasantries at various points in the conversation.

Grandmother leaned over to Mom and squeezed her hand. "He is a delightful young man, isn't he?"

My mother looked at her with joy and they both nodded their heads in approval. Oh the thrill of being so proud of Ross and watching his charm affecting my grandmother!

Ross talked at the table about our calling to be missionaries for life in Barbados. Mom communicated to Grandmother, "Mom, our personal faith is different than Ross and Ruth Mary's."

Grandmother smiled and said, "It'll just grow and carry them through in old age."

Mom told Grandmother, "They make a good team.'"

The brief statements of approval were like winning a state competition. Grandmother turned to Mom and said, "Ruth Mary will have to read a lot in order to keep up with him."

My grandmother and mother were amazed with how congenial my uncle was with Ross. I was so honored that Ross spent time with my uncle who was a professor at the local college and who was usually very quiet. From the kitchen we could hear him speaking, sharing and even asking Ross questions. That was nothing short of a miracle as my uncle was usually a man of few words. He was extremely intelligent but few people managed to attract enough interest for him to seek out any prolonged conversation. Ross spent several hours just listening and getting to know him. My uncle was happy, vibrant and even chuckled a few times.

When I hugged Grandmother good-bye, she said, "You've made a wonderful choice. He's so smart and experienced. I know he's only 19 but he acts like he's 25."

I was richly affirmed by my grandmother's words and I could see her joy as her eyes twinkled. She smiled as Ross warmly hugged her goodbye.

The only odd comment that came later was that Grandmother told Mom. "He is such a nice young man. But why does he always carry that gun around?"

When Mom related those words to me, I was confused. Then it all made sense and I laughed. "Oh, my goodness. Poor Grandmother. That wasn't a gun. It was his camera bag." Nevertheless, Ross made a deeply lasting positive impression on my grandmother and uncle.

Chapter 33

Revelation of God's Grace

$\mathcal{R}$oss talked to me about marriage being a blood covenant. The more he shared, the more I made the connection, which I hadn't quite grasped before. Then the gnawing fears and sadness of my past gripped my heart once again. The pangs of regret were sharp and quietly I asked him, "Will you forgive me for not waiting for you?"

"Yes, I forgive you."

Ross shared with me what he had asked God for, "a virgin, someone who loves me and someone I can love, and someone who likes to hear me talk." How special to know that I fit Ross' answer to his prayers.

The next day we prayed and knew that soon he was to go home and be with his family in South Carolina. My fear was that I wouldn't be on the bus. I didn't have sufficient funds and I didn't know where the money would come from. Ross said, "God will provide…you never know, He might even use your parents."

I didn't want to say good-bye to him. I knew that I needed and wanted to spend some quality time with just my parents but I was in love with Ross and separation even for a few days seemed to pull at my heart.

The next morning before he left, the passionate feelings were deep. Then he shared with me how some dear Christian friends found themselves going beyond the godly boundaries before they were married. He did not want us to fall into those traps and I was caught off-guard realizing that passion is a powerful emotion. We didn't desire to sin but we did know that we were going to get married and the natural pull of wanting to become one was something that we needed to guard against and hold each other in respect and honor.

That sobered both of us and I went to sing and cry out to God. I rejected Ross by leaving him alone as I went into another room to think about what he had just told me. I was so afraid of pushing the limits or stepping over the boundaries and I didn't communicate to him what I thought. I merely pulled away from his embrace and left him to wonder what was wrong with me. I didn't want to sin against God or Ross or in any way become a stumbling block to him.

I returned to the room and spoke to Ross. "Ross, I trust in your ability to be the spiritual leader. I trust in you to hear the voice of God. The fact that you've never given in is a stronghold—I take courage in that—it assures me that you won't give in now and God has so severely dealt with me that though the physical desire is there, anything below the neck is not a desire. Our hearts are tender before God." We both felt such peace and reassurance of the love of God and it was so much better for both of us.

The boundaries of hugging, holding hands and kissing on the cheek were sweet gestures of caring, love and commitment. They did not have to become passionate expressions and that was a safe guard for both of us. Our wedding wasn't set to happen until the following June and so we had over nine months before we would become husband and wife.

Later, I wrote in my journal, *"Although the sexual desires are there –oh Father God—help us to walk in holiness and in righteousness before You that we'll speak with authority through the tests of purification in Your Name, Jesus."* I was honest with God in our desires sexually but our much higher desire was to stay holy for God's sake and for each other.

I spent the last few days having good quality time with Dad and Mom. It was so good to be with them and just see all the changes that God had made in me and the healing of our hearts towards one another. They paid for my bus ticket to South Carolina to be re-united with Ross.

I was thrilled to be back with Ross. A few days later, I celebrated my 26th birthday. I reflected on my college days when the man "smelled spaghetti" and spoke over me the promise that the Lord would give me someone who would love me and that I would love. I remembered how I felt that I would be twenty-five when those things would happen and now to realize that God did bring Ross into my life when I turned 25 was a huge confirmation that I really did hear God's voice.

For my birthday, Ross gave me a pair of abalone heart shaped earrings. He said that they were like me. "Dainty with beauty, depth and intensity like the ocean in Barbados." He was so thoughtful. I loved the variation of colors. To be loved by receiving gifts was new to me but I enjoyed being cared for.

We returned to the talk about the physical temptations by which other godly couples had been ensnared and then Ross rose up with righteous indignation and declared, "Ruth, we will stand. We are aware of this pit in the road we're walking on and we won't fall in it. We aren't just going to survive our engagement—we're not just going to make it—but we're going to enjoy each other and we will teach and speak into other people's lives. Ruth, I love you. I will never touch you where it would be wrong, I will never force myself on you and I will never allow you to do anything to me that would be wrong. I've gone through some rough times and I'm not about to blow it now. On our wedding night—I won't lose it— I will give it.

"We aren't to judge or condemn our friends but to see our goal for purity as God's victory. Don't let satan rob you of your joy or feed you a bunch of lies. Satan would hate it if we got married because he sees the potential—why do you think he's fought it so hard the last six months, if not one way, then another—the tests, the trials, struggles, hurts, disappointments and the miscommunication? God has a call for us to be able to minister to restored marriages, dating and engaged couples—that's how determined I am, Ruth. I love you—but God is my number one priority."

My heart overflowed with respect and admiration as I knew this godly man was not about to succumb to fleshly desires. His words had such a prophetic quality in them and I sincerely hoped that someday God would use our story to bring Him glory and to encourage many people. It was another blow to the accusations and fears that the enemy of God tried to scream into my ears.

A few nights later at his house, we talked and just affirmed one another. "Ross, I approve of God's choice of who you are in every aspect."

He responded, "I have gotten the perfect mate. I am proud to say that I am going to marry you. I am going to spend the rest of my life with you. You are beautiful to me. Through all the testing and the trials, the good times and the bad times, through all the fun times and the silly times, through hell and high water—I will spend the rest of my life with you."

The sweetness of his words filled me with joy that no Hollywood script could mimic in sincerity and adoration.

Ross continued. "I want a son who will be both strong physically and spiritually—who will be handsome with blond hair and that can tan. He will be a man of God and he'll grow up to be a great man of God. I want a daughter who will be beautiful with long hair and will be an encourager like her mother. Who will be beautiful without as well as within and it will radiate—because she is a woman of God— like it does from her mother.

"I want our children to be trained in godly ways so that their best friend will be God. That they won't have to go through some of the struggles of their peers—because their best friend will be God. I want them to be able to come to their parents if they have a problem and that we'll be friends as well. Our children will be a great source of joy for us as they will be a great man and woman of God.

"When we grow old and grey together and we pass on from this life and we stand before God, He'll say, 'Well done, thou good and faithful servant. Enter into the joy of the Lord.' And then in heaven we'll see the thousands whose lives were changed through a personal relationship with Jesus Christ as their Savior—as marriages were restored, young people we ministered to –all the people whose lives we touched and these will be our rewards. And it shall be said of us, 'Look at the great man and woman of faith who believed God and left everything to follow Him. They loved the Lord their God with all their heart, with all their strength, and with all their minds—the great man and woman of God.' That is why we can say that we will make it because of the victory of what lies ahead."

Again I was deeply moved by his declarations. We talked about the name of our daughter to be and we agreed that she would be Rachel McElwee. I had already received Samuel's name in prayer over a year before I ever met Ross.

Wow! Jesus, such tears in my eyes, Samuel Ross McElwee and Rachel McElwee—still in seed form but God already has a destiny planned for them!

Chapter 34

A Night to Remember
and A New Course Ahead

*W*e drove the sixteen hours back to Texas and I stayed awake the entire time and either talked with Ross or interacted in some way so that he didn't fall asleep. A few days later it was September 16. Ross and I prepared to go out to dinner. I knew this was the night when he would officially ask me to marry him. I put on the beautiful shimmery black and silver gown while Ross dressed in black, as well. Someone took a picture of us. As we drove, neither of us spoke much. He said simple things, "I love you," and "you are the most beautiful woman I've ever seen."

He took me to an elegant Chinese restaurant. We had reservations and were seated at a table arrayed with a white linen tablecloth and napkins. The ambiance was romantic and sacred with the flickering candlelight, the succulent food and the quiet as we contemplated the significance of this night. We talked about Barbados and below us were a group of adults I recognized from church but I focused only on Ross.

Our delicious dinner consisted of egg rolls, fried rice and almond chicken. Occasionally, Ross reached across the small table and held my hand. Though we didn't speak much, our eyes and hearts communicated volumes. My heart fluttered as I drank in the depth of Ross' love for me as seen in his eyes. In typical fashion, once I finished my meal, I excused myself to go to the bathroom.

When I returned, I noticed a small plate with a nicely folded napkin sitting on it. I honestly thought that it was set up for the next customer, as I knew we hadn't ordered any dessert. I prepared to leave, but Ross gestured for me to sit down.

I removed the napkin and underneath was a beautiful diamond ring! Ross took my hand, and knelt on one knee, and proposed to me. "Ruth, will you marry me?"

Because I was so convinced that he would ask me in a private area of the Rose Garden, my first words were, "Not here!"

We both started laughing and smiling. Obviously, that's not the normal answer to a proposal. Then, I told him, "Yes," and I kissed his hand.

We held hands and there were tears in his eyes. He kissed my hand. Then I slipped the ring on my finger. Oh, I loved it! The most beautiful ring I ever saw. God had given him the design of the ring and he'd had it custom made. It had two diamonds of the same size, cut and quality. The white gold represented purity, holiness, a mixture of silver and gold. The diamonds spoke of durability, strength, endurance, beauty and unity as the two became one. Each of the diamonds represented us.

Ross paid for the meal and then we drove to the Rose Garden. He had considered proposing to me there, but he realized that I would see the ring better in the restaurant. When we arrived, a wedding had just finished. We walked out to the gazebo and the moon was beautiful. We kissed and I told Ross what a diamond he was to me. It was so special. *Yes, we're engaged!*

The next day at church, a few members asked us, "Were you that couple that was at the Chinese restaurant last night? We all commented, 'There's something really different about that couple. There is something special happening with them.' Ross and I laughed and smiled as he held up my hand and displayed my new ring. I was so moved that people who didn't even know us could tell that God was doing something special for us. What a confirmation of our engagement!

During the service, I felt the impression from the Lord, "Thank you for waiting for My best for you." He continued to speak to me about the physical aspect of our relationship. "Take that passion and turn it to passionate praying."

Our school schedule was demanding and grueling. We were in class all morning, ate lunch, had separate work duties, ate dinner and then Ross went to do his homework in his dorm and I went to my room to study. School of the Bible was intense—a complete two year program crammed into a nine-month course. Our school was only about seven students and I was the only single female. One other woman audited a few classes and the rest were Christian brothers— some married, some single and then Ross.

School of the Bible shared a campus with a K-12 private Christian school. It was their policy that there would be no public display of affection. Ross and I were admonished to follow that as well. It made it challenging to always feel like our engagement was shameful or embarrassing.

Ross and I were saddened that our engagement was made to feel "hushed" or ignored. We felt it would have been the perfect opportunity to encourage the high school students to wait on God's timing and to be assured that He knows how to match-make.

It was also painful that at times Ross and I hugged and some staff women who had been wounded in life made derogatory statements to us. One time there was a comment, "If you two want to do that there's a mattress under the gym." It shocked me and made me feel cheap as if only the sexual/physical side of the engagement was what we were interested in. I found myself frequently re-living the pain of my high school years, even though this relationship was holy and pure. I struggled with the way we were treated.

One day Ross held my hand at lunch while we were outside away from the other students and a male high school senior teased him and said, "Hey, Ross, don't you know we're not supposed to do that?" Ross took the perfect chance to challenge this young man and tell him, "Hey, when you can say, 'I love you,' to the woman and then the next words out of your mouth are, 'Will you marry me?' and you have the means to take care of her.....then you can put a ring on her finger and you can hold her hand, too."

In the middle of all the college courses, the work duties, home-work and mostly full weekends, Ross and I planned our wedding. Since I had never given much consideration to being a bride, I turned to the Lord for counsel, help and guidance. I prayed and asked God to show me the dress I was to wear. I looked at a magazine to get some ideas when I saw the dress. It had large puffed sleeves, lace neckline and lots of petticoats. It was stunning. I certainly couldn't afford it but at least now I knew what I wanted my dress to look like.

Ross and I prayed about minute details and it made all the deci-sions so much easier and more exciting. God was an integral part of our ceremony from the beginning. Our invitations had the traditional verses from Ruth. "Entreat me not to leave thee or to forsake from following after thee. For where you go, I will go and where you lodge I will lodge. Your people shall be my people and your God my God." We watched excitedly as every little thing came together. We planned to get married in the Tyler Rose Garden and figured that God would provide the flowers. After all, the first couple got married in a garden.

When I went to South Carolina with Ross for Christmas, we were finally able to spend some quality time together. There was still homework that we needed to do but there was a break from the daily classes and demands.

The Lord led me to serve Ross in a special way. I washed his feet, prayed over him and let my tears freely fall. I reaffirmed my love and my commitment to marry him and be his wife. He had tears in his eyes, too. He told me he had never had anyone wash his feet before.

Because we knew that we would have lots of time together, we chose once again to limit our physical expression of our love to only hold hands, hug and kiss on the cheek. For Christmas day, we gave ourselves the freedom to French kiss.

On a Sunday morning, Ross preached at a different church than his home church and God had me share some encouraging words. This preaching was part of our assignments over the break. During the singing, I prayed and re-committed myself to God and to move to Barbados. There were many blessings spoken over us and Ross and I came away refreshed in God.

We received powerful ministry at Ross' church. The Lord met us in a special service and a special speaker prayed over us. The words he spoke were statements of desires in our hearts that only God knew about. Some of those words were merely pondered in our hearts and others would take almost twenty years before they were fulfilled.

"Brother, God has taken away all your own desires and He has filled you with one desire only—to be a flaming evangel of the Gospel. Though you are a quiet man, God will give you a new voice, with a new timbre but when you speak it will be as an oracle of God. You desire to go to Barbados but keep it in the back of your mind that God is going to send you to other countries. There are a lot of young people who go with the idea of the "romance of missions" and when it doesn't work out, they have Plan B waiting in the wings. You have to be really sold out to this. There can't be a Plan B. It will be an adventure all right —one which you can never imagine. God is going to make you a shepherd and you will shepherd a flock. He has had His hand on you since you were a young boy and though you have sewn a few wild oats in your time your heart has been to please the Lord."

"Sister, the Lord is really going to use you in dance. You are going to lead people in worship. You two really need to study worship. Worship is key to your ministry. There is such potential in this couple."

Chapter 35

A Wedding Dress
and Personal Observations

*T*he night before we left, the Pastor's wife loaned me a wedding dress. I was overwhelmed. It was small and from the waist up it wasn't quite what I wanted. I prayed and asked God that if He wanted me to have it, that He would move on her heart to allow me to have it and alter it anyway I chose. Within a few minutes she called me back and said, "Ruth, I want to give it to you for you to use anyway that you would like." Oh, how my heart thrilled with her kindness and love but also with God's intimate answer to my prayer.

Earlier when my parents had discussed finances for the wedding, Mom said, "Normally the bride pays for her own wedding gown but since you have no job, your father and I will pay for that too."

When I let them know that I had been given a wedding dress, they were amazed and overjoyed at the lavish gift of the pastor's wife. What was so wonderful was they saw through God's provision of the dress that I worked for Him and He provided for His daughter. My dress was way beyond our budget but it wasn't beyond God's.

Once we returned to Texas, the schedule went back to classes and home-work. On one of the weekends, I made a special dinner for Ross as a "date." No girl had ever made dinner for him before! I loved how God guided me to do something for Ross and then I discovered that I was the only one who had ever blessed him like that.

Ross just looked at me with tears in his eyes and said, "I love you." It was special. I washed dishes and then we went to the classroom and prayed. Later we were romantic together as we kissed within the guidelines that God had given us. The romantic kisses usually occurred only after we focused on prayer first. We tried to leave the physical aspects of our relationship until the end of our time together and only spent a short amount of time kissing.

Many times we misunderstood each other. He desired to be romantic but I was tired; then I wanted to be romantic and he was busy. There were lots of hurts that occurred. I honestly thought that I would help Ross by encouraging him to change. I wanted people to take him seriously so I tried to tell him to dress and act differently. I had watched engaged couples as the woman helped her man become someone that others noticed because of her influence. Unfortunately the way I went about trying to change Ross was disrespectful and dishonoring.

I struggled with the expectation that we would study together throughout School of the Bible. As it became evident that Ross found me too much of a distraction to study with, I spent my nights in the dorm alone studying on my own. It was hard to handle the disappointment but I knew that I wanted to marry Ross and I honored him in that area. The enemy bombarded me and told me that my sexual past was why Ross couldn't study with me. I was too dangerous; I might cause him to fall sexually. I never told him my fears because again, I believed that my perceptions were true.

I wanted the idyllic engagement, complete with no conflict, happily-ever-after Hollywood style, but that was not reasonable if I wanted God to develop His character in me and to grow closer to becoming like Jesus. Honestly, I believed naively and with pride that "we loved God so much and we loved one another so much that there will never be any conflict." I wanted perfection and refused to see that we were both merely human. It took several years for that lie to break and that delusion in my heart to be exposed.

The petty arguments flared between us and finally I crawled into God's arms and wept. It was then that comfort and understanding began to come. God showed me that engagement is like a transition and character growth time. It is like when a mother is pregnant and the time draws nearer to delivery, her emotions and her excitement increase. If the baby were to stop growing—it would die. The baby is healthy and continues growing so that at the time of delivery both mother and baby are ready.

An engagement is like that as well. The relationship develops in a process of growth. If the emotions, feelings and desires stopped–the relationship would die. It wouldn't be healthy—it would be a cause for alarm. If the same feelings, emotions, desires, and commitment were to reverse that would not be healthy either. A relationship that moves too quickly is premature. A relationship that grows steadily stronger is healthy.

My small group leader, Lois, and I went and bought the material for my dress and ordered the lace and the buttons. In answer to prayer, she remade the top, the bodice, and the sleeves to be exactly what I wanted, to look like the dress I saw in the magazine. The many petticoats were already a part of the original dress. Ross took the cathedral veil and cut part of it, purchased silk flowers, two combs, and along with some white florist's tape and a wire hanger, made my wedding veil. The napkins were lavender with two candles, flowers and a Bible motif. I was so excited and happy because everything was coming together. There were only twelve weeks until the wedding!

Chapter 36

Fit to be Tied

*A*s our wedding date drew closer, we became more desirous of one another. In order not to fall into the traps of the enemy, we lovingly distanced ourselves and re-established our commitment to only hold hands, hug and kiss on the cheek. We were aware that there were times when we began to overstep safe and wise boundaries and when we did, we confessed to God and one another.

Then we repented and deliberately reinstated our commitment. Though we loved God, we also loved one another passionately and we recognized that we were merely human. At the end of another 30 day commitment in April, within a few days in May, we realized that we needed to keep the commitment in place until our wedding day.

My bridal shower was held May 18th. It was such a special time as I was given gifts but then the women prayed over me and different people shared encouraging words. *"God sees me as a rose— and I am going to blossom in marriage. I will have a sweet fragrance. A rose is dainty and delicate but it's also sturdy. It is significant that we are getting married in Rose Garden. People sensed the peace of God and that He was having fun and being delighted in our engagement and in helping us with the wedding. God is pleased with us."* Thank You, Lord!

My maid of honor, Anne, came to bless me. Anne was in the first training of my schools and the second phase of Ross' schools. She was a beautiful friend who loved and encouraged Ross and me early in our relationship. There was one night in particular when I was first seeking God about my feelings towards Ross and I asked Anne to pray for me. She did and then later that night she told me, "Ruth, it was phenomenal. I had such an amazing peace in my heart that God was putting you and Ross together. It felt like warm oil all over me when I prayed for both of you."

Anne told me that the Lord spoke to her, "You are to serve Ruth. You are to give her your hands and not withhold them and you are not to have them empty." It touched me to hear her share that. *Oh, Father, You are the Provider. I stand amazed at Your great love. Tomorrow I get my haircut—let it be so pretty. Anne's getting her dress ordered and she will sing, "Because of Who You Are." You are so faithful, God! Oh, my heart is so full of love and understanding.*

I wondered what gift I could give to Anne….and the tears came to my eyes as I realized that I could bless her with my wedding dress. The Barbados climate would only ruin it and I had no need to wear it again. She hoped to be married soon.

Ross finished my headpiece. Because we had just gone through School of the Bible together, our school leader said that Ross and I didn't need the "usual" premarital counseling. He said that the basis of a marriage is deep friendship with the teaching of the love of God, relationships, value and the truth of Jesus Christ dying on the cross in our place. These were all things we learned in class. Then add to that, kindness, tender-heartedness, forgiveness, even as God in Christ Jesus has forgiven us.

A friend gave me a hundred dollars towards Ross' ring but I still didn't have enough. The store-bought cake mixes that we had purchased so the cakes could be made early and then kept refrigerated all flopped so our friends willingly made the cakes from scratch. We bought gifts for our friends, finished finals and shopped for the various supplies we needed for the wedding.

I sold my school books to an upcoming student and then I had all the money I needed to buy Ross's ring. True to His word to me, God provided and I, personally, didn't pay for the ring. It was quite an act of faith for me because there were only seven days left! I prayed, *"Help everything work out as a testimony of Your Presence and blessing. Help me relax."*

Our last week was filled with so many details. Both sets of our parents and some of our family members came on Thursday. Susie flew in from Germany and I was thrilled to know she came all that way to see me get married. The Rehearsal Dinner was Friday. Our rehearsal was extremely short since there was another wedding getting ready to occur when we arrived at the Rose Garden to practice.

My Dad said, "This symbolizes an end of separation and her mother and I give our approval and our blessing on this marriage." After the dinner, Ross' Dad said, "As my mother used to say to me, 'Shalom,' so I say to you, "Shalom." (It was a traditional Jewish blessing of "Peace" but I didn't know if there was Jewish background in Ross' family.)

On the way back to the base, my mother asked if I would like to carry my Dad's Bible. I was so blessed and I was also going to carry my Grandmother's handkerchief inside the Bible. I found out that my grandparents, on my mother's side, also got married on June 30th, and their marriage lasted 50 years (until my grandfather's death a few days after their anniversary). We signed the marriage license and kissed each other a quick good-night as Ross was tired.

My journal entry, *I hope Ross isn't exhausted tomorrow night! I am trying to pack....help me Lord! Be still my soul, my heart— We made it— Virgins!—pure, chaste, white and clean! I am soon to be Ruth Mary McElwee!!!*

Chapter 37

Tying the Knot

I stayed awake until 3:00 in the morning. I woke up at 6:00 and Anne brought me breakfast. My stomach was in knots. The day was a beautiful, sunny morning in Texas. My Dad held my hand and let me know that he loved me. We walked down the steps together and I radiated with my smile and my heart full of love. Ross and I wrote our own vows.

Ruth,
I take you as a gift from God
To be my wife
I choose to love you
Even as God loves you
Seeking your highest good
For life.

I cherish you, Ruth
Above all others
Save God.

Ruth, I promise that I will do my best
To be a good and strong leader
And that I will be a leader
Even as Christ was a leader
Serving you as unto Him.

I will seek God's direction
For our lives
Because He is a loving and wise God
And He cares about us.

And I make a covenant with you
This day
For better or for worse
For richer or for poorer
In sickness and in health
From this day forward
Till death do us part.

Ross,
Entreat me not to leave you
Or to forsake from following you
For where you go,
I will go
And where you lodge
I will lodge
Your people shall be my people
And together we will serve our God.

Ross, I take you as a gift from God
To be my husband.
To have and to hold
To honor and cherish
To love and to serve.

I will passionately love you
With all my heart, soul, mind and strength
I will encourage, edify and strengthen you
In order that you may be
A man after God's own heart

In order that you may do His holy will
And in order that you may be a success
In His Kingdom.

I will obey you
I will submit to you
I will gladly give all that I have
And all that I am to you.

I acknowledge you as the spiritual head
And leader of our home
And I promise to help you
Fulfill this God-given role.

This day I dedicate myself to you
Even as unto the Lord
For better or for worse
For richer or for poorer
In sickness and in health
From this day forward
Till death do us part.

We shared our first communion together and prayed for our marriage. Everything seemed to go perfectly.

Oh, there were the little things.....like my train didn't get spread out so it was all bunched and Ross almost forgot to kiss me. I had teased him mercilessly throughout our engagement, "You'll be so nervous.....you'll probably forget to kiss me." I never imagined that it would happen. It brought a chuckle to the crowd watching us. He took a half-step before the words, "Now, you may kiss your bride."

At the reception, we had simple refreshments— cake, punch, mints and nuts. We drank from Styrofoam cups and used plastic silverware. The groom's cake was chocolate, made in the shape of Barbados.

When it came time for the garter, I was so nervous thinking about Ross touching my bare leg, that I put my foot on the chair, hiked my dress up, and hoped he would "get it over with." I had gone to many weddings growing up and I "knew" that normally the bride sat in the chair but at that moment, all sense of decorum was gone. Thankfully the many layers of petticoats prevented any real embarrassment.

My mother was the only person who took a picture of that pose….. The funny thing was that I was afraid the garter would fall down so I had put it on above my knee. It was only after we had been married for a year and we showed our pictures to a friend in Illinois who commented, "Oh, is that how they remove the garter, in Texas?"

Ross' car was really not decorated, though the girls had wanted to. He let me know that he didn't want things damaging the paint. So other than just a few streamers and some cans, the only sign was the one that was already in the back window: "God Rules." It summed up the story of our courtship and our lives.

We left the base and headed to our honeymoon time-share in Hot Springs National Park, Arkansas. That gift was from my parents. I teased Ross and said that it was good that he was married to me, since the regulations were that an adult must be 21 to stay there. He was only 20 but at least no longer a teenager. We stopped at a fast-food place to order hamburgers, fries and soft drinks and we drove on.

It was early evening when we arrived and we asked, "Where's the park?"

The receptionist responded, "You're in it. It's the city."

We both mistakenly thought we chose a week in a national park with lots of hiking trails, natural beauty and seclusion. Obviously, we were wrong.

We went into the bedroom and kissed. Ross leaned back with me on the bed and I immediately said, "Not yet!" He was tired so he took a nap. I stayed awake and emptied our suitcases and arranged our things. I looked for the candles that I brought, in order for us to have a romantic dinner. I realized I had neglected to bring matches and there were none in the timeshare. I prayed and asked God to provide.

I went outside and down to the pool. A small group of ladies were there. I asked, "Do any of you have some matches or a lighter? My fiancé and I just arrived for our honeymoon."

They all smiled at me and I honestly thought nothing of it. One woman said she had quit smoking a few weeks ago, but then she reached into her pocket and handed me her lighter. I returned to Ross and was thrilled at how God answered my prayer. I told Ross verbatim the story and he totally burst out laughing.

I was baffled. "What?"

"Did you really say that?"

"Yes. What did I say?"

"Honey, I'm not your fiancé, anymore. I'm your *husband*."

We both laughed and I understood the smiles at the pool. I had a running dialogue with the Lord, as I usually did. *"What is wrong with me? Why am I so nervous?"* The gentle, Fatherly voice broke into my thoughts… *"Uh, Ruth, you are on your honeymoon."* I almost laughed out loud.

I rejoined Ross in the living room and he asked me to massage his back. I focused on the massage and sang praise songs to God. There were no other sounds in the room. I was lost in thankfulness to God and love for Ross. After what might have been ten minutes or more, Ross spoke.

"Are you tuning me out?"

"Oh, no, Honey! I'm just praising the Lord."

Instantaneously, the Holy Spirit chided me. *"Ruth, that's exactly what you're doing."*

I countered, *I know….but God before the night's over, I'm going to be* <u>*naked*</u> *with this man!*

Ross was loving and gentle with me and we laughed so much. Our union was beautiful, romantic and special— the crowning touch of God's delight in bringing us together to become husband and wife. The next morning, I commented, "How come I was so nervous with you last night? We got married at the altar several hours before."

His smiling eyes and laughing voice lovingly and knowingly looked at me, "No, Ruth. We declared our vows publically to one another but we weren't *truly married* until we consummated our vows last night." Thus began the marriage that so far has seen the completion of over twenty-five years.

To God be the Glory!

~ Epilogue ~

Ross and I have been married for over twenty-five years. We served in Youth With A Mission (YWAM) for over seven years. We did move to Barbados, West Indies, thinking we would be there a life-time. But God had other plans. We lived there for six months and returned to the States as our life journey continued.

We moved back to Texas and continued raising our family. We did have Samuel and Rachel Joy. God also blessed us with Isaac and Leah. We lived on a family farm, built our own house and raised cows, sheep and chickens. I home-schooled all four of the children and Ross had his own cabinetry business.

After living on the farm for twelve years, God called us to move to Northwestern Alaska to a remote Iñupiaq Eskimo village. Ross served for almost seven years as a missionary pastor of the only church in the village. We currently live in Soldotna, Alaska.

~ Afterword ~

I add these pages to bring resolution. I attempted to indicate that the events were told through my perspective, feelings, knowledge and understanding at the time.

As I healed over the years, through training, understanding human behavior and studying the Bible, I learned more effective ways of viewing circumstances in my life. Learning the stages of grief was very insightful.

I believe you will see that my parents' reactions, as well as my own, in the light of trauma, were normal. I don't say that to diminish the pain, for indeed it was there for many decades, but that in looking back through the eyes of healing, I can share with you that their hearts were not intentionally malicious or evil in any way.

The stages of grief are sometimes broken down into five or ten categories, depending on whose references you look at. These stages include: Shock, Panic, Denial, Numbness, Anger/Rage, Anguish/ Despair, Bargaining, Forgiveness, Acceptance, Growth/Maturation and Helping Others. These emotions are all normal, natural and typical human feelings because we live in a fallen world. These emotions are not always in a neat little pattern or order and the feelings can be experienced so rapidly that it is merely seconds between stages.

Recall my mother's horror as her sweet, totally innocent little five-year-old girl tells her what the man did. Instantly, from Shock, Panic to the trauma breaking her heart, her words show her Denial, "Ruth Mary, I cannot believe that." Now, in my Mom's heart, she wasn't accusing me of lying—she just didn't know how to process that horrible information that someone could hurt her child like that.

To me, as a five-year-old, I was naïve. I did not have adult years of experience to comprehend the seriousness of the abuse. I only knew it wasn't right and I didn't like it. But in hearing my mother's words, all I heard as a five-year-old was, "You are lying."

I moved into Numbness. I merely shut down emotionally and to a large extent verbally. Then the Anger/Rage set in and the deep Anguish/Despair of feeling rejected and no longer loved.

My father went from his own stages of grief as several emotions warred inside of him. He decided not to show physical affection anymore, thinking that somehow that would keep me from remembering the abuse. He also told me when I was in my late teens, that he had struggled with wanting to kill the man. He fought feelings of murder. If you would have ever known my father, you would know that he was one of the most non-aggressive and non-violent men you would have ever met. To be a pastor and to wrestle with thoughts of Anger/Rage so intense that he wanted to kill the man must have been a terrible agony.

At the same time, what was he supposed to do? Already the church board wanted to fire him. Dad put his name into a pool to be chosen for another church but it was three years before an opening came.

In the meantime, the pain of his daughter rejecting him, the rage of his daughter, the lostness of his child who used to be so happy, carefree and affectionate, broke his heart. There seemed to be no remedy and taking an old, senile man to court didn't seem to be his answer. In many ways, there seemed to be no justice.

Later, when Dad told me that my abuser was dead, my mind blocked out the trauma. I went into Denial and because I forgot about the abuse itself, I had nothing to bring understanding as to why I hated myself so deeply and had such incredible low self-esteem.

Because my Dad didn't forget the abuse that happened to me, as my personality continued to fragment and then in my teenage years when I was so bitter and rebellious, all along he thought I had consciously remembered all that happened in Texas.

My mother did know that I had been abused but I think that she thought it was a small thing and had no idea the ramifications of that incident on my entire being. Her way of dealing with the trauma was in essence, to "forget about it," so Denial also played a major part in her relationship with me.

Because I did not consciously remember the abuse, it was a long time before I could heal. I stayed stuck moving from various stages of grief because I didn't know the source of my pain. Somehow I just knew to absorb insults, teasing, rejection and all the other negative experiences because there had been no protection for me when I was five and there was no one to defend me now. As a victim, especially a child, the abuse was against my will and as such, my will had been broken.

This is very important to understand because someone who's will has not been violated, often has an innate anger to self-protect, to speak up for themselves, to make the bullies stop hurting them, either verbally, emotionally or even physically. I did not have that kind of will-power. I felt defenseless and acted that way, without thoroughly understanding why.

I also didn't understand Anger/Rage. I absorbed negative experiences but eventually I was like a volcano, erupting in rage. Because I knew that social norms expected me to act morally or socially acceptable, the only ones who received my rage were in my own home. No one outside of our four walls would have ever imagined the level of verbal abuse, yelling, screaming or rage that my parents received. I never called them profane names to their faces, because profanity in our home was not tolerated but the intensity of hatred and disdain towards them engulfed the house.

At age 16, when I finally did remember the first abuse, I still had to pass through the stages of Shock, then Numbness and Anguish/Despair at what my life had become. I could see the pattern of what had happened but the lies that I had believed about myself were so ingrained into my being and lifestyle that I was broken on the inside. Years of promiscuity, unaware of abuse as a five-year-old, had developed a pattern in my life that was not easily broken. I had subconsciously been re-living the abuse but that realization didn't dawn on me until I had been married for several years.

Once I was no longer in Denial, I could begin to re-think my life, slowly, piece by piece, relationship by relationship. I gained some sense of power and choice as the healing of God continued in fragile moments and I started to come alive again.

By the time I repented in college on my knees out on the track field, I was in Bargaining with the Stages of Grief. I wept over my life full of sins and sought Forgiveness. In a moment that only God could do, He brought me through the reality of a sin-stained life, a broken heart and shattered dreams to a place of healing and Forgiveness.

Daily, I was able to move more into Acceptance of the grief that I had carried all those years. The stages of Growth and Maturation continued to bring forth the ability to forgive those who had sinned against me, those who I had sinned against, and to forgive myself and move on with life. Eventually, I reached a place where I am now Helping Others.

I would like to say that I feel that I am 98 % healed. I am a very free woman who occasionally has reminders of the pain that I carried. But most of the time, I am just a believer in Jesus Christ who has been saved from hell, shame, death and fear. I love Jesus and it is my greatest desire to share His love.

Healing is a journey and a process. I know that most of us would like instant healing and not have to go through the layers of pain. But that is not true healing. In order to forgive from the heart, one must feel the emotions of pain and loss, anger and abandonment and all the other emotions that one has managed to deny or hide behind false safe places.

Many people have broken hearts but their actions keep them and everyone else focused on their outward behaviors. These behaviors need to be addressed and changed but true transformation comes from getting to the heart of the matter.

Jesus Christ said that was part of His mission in coming to Earth. "To heal the broken hearted and to set the captives free." If no one was broken hearted or held captive to wrong beliefs, bondages, false safe places and lies, then Jesus would not have made that declaration from Isaiah to be part of His vision and mission statement.

In our churches, we often skirt the real issues because in order to heal the heart of an individual, that takes time. It is not a "quick fix." It is a part of discipleship, of walking through those places of pain, of examining the lies and of genuinely hating what the person did to you, but being able to genuinely love the person who hurt you. It is not a simple formula. We have to be willing to "bear one another's burdens." A burden by its nature is not easy; it is heavy. But oh, for the joy that awaits us as we heal and step into the beauty and freedom that Jesus Christ paid such a high price for on the Cross. This is to walk a victorious life in Christ, to be hidden in His love and held in His heart.

Oh, Precious Reader, do you know the Savior, Jesus Christ, the One Who loves you more than anyone else? Have you surrendered your life to Him? No one will ever take your place in the heart of God.

~ A Final Reconciliation ~

There are two miraculous stories that bring closure, healing and resolution to places of pain in my life. With both of my parents, I spent years after being married of having delightful, special times of phone calls and visits. I loved them both very dearly and the level of forgiveness and restoration was deep and rich in all of us.

Nevertheless, I had no idea the intense hidden pain that they each still carried. Sometimes towards the end of life, the deep wounds, fears and regrets are finally voiced in order to bring complete peace. I had these stories happen with both of my parents and I was blessed beyond words at the depth of healing that God had in store for me.

Dad was in Hospice, dying of throat cancer. I went to see him but honestly I had made my peace with Dad years before and I knew that there was no trace of bitterness, unforgiveness, shame or any other negative emotion in my heart towards him. I was assured of his love and of mine towards him and I knew that I would spend eternity with Daddy.

While I was visiting Mom and Dad in Florida, we talked freely about my childhood. I explained to them that I had recently received powerful ministry in my church bringing greater understanding and awareness of all the enemy's schemes to destroy me as a child. We talked specifically about the spiritual warfare, the demonic oppression and torment I experienced and about the rage I carried. It was through the ministry in my church that I had been set free of the intense, internal struggles with rage.

Even though I discovered that the rage had been a carryover in my life from the pain of sexual abuse, I had no idea that the enemy of God still tormented my Dad with memories from my past. Dad's voice began to break as he shook uncontrollably. "I was so stupid. I was so stupid with your diary. I was so stupid." (Dad never used the word, "stupid," and even that shocked me.) I hadn't seen him weep like that since I had been a teenager. His heart was breaking once again.

His tears poured and I was completely shocked. I had no idea the pain he still carried.

"Oh Ruth Mary, can you forgive me?"

My compassion gripped me as all I wanted to do was to comfort my precious father. I wanted to remove all the pain that he felt.

"Oh, Daddy, I forgave you years ago. There is nothing in my heart but love and gratitude for you. I love you, Daddy."

As he gained composure, I held his hands. "Dad, can you forgive me for all the hurt?"

"Oh, yes, Ruth Mary, I forgave you long ago."

We continued to talk about my past.

Dad said, "It was hell, living in the minister's house and I didn't know what to do."

I explained my recent ministry of deliverance and healing, including generational curses and spiritual warfare.

Dad replied, "Then you were like Legion, then?" (This is a reference in the Bible to the demon-possessed man who had a "legion" of demons).

I responded, "Yes, I was but we didn't know about stuff like that."

Dad said, "Every time you were with those boys, I knew you were reliving the abuse...."

I was shocked because I had never made any connection since I had blocked the memories until I was sixteen. When Dad said these words, I stopped him.

"Dad, Dad, the Holy Spirit just spoke through you..."

"Okay." He seemed somewhat puzzled, waiting for an explanation.

Various scenarios replayed themselves in my memory. Only this time, I connected all the dots. "Dad, I never understood that until now."

Dad replied sadly, "I did. I knew it."

The flood of insight of such past promiscuity took on a new understanding and another area of my heart healed.

Mom said something about my past and I looked at her. "Mom, will you forgive me?"

"Oh, Honey, I forgave you so long ago. I wasn't even thinking of that."

Dad asked, "Ruth Mary, is there still anything?"

"Oh Dad, I've been restored to you in my heart for over twenty years. No, there is nothing but love and gratitude. You and Mom never stopped loving me. You loved me unconditionally, even when I spurned you."

Mom said, "Well, I guess there were some things that needed to be said."

Then Dad gave me an amazing blessing that touched so many places in my heart. I felt like a fireworks display of love as the words burst and cascaded over the years of longing for affirmation. It was as if God, Himself, had my Dad give me His blessing before the Lord took my Dad home.

Dad gathered Mom and me on each side of him, as he sat in his chair. He placed his hand on my head and slowly spoke, "This woman praying — strong, godly, mature, beautiful woman — praying for me — and it's my daughter."

Daddy died before I ever wrote this book.

Periodically, over the years, when my story would arise in conversation, Mom always insisted, "Your father never told me." Now, for clarification, he eventually did tell her of the abuse but not until several months after it had happened. The truth was that she had lived in Denial about this particular part of the story and of course, I didn't even remember it myself until I was sixteen. But by that time, my relationship with my mother was horrendous.

But God had healed our relationship and from the time I was engaged, she and I had lovely times together. After Dad died, my family moved to Alaska to be missionaries in a village. During those years, Mom called me from Florida and we became best friends. She remembered stories from being in the ministry and she comforted me with her understanding and wisdom of being a pastor's wife.

I went to visit her for a few days while the rest of my family was in another state on vacation. Mom and I talked about her childhood and I listened to some of her stories. The very things that she used to say to me as a child in a negative way were very similar to some of her own painful memories. I did not tell her any of that, but the Lord allowed me to see that she had merely repeated her own insecurities from places of pain in her heart.

As we talked, my childhood past came up in the conversation. I wanted to just leave the conversation alone but somehow I sensed that the Holy Spirit was pushing us gently. So, as she talked, I heard the hurt in her own voice. "Ruth Mary, you wouldn't let me touch you. You pushed me away."

I had not realized until then that I had rejected my mother's physical affection after my father stopped displaying physical affection towards me. I had not recognized how deeply that hurt her for all those years of wanting to show love, hugs, tender touch and for me to consistently and vehemently reject her. My inner hatred and rage kept me from closeness.

Then once again, the painful admission, "Ruth Mary, your father never told me."

I cringed inside as I didn't want to be hurt over this anymore, but ever so gently I felt the Lord pressing me. So, I did something that I had never done in all the years prior when the conversation ended this way.

I gently placed my hands on my mother's hands and without any trace of bitterness, unforgiveness, anger, rage, criticism or anything negative I spoke each word slowly, with tears in my eyes.

"You're right, Mom. Daddy never told you. I did...and you didn't believe me."

The Shock came immediately on her face, the Panic of what the words meant and after all those years, Denial finally lost. Her voice cracked with pain and she wept with broken words as the truth penetrated her heart.

"Oh, Ruth Mary... I'm sorry....I beg your forgiveness....I beg you to forgive me....I am so very sorry."

"I forgive you, Mom." I broke into tears as well, and dropped my head into Mom's lap and bawled. The pain of all those years and the tears we both wept. She stroked my hair. I hadn't let her do that since before I was ever first abused. That action touched something deep inside me and I remembered how long ago, she used to stroke my hair when I rested my head in her lap at church. The healing of God was profound. I didn't know that this conversation would ever be held on this side of eternity.

Later that night as I was going to bed, she spoke these beautiful words. "Ruth Mary, you are beautiful — inside and out. There isn't anyone in your high school who wouldn't be proud to know you. They would say, "Is that Ruth Mary? She's marvelous. She's tremendous. She's powerful. I am proud to know her. Oh, Honey, they don't remember what you were — but what your life is like now. Look what the Lord has done!"

~ About the Author ~

$\mathcal{R}$uth McElwee was born the youngest of four into a pastor's family. She grew up in Texas and West Virginia and graduated from Marshall University, *cum laude,* with a Bachelor's degree in English and a double minor — one in Psychology and another in Counseling & Rehabilitation.

She served in YWAM, Youth With A Mission for over seven years, working in many parts of the U.S., Mexico, and Barbados. While in YWAM, she also received an Associate's Degree in Biblical Studies.

After living on a farm in rural East Texas for twelve years, the family moved to the beautiful Iñupiaq Eskimo village of White Mountain, in a remote part of Western "Bush" Alaska. Ruth worked along-side her husband, Ross, who served as the pastor of the only church in that village of 200. After living there nearly seven years, they moved to Soldotna, Alaska, in 2014.

Currently Ruth serves at Alaska Christian College. She has encouraged many in churches and women's conferences, in Alaska and beyond. She is also a state representative for AVA — Advocacy for Victims of Abuse.

To contact for speaking engagements, find us on the Web, check out our blog, or drop us a note:

Facebook:
www.facebook.com/HeartsHealed
Web: www.BrokenHeartsHealed.org
Email: RuthMcElwee@gmail.com